CHINA'S RESPONSIBILITY FOR CLIMATE CHANGE

Ethics, fairness and environmental policy

Edited by Paul G. Harris

First published in Great Britain in 2011 by

Policy Press
University of Bristol
1-9 Old Park Hill
Bristol BS2 8BB
UK
t: +44 (0)117 954 5940
pp-info@bristol.ac.uk
www.policypress.co.uk

North America office:
Policy Press
c/o The University of Chicago Press
1427 East 60th Street
Chicago, IL 60637, USA
t: +1 773 702 7700
f: +1 773 702 9756
sales@press.uchicago.edu
www.press.uchicago.edu

© Policy Press 2011

British Library Cataloguing in Publication Data
A catalogue record for this book is available from the British Library.

Library of Congress Cataloging-in-Publication Data
A catalog record for this book has been requested.

ISBN 978 1 84742 812 7 paperback
ISBN 978 1 84742 813 4 hardcover

Cover design by Qube Design Associates, Bristol.
Front cover: image kindly supplied by www.alamy.com
Printed and bound in Great Britain by Marston Book Services, Oxford.

Contents

List of tables and figures

Tables

Figures

Notes on contributors

Derek Bell is Senior Lecturer in Politics at Newcastle University, UK. His research interests are in environmental politics and political philosophy. He has published articles on environmental justice, environmental citizenship and liberal environmentalism in leading journals, including *Political Studies, Environmental Politics* and *Environmental Ethics*. He is co-editor (with Andrew Dobson) of *Environmental citizenship* (MIT Press, 2006). He is currently working on a book on global justice and climate change.

Olivia Bina is a research fellow at the Institute of Social Sciences, University of Lisbon, Portugal, and Adjunct Assistant Professor in the Department of Geography and Resource Management at the Chinese University of Hong Kong. She has published widely on the theory and practice of environmental governance mechanisms, especially strategic environmental assessment. Her current research focuses on Chinese and European conceptions of progress, growth and ecological sustainability, and on related themes of responsibility, happiness and wellbeing in economic and sustainability theory.

Christian Ellermann is completing his doctorate in Chinese climate policy at the Environmental Change Institute, Oxford University, UK. He is a consultant with Ecofys, where he works on projects in the area of post-Kyoto climate change policy, often involving extensive work on greenhouse gas data. During his latest assignment he was leader of a project team working on sectoral approaches in Beijing. He has a special interest in Chinese energy and climate change policy. He is fluent in Chinese.

Paul G. Harris is Chair Professor of Global and Environmental Studies, Head of the Department of Social Sciences, Director of the Social and Policy Research Unit, and Senior Research Fellow in the Centre for Governance and Citizenship at the Hong Kong Institute of Education. His work has appeared widely in scholarly journals. He is author or editor of a dozen books on global environmental politics, policy and ethics, most recently (as author) *World ethics and climate change* (Edinburgh University Press, 2010) and (as editor) *Ethics and global environmental policy* (Edward Elgar, 2011).

Niklas Höhne was responsible for negotiation of the 'Brazilian proposal' while a staff member of the United Nations Framework Convention on Climate Change secretariat from 1998 to 2001. Since 2005, he has been Director of the Energy and Climate Strategy Group of Ecofys in Germany, where he was previously a project manager working on international climate change negotiations and the Kyoto Mechanisms. He developed the WWF 'climate scorecard', and was a lead author of the Intergovernmental Panel on Climate Change's *Fourth assessment report.*

Michael C. MacCracken is Chief Scientist for Climate Change Programs with the Climate Institute, Washington, DC, USA. He was Senior Global Change Scientist with the Office of the US Global Change Research Program, also serving as its first Executive Director and as Executive Director of the National Assessment Coordination Office. In addition to numerous papers and reports, he is a senior co-author of *Confronting climate change: Avoiding the unmanageable and managing the unavoidable* and *Sudden and disruptive climate change: Exploring the real risks and how we can avoid them.*

Frances C. Moore is a doctoral student in the Interdisciplinary Program in Environment and Resources at Stanford University, California, USA, where she works on modelling climate change adaptation in rural communities. Her previous research focused on the construction and negotiation of adaptation policy in the Copenhagen negotiations. She is a Switzer Foundation Fellow and an NSF Graduate Research Fellow. She holds a Master's in environmental science from the Yale School of Forestry and a BA, *summa cum laude*, in earth and planetary science from Harvard University.

Benito Müller is Director (Energy & Environment) at the Oxford Institute for Energy Studies, Managing Director of Oxford Climate Policy and Director of the European Capacity Building Initiative, UK. He is Supernumerary Fellow at Wolfson College, a member of the Philosophy Faculty, Senior Research Associate at Queen Elizabeth House and Associate Fellow in the Environmental Change Institute and the Centre for Brazilian Studies at the University of Oxford, UK. He is also a Specialist Adviser on Climate Change to the International Development Committee of the UK House of Commons.

Andreas Oberheitmann is International Director of the Research Centre for International Environmental Policy and Visiting Professor in the Department for Environmental Science and Engineering at Tsinghua University, Beijing, China. His research on energy and environmental policy issues in East-Asia has been published in well-established and peer-reviewed journals, such as *Mitigation and Adaptation Strategies for Global Change, Energy Policy, China Perspectives* and *Utilities Policy*, as well as in books, some in Chinese. He is editor of a book on statistical analysis and empirical research in China.

Erich W. Schienke is Assistant Professor of Science, Technology and Society at Pennsylvania State University, USA, where he is also affiliated with the Asian Studies Program and is Research Fellow in the Rock Ethics Institute. His research interests include ethics in scientific research, particularly how ethics and environmental knowledge are produced, prioritised and communicated among scientists, policy makers and the public. He is developing the Ethical Dimensions of Scientific Research Program and writing a book on the history of Chinese ecological science and environmental governance.

Patrick Schroeder is International Adviser at the China Association for NGO Cooperation in Beijing, China. He supports the coordination and international cooperation of the China Civil Climate Action Network. He also works as a consultant on China projects for the United Nations Environment Programme/Wuppertal Institute Collaborating Centre on Sustainable Consumption and Production. He holds a Master's degree in international relations from Victoria University of Wellington, New Zealand, where he is completing doctoral work on 'environmental leapfrogging' in China.

Eva Sternfeld is a sinologist, geographer and Director of the Centre for Cultural Studies of Science and Technology in China at Technical University Berlin, Germany. She previously worked as Director of the China Environment and Sustainable Development Reference and Research Centre, a public environmental information centre administered by the State Environmental Protection Administration in Beijing. Her publications include articles on China's environmental and climate protection policies, urban water management in China and environmental education.

Jonathan Symons is Assistant Professor in the Department of Political Science at Lingnan University, Hong Kong. He has taught international relations and global environmental politics at La Trobe and Deakin universities in Australia. He was formerly a post-doctoral research fellow at Lingnan University and at the Hong Kong Institute of Education. He is contributing co-editor of *Energy security in the era of climate change: The Asia-Pacific experience*, and author of articles on environmental politics and the politics of climate change.

Preface

China is now the largest national source of the greenhouse gas pollution causing global warming and resulting changes to the Earth's climate. In coming decades, the growth in its emissions of carbon dioxide, the most significant greenhouse gas, will likely exceed that of the rest of the world combined. Therefore, on a very practical level, China is absolutely central to the world's efforts to address climate change. That said, it is quite a more complex and controversial question to ask whether, and to what degree, China is *responsible* for climate change. Certainly the question needs to be asked because the answer to it will be central to China's willingness, and indeed the willingness of the Chinese people, to be fully involved in global solutions to this problem. However, the question of China's responsibility for climate change is seldom posed, making this book possibly the first one devoted to it. No doubt more will be written in coming years.

I should state at the outset that the aim of this book is certainly *not* to single out China for blame. There is plenty of blame for causing climate change to go around, with the United States and most Americans foremost worthy of it. The received wisdom seems to be that China is *not* responsible for climate change, with justifications for this conclusion usually revolving around China's large population, relative poverty and low historical pollution relative to the world's wealthy countries. However, as the contributors to this volume demonstrate, the received wisdom, while having merit, may be too simplistic and increasingly anachronistic. The answer to the question of China's responsibility for climate change depends greatly on whether one is thinking in terms of practical contributions (for example, how much pollution comes from China's territory), time (for example, past, present and future contributions to the problem), ethics (for example, moral foundations and assumptions about what is right and wrong, just and unjust), agency (for example, whether it might be the Chinese state, Chinese people or Chinese corporations that are responsible) and so forth.

In other words, identifying whether China is responsible for climate change, and whether and how it will be involved in addressing the problem, is not a straightforward matter. Hence this book, which aims to address China's responsibility for climate change (or lack of it) from a range of theoretical, empirical and normative perspectives.

Contributors to this volume come from a variety of national and professional backgrounds. We try to take a generally disinterested look at China's place in the climate change debate and in the world's responses to this most-profound problem. Although we are 'outsiders' in so far as we are not Chinese nationals, many of us have experience of studying, living and working in China. My desire as editor was to include Chinese contributors, but this proved to be more difficult than anticipated. One reason was that, while Chinese experts often have in-depth knowledge of China's contribution to climate change, they overwhelmingly tend to reinforce the official view of the Chinese government, which is that China has no responsibility for climate change, apart from any that it is willing to take on for reasons of magnanimity or generosity. While a number of Chinese scholars are willing to challenge government policy in informal settings, I was unable to find any of them willing to do so for this book. This is unfortunate, because without substantial revisions quite soon, China's official policy will contribute to global environmental catastrophe. With this in mind, a central objective of this book is to analyse the official perspective, and more specifically to consider alternatives to it.

Work in this book was substantially supported by a grant from the Research Grants Council of the Hong Kong Special Administrative Region, China (General Research Fund Project no. HKIEd 340309). I wish to thank the contributors for agreeing to share their ideas in this volume. I am very grateful to anonymous reviewers for strongly supporting the project. I am indebted to the great team of people at The Policy Press, especially Emily Watt and Leila Ebrahimi, for their work to bring this book to readers. As always, I am most grateful for the daily support of K.K. Chan, who (after more than a decade) remains surprisingly tolerant of my long hours at the computer.

In an attempt to take some responsibility for climate change, especially its impacts on nature, all of the editor's royalties from the sale of this book will be paid by The Policy Press directly to Friends of the Earth. All people with the capability to do so – including those of us living in China – have a responsibility to behave as though our individual tiny acts can make a difference. Collectively they surely can.

Paul G. Harris
Hong Kong, China

Part One
Introduction

ONE

Diplomacy, responsibility and China's climate change policy

Paul G. Harris

Climate change is the most profound environmental problems facing the world. Attempts by governments to address it have been characterised by preoccupation with narrow and short-term perceived national interests rather than the pressing need to mitigate atmospheric pollution and respond aggressively to its impacts. This was amply demonstrated at the 15th Conference of the Parties (COP15) to the United Nations Framework Convention on Climate Change (UNFCCC) held in Copenhagen in December 2009. That conference failed to reach any formal or binding agreement on steps to reduce emissions of greenhouse gases (GHGs) or to deal with the consequences of global warming for societies and ecosystems. The Copenhagen conference revealed a fundamental flaw in the international management of climate change, namely underlying political norms and ethics that place nearly all value and importance in states and their national interests.

A major manifestation of this problem is recurring debate over the historical responsibility of the developed countries for GHG pollution. While developed countries surely deserve most of the blame if we think only in terms of states, this focus on state responsibility fails to account for rising GHG emissions among industrialising countries in the developing world and, importantly, among affluent people in those countries. These changes are manifested profoundly in the case of China, which is seeing explosive growth in its GHG emissions and a rapid expansion in the sizes of its middle and upper classes. Given the misfit between historical national responsibility and current emissions, the predominant emphasis on responsibility of developed countries for climate change will have to be overcome if the world is to take the extraordinary steps necessary to combat the problem aggressively in coming decades.

We can find no greater support for this argument than in the case of China. China is now the largest national source of GHG pollution. This pollution must be limited and eventually reduced if the most catastrophic consequences of climate change are to be avoided or at least mitigated. Thus, addressing climate change effectively will require China's participation. However, the Chinese government rejects internationally binding limits on its GHG emissions for two very good ethical reasons: the developed countries polluted the atmosphere as they became wealthy, so they ought to reduce their emissions before expecting China to do so; and China is a developing country with millions of poor people, meaning that it should be allowed to raise living standards before being required to limit GHG pollution. Put simply, the Chinese government's perspective is that it need not accept any formal obligation to limit its contribution to climate change, let alone agree to *reduce* its GHG emissions, before the West does so *and* behaves accordingly. In short, China has decided that much of its environmental policy, and its response to climate change in particular, will be subject to what Western countries do first.

China's position is not new. The Chinese government has refused to be bound by commitments to limit the country's pollution of the atmosphere since the start of international negotiations on climate change in the 1980s. President Hu Jintao has reaffirmed that China will not commit to mandatory emissions-reduction targets before the world's wealthy countries take the lead in addressing global climate change. He has also called on affluent countries to pay for emissions limitations in China and other developing countries (Hu, 2009). Alongside these Chinese concerns about justice and historical responsibility is the new reality that China has become the largest national source of pollution causing climate change. Without China's involvement, notably through limitations in its future GHG emissions, international efforts to mitigate global warming substantially are very unlikely to succeed. Indeed, we can almost certainly conclude that they *cannot possibly* succeed without China's robust participation. This conclusion comes against the backdrop of increasing concerns among atmospheric scientists that global warming is happening more quickly than predicted, that climate change will be more severe than anticipated and that the poorest countries and poorest people of the world will experience monumental suffering in coming decades as a consequence (UNEP, 2009).

With the increasingly central role of China very much in mind, this book aims to assess how China's longstanding concerns about international fairness and justice can be squared against the pressing need for an effective international regime and effective domestic policies that limit GHG emissions – including those from China – and that respond efficaciously to the inevitable consequences of climate change. The main objectives of the book are:

- to describe and analyse China's contribution to climate change and its domestic and foreign policy responses to this problem;
- to critically explore China's responsibility for climate change from a variety of perspectives;
- to explore some of the policy scenarios that might mitigate China's contribution to climate change while promoting its own interests, its stated policy goals and the international community's expectations; and
- to address all of these objectives in a single volume, thus making for easy access to a wide spectrum of readers, such as policy makers, experts, activists, university students and concerned members of the public.

This chapter lays a foundation for the chapters that follow. I begin by describing very briefly some of the science and international diplomacy of climate change before summarising some key aspects of Chinese climate policy and providing some possible explanations for that policy. I then summarise selected findings of subsequent chapters.[1]

Climate diplomacy in brief

To put the problem of climate change in perspective, and to show how much climate diplomacy and resulting national policies lag climate science, it is worth bearing in mind that anthropogenic global warming was first theorised in the 19th century. By the 1970s, climate change was receiving serious international attention from scientists, and the First World Climate Conference was held in 1979. The Intergovernmental Panel on Climate Change (IPCC) was created in 1988 as part of governments' efforts to study the problem, and in 1990 the Second World Climate Conference was held. International concern was manifested in the 1992 UNFCCC, the 1997 Kyoto Protocol and myriad subsequent agreements that have been reached during the intergovernmental negotiating process. The upshot is that the problem is far from new, and more importantly that scientists and governments have been very actively engaged in it for over three decades.

The latest science of climate change paints a bleak picture of the future. In its most recent assessment, the IPCC reported that climate change will result in a range of unwanted impacts, such as more widespread and severe droughts and floods, an increasing number of severe weather events, loss of biodiversity and damage to vulnerable ecosystems, and many adverse impacts for human communities, such as water shortages, spread of disease-carrying pests, adverse effects on fisheries and loss of inhabited areas and farmland to the sea (IPCC, 2007). While the IPCC predicted that many of these adverse impacts would occur much later in the century, more recent science suggests that they will occur much sooner – and in many cases may be happening already – and will likely be more severe than the IPCC has predicted (see, for example, McCarthy, 2009; McMullen and Jabbour, 2009). In short, the IPCC science underlying the international negotiations has been, if anything, too optimistic.

We can take at least three messages away from this evolution of climate science and the political response to it. First, the world has known about the problem for decades, with the dangers to humanity having been widely discussed for about two of those. Second, the science is telling us that the future will likely be bleak for many ecosystems and for many millions (possibly billions) of people in the future. The more we learn about climate change, the more bleak the future appears to be and the more confident we become of that bleakness. The science will always contain uncertainties, but the danger is clear (see Hamilton, 2010). Third, the international politics, diplomacy and domestic policies surrounding climate change are grossly inadequate to the task. The science improves by leaps and bounds, the dangers of climate change become more profound each year, but the diplomacy and national responses to climate change plod along at a diplomatic pace, resulting in agreements and policies that are too little, too late. The 2009 Copenhagen conference was but one of many examples of this: even if fully implemented, the voluntary GHG emissions cuts pledged there will be insufficient to avert dangerous global warming (UNEP, 2010).

As with previous major international conferences on climate change, some people characterised the 2009 Copenhagen conference as an important first step towards serious action. For example, in a joint letter, Danish Prime Minister Lars Lokke Rasmussen and United Nations (UN) Secretary General Ban Ki-moon told heads of state that the 'Copenhagen Accord represents the essential first step in a process leading to a robust international climate change treaty' (Rasmussen and Ban, 2009, p 2), and German Chancellor Angela Merkel described it as a 'step, albeit a small one, towards a global climate change architecture' (quoted in den Egenhofer and Georgiev, 2009, p 1). However, given the science and a quarter-century's international negotiations, we must ask when the world will take the second, third and fourth steps of actually slowing, eventually stopping and ultimately reversing GHG emissions causing global warming, in addition to taking further steps of responding with necessary vigour to the inevitable impacts.

International negotiations surrounding climate change now encompass almost all of the world's governments, and indeed many sub-state and non-state actors. The Copenhagen conference was remarkable for its unprecedented international participation. It involved 192 countries, including 119 heads of state and government, making it almost certainly the largest gathering of state leaders in modern history. What is more, tens of thousands of non-governmental delegates and activists participated in the event (IISD, 2009). From this perspective, the response to climate change has been unprecedented and truly 'global' in scope. This is an important historical development. However, the scale of the failure at Copenhagen was as great as was participation in discussions held there. The result was a relatively feeble statement – the Copenhagen Accord (UNFCCC, 2009) – which repeated some aims discussed at the conference but did not require any governments to comply (and, unusually for such UN meetings, was not endorsed by all delegates), much as the 1992 UNFCC did not require compliance, with predictable results. A growing global catastrophe has emerged from scientific circles to catch the attention of the world's leaders, yet they effectively stand frozen, like deer in an car's headlights, unable or unwilling to move despite knowledge of what is to come. Admittedly, the conference did result in some progress on negotiations for long-term cooperative action, the post-Kyoto Protocol process and other issues, but, as in past conferences, progress comes at a snail's pace even as the Earth grows warmer at an accelerating pace. Copenhagen thus revealed a proportional relationship between participation of leaders in climate change conferences and the lack of success. Part of the problem is the myopic attention that governments of states arrogate to themselves. Arguably, the Chinese government is among the governments of several major countries most guilty of this myopia.

China's growing contributions to climate change

Despite a swelling of expectation around the world that the Copenhagen conference would result in a binding agreement among governments to substantially reduce pollution causing climate change, the outcome was little more than the voluntary Copenhagen Accord and hope that a robust agreement might be achieved in time for the 16th Conference of the Parties (COP16) in Cancun, Mexico, in December 2010. Many observers, and indeed some government officials in the West, blamed China for the failure of the Copenhagen meeting, in particular for China's opposition to a binding agreement to reduce global emissions of GHGs by 50% by mid-century (for example, Miliband, 2009).

China was especially strident in opposing any binding cuts in GHGs for any developing countries, although it pledged voluntary efforts to improve its own energy efficiency. Whether China was to blame for the outcome at Copenhagen remains subject to debate, and of course the Chinese strongly denied the accusation (Shi, 2010). What was beyond question, however, was that China had become the largest national source of pollutants causing global warming, thus making its policies and actions central to efforts by governments, industry and individuals to address climate change.

China has been taking steps domestically that will limit its aggregate GHG emissions over business-as-usual scenarios. However, these limitations are far too little compared to the scale of global cuts that will be needed to avert catastrophic climate change. Accordingly, developed countries have pushed China to be more aggressive in limiting its emissions, and to submit to external auditing of the implementation of those limits, ideally to be followed by measurable reductions. These sorts of demands have run up against China's profound sense of grievance generally vis-à-vis the outside world for 20th-century intervention in Chinese affairs (for example, invasions during the first half of the century and perceived efforts to hold back China's development in the second half), and more specifically those demands contradict the argument that the developed countries are to blame for climate change. Consequently, China's diplomatic position does not reflect its new status as the world's largest polluter, nor does it account for the hundreds of millions of newly affluent consumers in China's cities who are consuming and polluting at near-Western levels. Put another way, China's policies on climate change are those of a relatively poor developing country that wishes to focus intently on domestic economic growth and which sees the developed world, particularly the West, as responsible for addressing climate change. China expects wealthy countries to take robust action to limit their own GHG emissions, to reimburse China for the extra cost of more sustainable development practices that it adopts beyond its own domestic plans, and to compensate developing countries for the suffering that will accrue from historical atmospheric pollution.

It was in 2006 that China overtook the United States (US) to become the largest national source of carbon dioxide (CO_2) emissions (Netherlands Environmental Assessment Agency, 2007). China now accounts for a quarter of carbon emissions globally, and in 2008 two thirds of the total global increase in emissions came from China alone (Netherlands Environmental Assessment Agency, 2008). While China's average per-capita emissions remain far below those of the US, in that same year its per-capita emissions surpassed the global average, placing emissions well above those of most developing countries (Boden et al, 2009). Per-capita emissions are levelling off in the developed world, but in China they are increasing rapidly; for example, China's CO_2 emissions are increasing four to six times as fast as US emissions (Asia Society and Pew Centre on Global Climate Change, 2009, p 18). Despite attempts in China to improve energy efficiency, the country's CO_2 emissions from fossil fuel use alone increased by nearly 80% in just the past decade, with most of this coming from the burning of coal (Boden et al, 2009). Indeed, China's coal-fired power sector is the world's largest anthropogenic source of CO_2 emissions (Lewis and Gallagher, 2011, p 259), and by 2009 the country's CO_2 emissions were 24% of the global total, despite China having substantially less than a quarter of the world's population (Friedlingstein et al, 2010).

China's GHG intensity (emissions per unit of economic output) has improved in recent years, but it is nevertheless among the highest in the world, above averages for other developing countries and well above averages in the developed world (Pew Centre on Global Climate Change, 2007, p 1). This is driven to a significant degree by the use of coal to power the country's export-oriented industries. More generally, a significant source of growth in China's emissions is the production of exports, although the majority of production is consumed domestically, with this consumption almost certainly to increase greatly in the future as more Chinese join the global middle class (Asia Society and Pew Centre on Global Climate Change, 2009, pp 18-20). In the run-up to the Copenhagen conference, China agreed to voluntarily implement a 40-45% reduction in the country's carbon intensity by 2020 (referenced from 2005 emissions). However, from 1991 to 2006, the country's total CO_2 emissions doubled even as carbon intensity dropped by 44% (Lewis and Gallagher, 2011, p 273). In just the four years up to 2006, demand for energy in China grew more than it had in the preceding 25 years put together (Asia Society and Pew Centre on Global Climate Change, 2009, p 19). Thus, if recent trends in economic growth continue, even with the Chinese government's Copenhagen pledge, the country's total emissions will increase, possibly sharply.

Cumulative historical carbon emissions from China are about one fourth those of the US (Pew Centre on Global Climate Change, 2007, p 1), which is by far the largest polluter of the atmosphere historically. However, China is expected to overtake the US in this respect as well by mid-century (Botzen et al, 2008). Consequently, it becomes clearer with time that the world cannot possibly address climate change effectively without China's participation in global cutbacks in GHGs, something that has always been said about the US and some other Western countries (and which remains true), but which in the case of China is a new phenomenon that has occurred alongside its rapid economic development over the last three decades.

China's climate-related objectives

What explains China's climate change policies, and what is the government trying to achieve through them? China first became involved in international discussions on climate change in the 1980s when it collaborated with the US to study the impacts of CO_2 emissions (Schroeder, 2009, p 57), thus beginning a process of growing Chinese involvement and interest in climate diplomacy and its impact on international relations, economics and the environment. China's climate change diplomacy became more proactive in the 1990s when it joined with other developing countries to influence negotiation of the 1992 UNFCCC and the 1997 Kyoto Protocol. These negotiations affirmed the principle of common but differentiated responsibility (CBDR) of states for climate change. This principle established that the world's developed countries were most responsible for climate change and thus should take the lead in reducing GHG emissions and helping developing countries address the problem. Generally speaking, for China climate change went from being a scientific issue in the 1980s to being a developmental (and highly politicised) issue by the 1990s (Lewis and Gallagher, 2011, p 269), where it remains today. As a developing country, China is not legally required to limit its GHG emissions in any way. It defends this position and, as demonstrated at Copenhagen, has shown few signs of allowing change in successor agreements to the Kyoto Protocol. Nevertheless, it is taking steps domestically to become more energy efficient, in effect limiting what would otherwise be a larger contribution to global warming.

China's policies on managing climate change are officially guided by six principles (NDRC, 2007, pp 24-5):

- addressing climate change within the broader framework of the country's 'national sustainable development strategy';
- adhering to the principle of CBDR;
- addressing both climate change mitigation and adaptation;
- integrating climate change-related policies with programmes for 'national and social economic development';
- relying on technological advancement for effectively mitigating and adapting to climate change; and

- 'actively and extensively' participating in international cooperation on climate change.

Generally speaking, what comes from these principles is a clear indication that climate change is taken seriously, but also that it does not take priority over China's other national objectives. If climate change mitigation and adaptation can be made consistent with those objectives, China will act forthrightly. If advantages for development and other objectives can be rung from the climate change issue, China will exploit them (for example, in extracting funding and technology for both economic development and GHG mitigation).

The second of these objectives – CBDR – largely determines how far China is willing to go in meeting the demands of outsiders for greater domestic action, particularly with regard to GHG limitations. It is important not to underestimate the extent to which Chinese officials take the principle of CBDR. They interpret it very strictly as requiring that:

> developed countries take the lead in reducing greenhouse gas emissions as well as providing financial and technical support to developing countries. The first and overriding priorities of developing countries are sustainable development and poverty eradication. The extent to which developing countries will effectively implement their commitments under the [UNFCCC] will depend on the effective implementation by developed countries of their basic commitments. (NDRC, 2007, p 24)

A clear statement on China's minimum position with regard to climate change negotiations and obligations can be derived by simply replacing 'developing countries' in this statement of principle with 'China'.

This leads to the Chinese government's overriding short- and medium-term priority in the context of climate change (and in most other policy contexts): economic growth. To be sure, there are a number of other fundamental concerns underlying China's positions, notably:

- sovereignty and non-interference in internal affairs (see Zhang, 2003);
- social stability and regime vitality;
- propaganda and support for the party and the government;
- demonstrating leadership among developing countries and challenging the international authority of the US;

- environmentally sustainable development as a medium- and long-term objective; and
- obtaining aid and technology from developed countries (see Kobayashi, 2003).

Although China's leaders are increasingly concerned about climate change, in terms of both its impacts on the country and its international political ramifications, the issue 'has not surpassed economic development as a policy priority' (Lewis and Gallagher, 2011, p 269). Economic development is in turn tied to the ruling party's policy objectives (for example, lifting the Chinese out of poverty and using growing economic strength for national defence and to ensure territorial integrity) and, very fundamentally, the party's apparent assumption that economic growth is essential to regime survival and more generally to political stability (see Shirk, 2007). In particular, according to Abebe and Masur (2010), the regime is focused on developing the Western provinces to avoid unrest: 'The social and economic disparities between East[ern China] and West[ern China] have made rapid western growth a political imperative for the Chinese Communist Party, which will be loath to sign any climate agreement that might stunt this growth' (Abebe and Masur, 2010, p 388).

While China has many domestic policies related to climate change, such as increasingly significant efforts by the central government to encourage energy efficiency and to provide support for alternative energy production (see Government of China, 2008), those policies are driven by objectives other than fighting climate change, such as energy security, technology innovation to enhance economic competitiveness, and profiting from the Kyoto Protocol's Clean Development Mechanism. In other words, China's climate change policies are only incidentally or at best indirectly related to climate change.[2] This may change as the impacts of climate change to be experienced in China become more immediate, although even then the official calculus may be that economic growth is more desirable given its political and social benefits in the short term and its potential to provide resources to aid adaptation to climate change in the future. In short, the calculus may continue to be that mitigation is more costly for the regime and for the economy than is adaptation. This would help to explain China's focus on adaptation over mitigation in international negotiations over the last decade.

Some scholars argue that the 'norm of climate protection [has] become internalized in Chinese politics' (Schroeder, 2009, p 52), while others focus on the extent to which the Chinese government's rhetorical claims to care about environmental issues are not matched by policy implementation, often due to local corruption (Economy, 2007). What is clearer is that the Chinese government is opposed to outside monitoring of its GHG emissions, an issue that exercised world leaders at the Copenhagen summit. China's policy in this respect is driven first by its obsession with sovereignty and its total opposition to 'intervention' in its internal affairs (see Drexhage and Murphy, 2009, p 3), but also by concerns that the central government simply cannot guarantee that its pledges will be fully implemented. In short, the Chinese government will oppose international policies that could be interpreted by Chinese officials as intervention. China's reticence about allowing outside monitoring of its emissions is also a function of the central government's weak capacity in this respect, exacerbated by the longstanding problem of lack of transparency related to statistics of almost any kind. Thus, the seemingly reasonable demand from the US and some other countries at Copenhagen for China to agree to monitoring of its emissions targets is, from the Chinese perspective, partly unreasonable and partly unworkable.

Until very recently, China stood alongside developing and very poor countries in international negotiations related to climate change. Indeed, experts have argued that its positions rarely deviate from those of the developing world (see, for example, Lewis, 2007-2008, p 163; Harris and Yu, 2009, p 62). However, this changed quite dramatically at the Copenhagen conference when China joined forces with a number of large and relatively well-off developing countries — the so-called BASIC states, comprising Brazil, South Africa, India and China — to refuse binding limitations on these countries' GHG emissions despite pleadings from extremely vulnerable poor countries, especially small-island states, for China to accept GHG limitations that might help mitigate what for them is an existential threat. To this extent, China is no longer a champion of the developing world; like many rich countries, it is now unquestionably a champion of its own national interests regardless of the costs for those countries that are most vulnerable to climate change.

China's position in future international negotiations on climate change could go in one of three directions. It is possible, perhaps likely in the near term, that the government will dig in its heels (alongside some other large developing countries, such as the BASIC states) and refuse to alter the position it took in Copenhagen. Alternatively, China may surprise analysts by becoming much more proactive in agreeing to limits on its GHG emissions. Also possible is something in between, but close to its historical position — reaffirmed so forthrightly at

Copenhagen – to refuse binding emissions limitations while gradually agreeing to voluntary emissions measures, perhaps starting with a stronger energy-intensity target (given that the one agreed in the context of Copenhagen lacked ambition) and eventually agreement on a firm date when China's emissions will peak and begin to decline. China probably will not agree to economy-wide limitations on GHG emissions, but it is likely to agree to limitations within specific programmes and projects, especially when those can benefit from deployment of alternative energy sources coming on line and already planned. At the same time, China will continue to enact and try to implement policies domestically that move more or less in the direction of GHG limitations, consistent with broader national developmental goals (cf Lewis and Gallagher, 2011, p 273).

What is clear at this point in time is that the Chinese government is not planning to make major concessions on climate change in the near future. Indeed, Su Wei, China's top official on climate change matters, said in early 2010 that the country's emissions would have to increase, that the government will continue to be guided by the CBDR principle and that 'China "could not and should not" set an upper limit on greenhouse gas emissions' (Xinhua, 2010). Consequently, agreement from China to take on new binding obligations to cap or limit – least of all reduce – its GHG emissions, or to submit to independent verification of those emissions, seems unlikely at present (see Shi, 2010). Bold moves by developed countries towards reducing their own GHG emissions are almost certainly a *prerequisite* for such a change in Chinese policy in the medium term.

China's climate change policy will be influenced by events in the US. If a compromise on climate change-related energy legislation can be reached in Washington (a possibility, albeit with many compromises and thus relatively meagre US emissions cuts), it is likely that the medium-term outcome will be trade-related measures (that is, tariffs) by the US and indeed other Western countries to address China's relatively high emissions per unit of production (see Pew Centre on Global Climate Change, 2009). If not handled properly, pressure on China from these measures could result in a backlash whereby China actually delays climate-related policies to avoid the appearance of giving in to outside pressure, such is the importance of its historical grievance vis-à-vis the outside world.

Domestic policies related to management of climate change (but not directly driven by the problem) are easier to predict. China will continue to become more energy efficient relative to economic output, and new energy-efficient technologies will be adopted in so far as they are consistent with overall development objectives (that is, the cost–benefit analysis of adopting them is favourable relative to less efficient technologies) and when they bring in additional funding, investment and access to technology from abroad. In short, China's GHG emissions will not be as high as they might be without conscious efforts by the government and international partners to encourage more environmentally sustainable development domestically. Whether this will be enough to actually bring the increase in China's emissions to a halt anytime soon, and then to start reducing them, is an open question – but this is unlikely to start happening soon enough to avert many of the severe consequences of climate change.

Exploring China's responsibility for climate change

Contributions to this volume help to answer the question of whether and how China is responsible for climate change. The chapters are arranged into three additional parts. Part Two of the book assesses responsibilities for climate change and related considerations of fairness and rights. Part Three examines the implications of climate-related responsibilities for climate policy. Part Four concludes the book, focusing especially on the role of individuals in causing and responding to climate change.

Determining responsibility

We begin in Chapter Two with Derek Bell's analysis of historical emissions, climate duties and human rights. As we have seen, like the governments of many other developing countries, the Chinese government adheres to two fundamental principles. The first principle is that of historical responsibility or 'polluter pays', which affirms that developed states of the global North should bear the costs of addressing climate change because they are historically responsible for most GHG emissions that have causally contributed to problem. According to the Chinese interpretation of this principle, current and future allocations of costs associated with dealing with climate change should be based on each state's cumulative or historical emissions of GHGs. The second principle is that developing countries of the global South have a right to development. They should not be required to sacrifice their development to address problems arising from climate change. Consequently, the costs of climate change should be borne by those who can afford to bear them, namely the developed countries. With this in mind, Bell outlines an account of 'climate justice' that addresses the question of how to fairly allocate the costs of climate change. Drawing on the 'Greenhouse Development Rights' framework, he arrives at a human rights-based approach to climate justice, albeit one that rejects the principle of 'equal per-capita emissions' and focuses instead on duties of rectification that anyone who fails to comply with a general climate duty should incur. Bell argues, consistent with the Chinese position, that citizens of developed countries have duties to pay compensation for their excessive and unjust GHG emissions during the last 20 or 30 years. However, Bell concludes that earlier historical emissions are not relevant in the straightforward way that Chinese officials may assume.

In Chapter Three, Olivia Bina looks more deeply at climate change and the rights to development often asserted by China. She believes that, particularly in the case of China, economic growth and environmental protection have never been in such conflict as they are now. She argues that 'the climate change crisis is the ultimate expression of unsustainable patterns of growth'. The tension surrounding climate change negotiations is closely linked to the unresolved question of how to reconcile aggressive pursuit of economic growth with the Earth's ecological limits. The use of energy is illustrative, with Bina describing in some detail China's enormous contribution to the global growth in the use of fossil fuels. Indeed, she points out that three fourths of the increase in energy-related CO_2 emissions to 2030 will come from China. After linking climate change to economic growth, Bina explores the question of responsibility for limiting GHG emissions as it relates to the pursuit of economic development. According to Bina, China's leaders have an opportunity to embark on a development path that avoids 'undifferentiated irresponsibility' of *all* countries, rather than the common but differentiated responsibility that has been agreed in international climate negotiations. For Bina, the promise of a 'new path for development' can be realised if China pursues bold alternatives to so-called 'efficient growth'.

Following a theme that permeates the book, in Chapter Four Christian Ellermann, Niklas Höhne and Benito Müller examine historical responsibilities for climate change. Like other contributors, they pull apart the notion of historical responsibility and challenge common assumptions about it, doing so through rigorous analysis of data. Their chapter delves into a politically sensitive aspect of past GHG emissions, namely the issue of *differentiating* historical responsibility. In so doing it shows that *contributions to* climate change and *responsibility for* it are fundamentally different. Ellermann, Höhne and Müller describe a methodology for calculating 'shares of responsibility' – rather than 'shares of causal contribution', which are more commonly addressed in analytical models. They apply their methodology to the case of China, using two conceptions of responsibility – 'strict' and 'limited' – to help operationalise the CBDR principle in the Chinese context. The key message resulting from Ellermann, Höhne and Müller's calculations is that causal contributions to climate change, while an important indicator of environmental impact, ought not be confused with moral and legal responsibility for the problem. The significant difference between *contribution to* climate change and *responsibility for* it requires us to think in new ways about the sorts of burdens that can justly be demanded when applying the CBDR concept, notably in the case of China.

In Chapter Five, Jonathan Symons looks at China's responsibility for climate change in a new way, basing his analysis on whether China is cooperating with other countries to solve the problem. Given the divergent conceptions of fairness held by different countries, Symons argues that *cooperation* should be accepted as an independent normative goal within climate negotiations, and that each government's negotiating position should be assessed against the pragmatic standard of its contribution to effective international cooperation. As a measure of the point at which fairness concerns become an obstacle to cooperation, he draws on the distinction between 'equitable CBDR', which tilts the distribution of cooperative surplus towards certain parties, and 'inefficient CBDR', which allocates more than the entire net surplus of cooperation to certain parties and so strips states of their incentive to cooperate. Symons argues that the emissions-intensity targets that China promised at Copenhagen were consistent with both equitable CBDR and a cooperative outcome. However, China's refusal to accept the targets as *binding* totally undermines its positive contribution, making the country a central obstacle to international cooperation. Symons develops a 'non-cooperator pays' principle, which states that 'actors negotiating to secure an essential public good that cannot be provided without widespread cooperation are justified in seeking to induce cooperation by imposing costs on non-cooperators, even if this cost allocation would be considered unjust in the absence of the collective action problem'. Given that Symons argues for a country's responsibility for climate change to be assessed in terms of both its contribution to international cooperation and its actual emissions, it might be fair for future international agreements to penalise China for its failure to be more cooperative. Controversially, one way to do this might be border tax adjustments or carbon tariffs that equalise the costs of GHG emissions that are embodied in China's exports.

Policy implications

Part Two of the book continues to assess China's responsibilities related to climate change, in the process looking more intently at related implications for the country's domestic and international policies. In Chapter Six, Erich W. Schienke looks at the many ways in which ethical obligations related to climate change play out across various sectors inside China. He considers China's obligations according to eight 'ethical dimensions': responsibility for damages, atmospheric targets, allocation of emissions, uncertainty, economic costs, responsibility to act, technology and procedural fairness. Schienke describes the ethics of what he calls 'China's climate problem' as a series of interrelated issues at multiple 'scales of governance'. Schienke argues that a normative analysis of China's obligations may not fully reveal that what seems to be ethically coherent at the scale of national governance is something that becomes quite difficult to interpret as clear ethical directives at the levels of regional, local or urban governance. Although the nation of China may have a clear directive as to how much it needs to mitigate to reduce emissions, how to implement the distribution of mitigation efforts to regions with diverse geography and distribution of wealth is less clear. The problem of distributing China's mitigation costs and efforts internally is made even more ethically complex when one takes into account mismatches between scales of governance, such as the size and scope of institutions and the scales of certain ecosystems, such as carbon sinks in forests that may cross multiple municipalities or regional authorities. That is, saying what China's ethical obligations should be to address global climate change is much more straightforward than determining how it should actually address climate change as an internal matter of governance.

Another approach to the question of China's climate-related responsibilities is found in Chapter Seven. Instead of the much more common analysis of long-term greenhouse gases, such as CO_2, in this chapter Frances C. Moore and Michael C. MacCracken look at questions of climate fairness from the perspective of so-called 'short-lived' GHGs, in particular black carbon. Short-lived GHGs, which also contribute to general air pollution, have a major role in global warming; black carbon alone is probably the second or third most important GHG. Unlike cutting CO_2, reducing emissions of these short-lived GHGs results in a rapid reduction in their contribution to global warming. The short-lived pollutants also have significant adverse impacts on human and environmental health at regional and local levels. Significantly, technologies to reduce emissions of these gases are readily available, cost-effective and already widely deployed in developed countries. Reducing these pollutants is therefore a relatively easy mitigation pathway for developing countries that is both appropriate to their level of development and highly effective from the perspective of climate. It is also consistent with principles of fairness based on responsibility and capability that have been important in international negotiations on climate change. As such, cutting short-lived GHGs offers a pathway out of the current deadlock between developed and developing countries in which each group asks for more substantial emissions–reduction commitments from the other before taking action. As the world's largest black-carbon soot emitter, China could push for substantial CO_2 mitigation commitments from the developed countries in return for more aggressive action than it is presently taking to reduce its soot emissions. Such an approach would be consistent with China's own development strategy, would contribute substantially to the mitigation of climate change and would lower the likelihood of passing serious and potentially irreversible tipping points in the coming decades.

In Chapter Eight, Patrick Schroeder looks at China's responsibility for climate change from the perspective of 'sustainable consumption and production' (SCP). The SCP approach is an integrative analytical perspective that captures the complex relationship between economic activity, human wellbeing and environmental degradation. It is what Schroeder describes as an 'international political process to promote and support policies and actions necessary for systemic transition towards sustainable consumption and production patterns'. SCP encompasses a set of practical solutions or tools for addressing social, economic and environmental problems arising from unsustainable production and consumption. Drawing on the SCP perspective, the chapter discusses the responsibilities of a range of stakeholders in China's consumption-and-production systems that are connected through global value chains. Schroeder shows that attributing responsibility for China's growing impacts on global climate is a complex issue because responsibility should be shared between producers and consumers within China *and* in other countries. The chapter identifies opportunities for using the SCP approach to undertake 'environmental leapfrogging' in the areas of energy, industrial manufacturing, urban development and consumer behaviour. According to Schroeder, the application of the conceptual and practical approaches of SCP is necessary if China is to address the underlying causes of climate change and move towards a low-carbon economy and society.

In the penultimate chapter of the book, Andreas Oberheitmann and Eva Sternfeld analyse the implications for China of a new post-Kyoto climate change regime based on cumulative per-capita CO_2 emissions. They begin by reminding us that nearly half of the global increase in carbon emissions over the last decade has come from China alone. Consequently, they argue that great importance must be attached to China's environmental and energy policies and its involvement in shaping the post-Kyoto climate change regime. Oberheitmann and Sternfeld's chapter aims to start devising such a regime and to analyse the role that China might play in it. They describe several proposals for post-Kyoto regimes that have been discussed internationally, showing that all of them have drawbacks. For example, the biggest disadvantage of approaches taken so far is that they fail to make allowance for the fact that China (and other newly industrialised countries) are becoming increasingly responsible for future concentrations of CO_2 that are now accumulating in the atmosphere. Nevertheless, those approaches employ a fair mechanism for allocating emissions rights in terms of per-capita allowances. With this in mind, Oberheitmann and Sternfeld propose a new climate regime based on *cumulative* per-capita CO_2 emission rights measured in a way that they believe resolves the disadvantages inherent in other approaches. Environmental equity in responsibility for climate change can be achieved if historical carbon emissions of developed countries since 1750 are taken into account *along with* the growing emissions since the 1980s of China and other developing countries. An international trading system based on their new regime might encourage low-carbon technology transfer, and it might provide financial support to help China develop more sustainably.

In Part Four and Chapter Ten, I return to some of the major themes of the book in a final attempt (in this book) to answer the underlying question at hand: is China responsible for climate change? Not surprisingly, the answer must always be prefaced by 'it depends'. It depends on whether we are looking only at the Chinese state or also at the Chinese people. Arguably, the responsibility of the former is less from the perspective of the past and greater from a future perspective. What seems beyond doubt is that some people in China are already responsible for their contributions to future climate change, and for doing something about it right now.

Notes

[1] Parts of this chapter build on Harris (2010a, 2010b).

[2] Arguably, it does not matter from whence the motivation for implementing climate-friendly policies originates. What matters is the effect. However, the policies might be far more robust, and more routinely implemented, if they were motivated by a strong official desire to mitigate the causes and consequences of climate change.

References

Abebe, D. and Masur, J.S. (2010) 'International agreements, internal heterogeneity, and climate change: the "two Chinas" problem', *Virginia Journal of International Law*, vol 50, no 2, pp 326-89.

Asia Society and Pew Centre on Global Climate Change (2009) *Common challenge: A roadmap for U.S.–China cooperation on energy and climate change*, Arlington, VA: Pew Centre on Global Climate Change and Asia Society.

Boden, T.A., Marland, G. and Andres, R.J. (2009) *Global, regional, and national fossil-fuel CO_2 emissions*, Oak Ridge, TN: Oak Ridge National Laboratory.

Botzen, W.J.W., Gowdy, J.M. and Van Den Bergh, J.C.J.M. (2008) 'Cumulative CO_2 emissions: shifting international responsibilities for climate debt', *Climate Policy*, vol 8, pp 569-76.

den Egenhofer, C. and Georgiev, A. (2009) *The Copenhagen Accord: A first stab at deciphering the implications for the EU*, Brussels: Centre for European Policy Studies.

Drexhage, J. and Murphy, D. (2009) 'Copenhagen: a memorable time for all the wrong reasons?', *IISD commentary*, Winnipeg: International Institute for Sustainable Development.

Economy, E. (2007) 'The great leap backward?', *Foreign Affairs*, vol 86, no 5, pp 38-59.

Friedlingstein, P., Houghton, R.A., Marland, G., Hackler, J., Boden, T.A., Conway, J., Canadell, J.G., Raupach, M.R., Ciais, P. and Le Quéré, C. (2010) 'Update on CO2 emissions', *Nature Geoscience*, vol 3, no 11 (doi: 10.1038/ngeo1022).

Government of China (2008) *China's policies and actions for addressing climate change*, White Paper, Beijing: Government of the People's Republic of China.

Hamilton, C. (2010) *Requiem for a species: Why we resist the truth about climate change*, London: Earthscan.

Harris, P.G. (2010a) 'China and climate change: from Copenhagen to Cancun', *Environmental Law Reporter: News & Analysis*, vol 40, no 9, pp 10858-63.

Harris, P.G. (2010b) 'Misplaced ethics of climate change: political vs. environmental geography', *Ethics, Place & Environment*, vol 13, no 2, pp 215-22.

Harris, P.G. and Yu, H. (2009) 'Climate change in Chinese foreign policy: internal and external responses', in P.G. Harris (ed) *Climate change and foreign policy: Case studies from East to West* (pp 52-67), London: Routledge.

Hu Jintao (2009) 'Join hands to address climate change', Statement by H.E. Hu Jintao, President of the People's Republic of China, at the Opening Plenary Session of the United Nations Summit on Climate Change, New York, 22 September.

IISD (International Institute for Sustainable Development) (2009) *A brief analysis of the Copenhagen climate change conference*, New York, NY: IISD Reporting Services.

IPCC (Intergovernmental Panel on Climate Change) (2007) *Climate change 2007: Synthesis report*, Cambridge: Cambridge University Press.

Kobayashi, Y. (2003) 'Navigating between "luxury" and survival emissions: tensions in China's multilateral and bilateral climate change diplomacy', in P.G. Harris (ed) *Global warming and East Asia: The domestic and international politics of climate change* (pp 86-108), London: Routledge.

Lewis, J.I. (2007-2008) 'China's strategic priorities in international climate change negotiations', *Washington Quarterly*, vol 31, no 1, pp 155-74.

Lewis, J.I. and Gallagher, K.S. (2011) 'Energy and environment in China: achievements and enduring challenges', in R.S. Axelrod, S.D. Vandeveer and D.L. Downie (eds) *The global environment: Institutions, law and policy* (pp 259-84), Washington, DC: CQ Press.

McCarthy, J.J. (2009) 'Reflections on our planet and its life, origins, and futures', *Science*, vol 326, no 5960, pp 1646-55.

McMullen, C.P. and Jabbour, J. (eds) (2009) *Climate change science compendium 2009*, Nairobi: United Nations Environment Programme.

Miliband, E. (2009) 'The road from Copenhagen', *The Guardian*, 20 December, www.guardian.co.uk/commentisfree/2009/dec/20/copenhagen-climate-change-accord

NDRC (National Development and Reform Commission) (2007) *China's National Climate Change Programme*, Beijing: NDRC.

Netherlands Environmental Assessment Agency (2007) 'China now no. 1 in CO$_2$ emissions; USA in second position' (press release), The Hague: Netherlands Environmental Assessment Agency.

Netherlands Environmental Assessment Agency (2008) 'China contributing two-thirds to CO$_2$ emissions' (press release), The Hague: Netherlands Environmental Assessment Agency.

Pew Centre on Global Climate Change (2007) 'Climate change mitigation measures in the People's Republic of China', *International Brief*, no 1, www.pewclimate.org/policy_center/international_policy

Pew Centre on Global Climate Change (2009) 'Addressing competitiveness issues in climate legislation', *Climate Policy Memo*, no 5, www.pewclimate.org/acesa/addressing-competitiveness

Rasmussen, L.L. and Ban, K.M. (2009) 'Letter from the Prime Minister of Denmark and the United Nations', www.stm.dk/_p_12544.html

Schroeder, M. (2009) 'The construction of China's climate politics: transnational NGOs and the spiral model of international relations', in P.G. Harris (ed) *The politics of climate change: Environmental dynamics in international affairs* (pp 51-71), London: Routledge.

Shi, J. (2010) 'Wen offers his personal account of Copenhagen climate summit snub', *South China Morning Post*, 15 March, pp A5-A6.

Shirk, S. (2007) *China: Fragile superpower*, Oxford: Oxford University Press.

UNEP (United Nations Environment Programme) (2009) *Climate change science compendium*, Nairobi: UNEP.

UNEP (2010) *The emissions gap report: Are the Copenhagen Accord pledges sufficient to limit global warming to 2° C or 1.5° C? – a preliminary assessment* (November 2010 advance copy), Nairobi: UNEP, www.unep.org/publications/ebooks/emissionsgapreport/

UNFCCC (United Nations Framework Convention on Climate Change) (2009) *Copenhagen Accord*, New York, NY: United Nations, http://unfccc.int/resource/docs/2009 /cop15/eng/l07.pdf

Xinhua (2010) 'China has "no intention" of capping emissions', Xinhua News Agency, 25 February, http://news.xinhuanet.com/english2010/china/2010-02/25/c_13187687.htm

Zhang, Z. (2003) 'The forces behind China's climate change policy: interests, sovereignty and prestige', in P.G. Harris (ed) *Global warming and East Asia: The domestic and international politics of climate change* (pp 66-85), London: Routledge.

Part Two
Determining responsibility

TWO

Climate duties, human rights and historical emissions

Derek Bell

The 15th Conference of the Parties (COP15) to the United Nations Framework Convention on Climate Change (UNFCCC) did not produce the hoped-for successor to the Kyoto Protocol. Instead, 'Decision 2' of COP15 *takes note* of the Copenhagen Accord of 18 December 2009' (UNFCCC, 2009, p 4; emphasis in original). The Copenhagen Accord is an agreement among 'Heads of State, Heads of Government, Ministers, and other heads of ... delegations' present at COP15, but it is not a protocol to the UNFCCC (UNFCCC, 2009, p 5). Instead, it is a voluntary agreement that sets no emissions targets for states but rather asks them to submit to the UNFCCC secretariat details of their own planned voluntary emissions reductions or mitigation actions. So, while the signatories recognise that 'climate change is one of the greatest challenges of our time', they have not signed up to mandatory emissions reductions (UNFCCC, 2009, p 5).

China's submission to the secretariat states that:

> China will endeavor to lower its carbon dioxide emissions per unit of GDP [gross domestic product] by 40-45% by 2020 compared to the 2005 level, increase the share of non-fossil fuels in primary energy consumption to around 15% by 2020 and increase forest coverage by 40 million hectares and forest stock by 1.3 billion cubic meters by 2020 from the 2005 levels. (NDRC, 2010)

These commitments impose no absolute limits on China's greenhouse gas emissions. Moreover, the Chinese submission emphasises that 'the above-mentioned autonomous domestic mitigation actions are voluntary in nature and will be implemented in accordance with the principles and provisions of the UNFCCC, in particular Article 4, paragraph 7' (NDRC, 2010). The voluntary character of the Chinese mitigation actions is important, but the reference to Article 4, paragraph

7 of the UNFCCC may be even more important. This paragraph states that:

> The extent to which developing country Parties will effectively implement their commitments under the Convention will depend on the effective implementation by developed country Parties of their commitments under the Convention related to financial resources and transfer of technology and will take fully into account that economic and social development and poverty eradication are the first and overriding priorities of the developing country Parties. (UNFCCC, 1992, Article 4, paragraph 7)

The reference to this paragraph suggests that China's voluntary commitments are contingent in two respects. First, they are contingent on funding and technology transfer from developed states. If developed states do not provide finance and technology, China should not be expected to undertake its voluntary mitigation actions. Second, they are contingent on their compatibility with China's 'first and overriding priorities' of 'economic and social development and poverty eradication'. If China must compromise either its economic and social development or poverty eradication to undertake successfully its voluntary mitigation actions, it should not be expected to undertake those actions.

China's submission to the UNFCCC secretariat reflects the government's more general position on the allocation of the costs of mitigation and adaptation – or, more generally, the allocation of 'climate duties'. China recognises the significance of the threats posed by climate change but it insists that the costs associated with climate change should be borne primarily by the developed states. The Chinese position, like the position of many states in the global South, affirms two important principles. First, the principle of historic responsibility – or the polluter pays principle – affirms that the costs associated with climate change should be met by the developed states (or the global North) because they are historically responsible for most of the greenhouse gas (GHG) emissions that have causally contributed to anthropogenic climate change. The current and future allocation of the costs associated with anthropogenic climate change should be based on each state's cumulative historical emissions. Second, the developing states have a right to development. They should not be required to sacrifice development to address the problems associated with climate change. Therefore, the costs associated with climate change should be borne only by those who can afford to bear those costs – namely the developed states.

In this chapter, I will outline an account of 'climate justice' that addresses the problem of fairly allocating the costs associated with climate change. In the first section, I begin from a particular interpretation of the notion of a right to development. The proposed interpretation is based on the 'Greenhouse Development Rights' approach suggested by Paul Baer and his collaborators. I suggest that Baer's individualistic interpretation of the right to development leads us to a human rights-based approach to climate justice. I outline two further rights that follow from the human right to development. In the following sections, I consider how an account of climate duties might be developed from these rights-based commitments. In the second section, I consider Onora O'Neill's well-known objection to rights-based theories of justice, namely that they do not tell us how to allocate the correlative duties. I consider a response to this objection and I propose an account of climate duties that distinguishes three kinds of duty that should be included in a full theory of climate duties.[1]

In the remaining sections of the chapter, I consider these three kinds of duty in more detail and in relation to historical emissions. In the third section, I consider what I call the 'general climate duty', namely the duty to promote effective institutions for the fair specification and allocation of particular climate duties. More specifically, I consider when this duty might have been first acquired by citizens and states in the global North. In the fourth section, I consider principles for specifying and allocating climate duties under just (fair and effective) institutions. In particular, I consider the claim that the global North should be held responsible for historical emissions because its citizens have exceeded their equal per-capita share of emission rights. I argue that the principle of equal per-capita emissions should be rejected. In the fifth section, I outline an account of the duties of rectification that anyone who fails (or has failed) to comply with the general climate duty should incur and I suggest that this has important implications for how we think about arguments from historic responsibility. The final section summarises the arguments of the chapter.

The right to development and basic human rights

The right to development is a controversial idea, which may be interpreted in various ways. Paul Baer et al (2007, p 16) have suggested a way 'to make the abstract notion of a right to development a reality' in the context of climate change. They argue (2007, p 16) that:

> In our climate–constrained world, the right to development
> is not a right to growth, as such, in the quest for indefinitely
> expanding wealth. It is, rather, a right to a particular level
> of development, a modest but dignified level of well-being.
> We define this level by way of a *development threshold*. Below
> this threshold, individuals must be allowed to prioritize
> development.

Baer et al make clear that they understand the right to development as
'a right of individuals, not countries' (Baer et al, 2009, p 269; see also
Baer et al, 2007, p 18). In other words, the right to development is an
individual human right to a 'modest but dignified level of wellbeing'.
Baer et al recognise that any particular claims about the level at which
the 'development threshold' should be set, or about what constitutes
'a modest but dignified level of wellbeing', are likely to be 'somewhat
arbitrary' (Baer et al, 2007, p 17). However, they suggest that individuals
with an income of less than US$7,500 (purchasing power parity
adjusted) have the right to prioritise their own development over
other issues (Baer et al, 2009, p 269). In other words, they suggest
that a 'modest but dignified level of wellbeing' may not be available
to individuals with an income below this level but will normally be
available to individuals with an income above this level.

Baer et al's individualistic understanding of the right to development
may not be in keeping with more common statist conceptions of the
right to development. However, it seems difficult to resist the claim that
we care about development because we care that individuals are able to
achieve a 'modest but dignified level of wellbeing'. If it is plausible to
understand the right to development as an individual human right to
a 'modest but dignified level of wellbeing', we might usefully consider
the implications of this right for a theory of climate justice.

I want to suggest that there are two important climate–related rights
that follow from this understanding of the right to development. First,
the right to a 'modest but dignified level of wellbeing' implies a right
to the necessary means to achieve that level of wellbeing. For example,
if burning fossil fuels is the only available means for a person to keep
warm or to meet other important 'needs' (which are constitutive of a
'modest but dignified level of wellbeing'), the right to development
implies that they have a right to burn fossil fuels. In other words, the
right to development implies that individuals below the development
threshold should not be required to limit their GHG emissions unless
they have alternative means readily available to them that would allow
them to achieve a 'modest but dignified level of wellbeing' without

burning fossil fuels. As Baer et al suggest, the right to development implies that those below the development threshold 'should be exempt from any requirement to pay for climate policy' (Baer et al, 2009, p 269).

Second, the right to a 'modest but dignified level of wellbeing' implies a right not to be reduced below a 'modest but dignified level of wellbeing' by the adverse effects of anthropogenic climate change. The fourth assessment report of the Intergovernmental Panel on Climate Change states that '[t]he health status of millions of people is projected to be affected through, for example, increases in malnutrition; increased deaths, diseases and injury due to extreme weather events; increased burden of diarrhoeal diseases; ... and the altered spatial distribution of some infectious diseases' (IPCC, 2007, p 48). We can expect that climate change will cause many people to die from malnutrition, extreme weather events (including flooding, heat waves, wildfires and hurricanes), diarrhoeal diseases, infectious diseases and lack of water. We can expect that the wellbeing of billions of other people will be affected very adversely by climate change. Human emissions of GHGs will make (and already have made) a significant causal contribution to many people remaining or being brought below the development threshold throughout the world (IPCC, 2007, p 33), particularly in some areas of the global South. In short, anthropogenic climate change might now be considered to be a 'standard threat', against which individuals should be protected, to the right to a 'modest but dignified level of wellbeing' (Shue, 1980, p 13).[2]

So far, I have outlined a human rights interpretation of one of the two key principles advocated by China and other developing states, namely the right to development. Building on the work of Paul Baer and his colleagues, I have suggested that the human right to a 'modest but dignified level of wellbeing' implies two further climate-related rights: first, the right of those below the development threshold to be 'exempt from any requirement to pay for climate policy'; and second, the right not be held or forced below the development threshold as a consequence of the adverse effects of anthropogenic climate change. In the remainder of this chapter, I propose to explore the implications of this rights-based approach for a theory of climate justice. In particular, I consider how we might develop an account of climate duties that are correlative to the second derivative right that we have identified (that is, the right not to be held or forced below the development threshold as a consequence of the adverse effects of anthropogenic climate change) while also respecting the first derivative right (that is, the right of those below the development threshold to be 'exempt from any requirement to pay for climate policy'). In other words, my aim is to develop an account of climate duties that begins to tell us who is required to do what to prevent the harms associated with climate change. This account will help us to judge China's responsibility, or lack of it, for climate change. I will pay particular attention to the place of the principle of historic responsibility – the other key principle advocated by China and other developing states – in a theory of climate duties. Does a theory of climate justice grounded in the right to development support the Chinese claim that the costs associated with climate change should be borne primarily by the global North because the global North is historically responsible for climate change?

The general duty and particular duties

O'Neill has argued that the problem with rights-based theories is that they do not tell us who has the duty to protect rights (see, for example, O'Neill, 1986, pp 101-3, 1996, pp 129-35). O'Neill's particular target is positive rights, such as rights to welfare or education, because she assumes that we can specify the duties that are correlative to negative rights, such as the right *not* to be killed or injured. However, O'Neill's concern about unspecified duties extends to negative rights when those rights can be violated by the cumulative actions and collective practices – working through complex causal chains – of many millions of people.[3] In the context of anthropogenic climate change, a human rights-based theory does not seem to tell us what we most need to know: Who has a duty to do what? When do a person's GHG emissions, or other actions, violate the human right to development of victims of anthropogenic climate change?

In reply to O'Neill's concerns, Ashford (2007, p 217) has suggested that we can identify a duty that is correlative to human rights – namely the duty to promote and maintain effective institutions that will fairly 'specify and allocate' the particular duties needed to ensure the protection of human rights. If we take human rights seriously and we do not have clear and widely acknowledged criteria for specifying and allocating correlative duties, then we should recognise a duty to promote and maintain effective institutions that will fairly specify and allocate the duties needed to ensure the protection of human rights. Let us call this the 'general duty'. In the context of climate change, we might recognise a 'general climate duty' – namely the duty to promote and maintain effective institutions that will fairly specify and allocate the particular duties needed to ensure the protection of the human right to development *from the threat posed by anthropogenic climate change*. The general climate duty is implicit in the broader general duty once we recognise climate change as a 'standard threat' to the human right to development (Shue, 1980, p 13).[4]

The main problem with both the general duty and the general climate duty is that they still do not specify or allocate particular duties to individuals. Instead, they attempt to defer the problem by requiring us to promote institutions that will solve the problem for us by fairly specifying and allocating particular duties to individuals. However, the problem cannot be so easily deferred for two reasons. First, the duty to promote institutions that will fairly specify and allocate particular duties to individuals might plausibly be re-described as a duty to promote just institutions. However, I can only fulfil my duty to promote just institutions by promoting a particular substantive conception of justice. However, a particular substantive conception of justice will be (or will entail) an account of how particular rights and duties should be specified and allocated to individuals. In other words, we can only fulfil our duty to promote substantively just institutions if we already have an account of how particular duties should be specified and allocated to individuals. The general climate duty cannot be fulfilled unless we have a prior account of (or principles for) the fair specification and allocation of particular duties.

The second problem with the general climate duty is that it produces an additional problem of specification and allocation – namely the problem of specifying and allocating the general climate duty itself. If the promotion of fair and effective (or just) institutions is a collective endeavour, we will need to work out what the duty to promote just institutions requires from particular individuals at particular times and places. It is, for example, plausible that the general duty requires different actions from President Obama than it does from the average citizen of the United States. Similarly, it might require different actions from the average citizen of the United Kingdom than it does from a person living on less than $1 per day in a developing nation. In other words, a full account of the general climate duty will include an account of the fair specification and allocation of the duty to promote just institutions.

These important concerns about the general climate duty might lead us to the conclusion that we should look for an alternative response to O'Neill's criticism of rights-based theories. However, I think that would be premature. We have seen that the general climate duty cannot offer a complete solution to the problem of identifying the duties that are correlative to basic human rights. However, it does offer us a useful way of approaching the problem. The general climate duty suggests a particular structure for an account of each person's particular duties. It points us towards two sets of particular duties that a theory of human rights-based duties will need to specify and allocate. First, we need principles for the allocation of the duty to promote just institutions. These principles will tell us how to determine who should do what to promote just institutions. Second, we need principles for the specification and allocation of particular duties (to protect the human right to development from the threat posed by anthropogenic climate change) under fair and effective institutions. These principles will tell us who should do what when we have just institutions to protect the human right to development.

In addition, a theory of human rights-based duties may need to specify duties of rectification if our duty to promote just institutions is not fulfilled.[5] So, the third part of an account of human rights-based duties should include principles for the specification and allocation of duties that arise from the failure of some people to comply with their particular duties to promote just institutions. For example, if the failure of some of us to comply with our duty to promote just institutions prevents or delays the development and implementation of just institutions, we need to work out how (if at all) this affects the future duties of both the compliers and the non-compliers.

In the next three sections, I consider how we might begin to develop these three parts of an account of human rights-based duties in the particular context of climate change. More specifically, I consider the role and relevance of historical emissions in the proposed account of climate duties. In the third section of this chapter, I consider when we might first have acquired the general climate duty. I relate this discussion to the claim that the global North should pay the costs of anthropogenic climate change because it is morally culpable for its historical emissions, as argued by Chinese diplomats. In the fourth section, I consider one account of how climate duties should be allocated under just institutions. I argue that we should reject the idea of a universal right to equal emissions (or 'equal emissions over time') and, therefore, I suggest that all historical emissions should not be counted equally. In the fifth section, I consider duties of rectification. I outline some important duties of rectification and I suggest that it is the *recent* historical emissions of the global North that are likely to generate the most significant duties.

The duty to promote fair and effective institutions

The general duty to promote fair and effective institutions for the protection of human rights is a duty that has existed for as long as human rights have existed. However, the general *climate* duty to promote fair and effective institutions for the protection of the human right to development from the threat posed by climate change may be better understood as a newer duty. The human right to development, which is threatened by climate change, is not a new human right that has only come into existence with this environmental problem. It is a human right that can be violated in many different ways. Anthropogenic climate change is a new threat to – or a new way of violating – that right. Therefore, the original formulation of human rights, or the human right to development, could not plausibly have identified climate-related duties. This is a case where changes in 'circumstances which were not predicted ... give rise to a new duty which was not predicted in advance' (Raz, 1986, p 185). The duties that are correlative to human rights, including the right to development, will change over time because the 'typical major threats' will change over time (Shue, 1980, p 33). Anthropogenic climate change is a new way of violating human rights, which gives rise to new duties, including a new general *climate* duty to promote fair and effective institutions for the protection of the human right to development *from the new threat posed by anthropogenic climate change*. This is a normal result of the 'dynamic character' of human rights (Raz, 1986, p 185).

The general climate duty is a relatively new duty, but when did it come into existence? I want to suggest that two conditions are relevant to determining when the general climate duty came into existence. First, we have seen that the general climate duty is a response to the new 'standard threat' posed by climate change to the human right to development. Therefore, the general climate duty cannot have come into existence before climate change posed a 'standard threat' to that right. Two points of clarification are in order here. First, we should distinguish between the time at which climate change became a 'standard threat' to the human right to development and the time at which humans could reasonably have recognised climate change as a 'standard threat' to the human right to development. It is, at least, possible that climate change posed a serious threat to human rights before humans knew or could reasonably have been expected to know about it. Second, any judgement about when climate change became a 'standard threat' to human rights is likely to be contestable. It is clear from the evidence that climate change should now be recognised as a 'standard threat' to the human right to development. We know that the effects of climate change have already violated the human rights of some people and are likely to violate the human rights of many millions of people in the near (and far) future. It is less clear when anthropogenic climate change first posed a 'standard threat' to the human right to development.

When did climate change first pose a 'standard threat'? Was it at the very beginning of the Industrial Revolution when humans developed the capacity to emit large quantities of GHGs? Was it early in the 20th century when the mass production of motor vehicles began? Was it shortly after the Second World War when the global population exceeded 2.5 billion? Perhaps, the most plausible way of approaching this question is to consider when the probability of climate change causing widespread violations of the human right to development (and, thereby, posing a 'standard threat') exceeded some threshold. So, for example, we might imagine that the probability in the 1750s that humanity would take the route that it has taken since the Industrial Revolution (for example, the technological change, the population increases, and the social and economic changes) may have been quite low so that the likelihood of anthropogenic climate change violating human rights might also have been quite low. We might, therefore, conclude that climate change did not pose a 'standard threat' to human rights until more recently. A more detailed empirical argument would be required to make a plausible case for any particular date. However, we might reasonably conclude that some of the more ambitious claims about the historic responsibility of the global North might not be consistent with this understanding of when an agent's GHG emissions can legitimately be understood as rights-violating.

I have suggested that the first condition on the existence of the general climate duty is that it cannot have come into existence until anthropogenic climate change posed a 'standard threat' to human rights. The second condition is that the general climate duty – like all duties – should not be unreasonably demanding. We might distinguish two ways in which the general climate duty might be too demanding. First, it might be too demanding because it might ask people to sacrifice too much. The general climate duty asks us to make two kinds of sacrifice. First, it asks us to pay the opportunity costs of devoting time to promoting just institutions. In some circumstances, this might be too much to ask of an agent. For example, a person living below the development threshold is likely to have more urgent demands on their time, energy and resources; therefore, they should not be required to devote their limited time, energy and resources to promoting institutions that secure climate justice. Second, the general climate duty asks us to pay the opportunity costs of living under and complying with just institutions (after they have been successfully promoted and implemented). If institutions are genuinely just, they should not ask too much of individuals. On our account, just institutions will exempt those below the development threshold from paying the costs of climate policy. I think we might reasonably argue that neither the duty to promote just institutions nor the duty to comply with just institutions, properly interpreted, should demand too much from most citizens in the global North. Moreover, neither duty should demand anything from any person – in the global South or the global North – who is living below the development threshold.

The second way in which the general climate duty might be too demanding is that it might require us to promote fair and effective institutions for tackling climate change before we could reasonably be expected to know about the problem and its effects. If at time *t* we are excusably ignorant of the effects of our use of fossil fuels, it seems unreasonable either: at *t*, to claim that we have the general climate duty; or at *t+1*, to claim that we should be held morally responsible for our 'non-compliance' at *t* with the general climate duty. So, the general climate duty can only be imputed to an agent that is either knowledgeable or *in*excusably ignorant about the link between fossil fuel use and the rights-violating effects of anthropogenic climate change. Judgements about excusable ignorance will, of course, be contestable. However, I think we might reasonably argue that most ordinary citizens in the global North were excusably ignorant of the effects of fossil fuel use until (at least) the mid-1980s.

In this section, I have discussed the general climate duty.[6] I have considered how we might determine when the general climate duty should be understood to have come into existence. I have argued that the general climate duty could not have come into existence until the probability of anthropogenic climate change violating the human right to development became significant. I have also suggested that the general climate duty should only be imputed to an agent when (a) that agent has knowledge of, or is *inexcusably* ignorant of, the link between fossil fuel use and rights-violating anthropogenic climate change and (b) complying with the general climate duty (and complying with the proposed just institutions) does not make unreasonable demands on the agent.

This understanding of the 'birth' of the general climate duty is significant because it poses an important obstacle to historic responsibility arguments, including those made by Chinese officials. On one understanding of the historic responsibility argument, Northern states and their citizens should pay the costs of tackling anthropogenic climate change because they are morally responsible for the problem. However, my proposed theory of human rights and duties suggests that only the current generation of ordinary citizens in Northern states might be considered guilty of any climate-related moral failure. The general climate duty cannot reasonably be imputed to ordinary citizens before the mid-1980s. Therefore, the most ambitious arguments by Chinese officials and others for historic responsibility – grounded in moral responsibility or moral failure and extending back to the beginning of the Industrial Revolution – should be rejected.[7]

The specification and allocation of particular duties under fair and effective institutions

How should fair and effective institutions specify and allocate particular duties to protect the human right to development from the threat posed by climate change? What principles for the specification and allocation of climate duties should people who comply with the general climate duty be trying to promote? In particular, I want to consider the possibility that fair principles will allocate climate duties based on historical emissions. We have already seen that there are good reasons for thinking that the North's moral failure with respect to climate change is relatively recent. Therefore, if we want to allocate climate duties based on historical emissions over a longer period of history, we will need a different kind of argument to support that claim. In this section, I consider one important argument that has been offered to support the claim that the allocation of particular climate duties should be proportionate to historical emissions.

The central claim of this argument is that there is a universal right to equal GHG emissions irrespective of the time and place that a person lives. We might call this 'equal emissions'. Let us assume that we are seeking to promote fair and effective institutions for the specification and allocation of climate duties from time t onwards. If we accept equal emissions, we will take into account the historical emissions of each person before time t in allocating their current and future emissions to ensure that over their lifetime they do not exceed their 'equal emissions' allowance. Moreover, if we find that some persons have already emitted more than their 'equal emissions' allowance, we may reasonably require them to compensate others (assuming that there is some commensurability between emissions permits and other 'goods') by, for example, paying for adaptation.

There are several problems with 'equal emissions'.[8] I want to highlight two important problems. First, it is not at all clear why there should be a universal right to equal emissions. We do not normally distribute particular resources – even newly discovered resources – in an egalitarian manner (Beckerman and Pasek, 1995). Indeed, there are very few resources that are distributed equally in the contemporary world. Of course, we need not endorse the distributive principles that appear to operate in, or between, contemporary societies (even so-called 'liberal-democratic' societies). Instead, we might, and probably should, adopt a more egalitarian theory of global justice.

However, the second problem with equal emissions is that there are good reasons for advocates of egalitarian theories of global justice to support an unequal distribution of emissions. I will suggest two reasons. First, different persons may need different resources to achieve the same levels of development or wellbeing. Emission permits are a resource just like the fossil fuels that produce emissions. Some persons may need to use more energy (and emit more GHGs) than other persons to achieve the same level of development. If we are concerned about everyone achieving a 'modest but dignified level of wellbeing', we may reasonably reject equal emissions. Second, circumstances may vary between different times and places such that the marginal opportunity costs of not emitting GHGs vary considerably. This variation may be due to a range of factors, including the availability and cost of non-fossil fuel energy and the energy required to achieve a 'modest but dignified level of wellbeing' given the social, economic and technological structure of one's society. For example, it may be reasonable to suggest that current generations in the global North should not be entitled to emit such large quantities of greenhouse gases as previous generations because we have non-fossil fuel energy technology available to us, which would enable us to maintain a 'modest but dignified level of wellbeing' without burning such large quantities of fossil fuels. Therefore, we might reasonably reject 'equal emissions' between contemporary citizens in the global North and both previous generations in the global North and current generations in the global South.

If we reject 'equal emissions', we cannot treat all emissions at all times and places equally. Therefore, we will need to be rather more careful about how we take historical emissions into account in determining current and future responsibilities. In particular, one unit of emissions from the global North at the beginning of the 21st century should not count equally with one unit of emissions from the global South at the same time or with one unit of emissions from the global North at the beginning of the 20th century. The marginal opportunity cost – measured in an appropriate metric, such as impact on wellbeing – of reducing GHG emissions should be considered when we try to determine a fair allocation of climate duties. In other words, historical emissions may be relevant in determining the fair allocation of climate duties under just institutions but historic 'subsistence emissions', which could only have been limited at a high opportunity cost, should not be treated in the same way as historic 'luxury emissions', which might have been limited at a low opportunity cost (Shue, 1993).

Duties of rectification

So far, I have discussed the general climate duty to promote just institutions and the specification and allocation of climate duties under just institutions. In this section, I briefly discuss duties of rectification. The general climate duty assumes that the specification and allocation of more specific duties must be done by effective institutions that aim to protect human rights from the effects of anthropogenic climate change. This suggests that we have no specific duties – for example to limit our individual GHG emissions – until there is 'an actual [and "authoritative"] allocative scheme, operative and in force' (Feinberg, 1984, p 30). This is morally problematic because it suggests that we can continue with 'business-as-usual' GHG emissions until there are fair and effective institutional regulations in place that specify the level at which we are required to limit our emissions. This creates a perverse incentive for continuing non-compliance with the general climate duty: if we do not comply with the general climate duty and just institutions are not created, we do not violate any human rights-based duties by continuing to emit high levels of greenhouse gases.[9] If we want to avoid this problem, we need to go beyond the general climate duty.

I want to suggest two further duties, which follow from the general climate duty. First, we have a duty to rectify the wrong that we have done if we fail to comply with the general climate duty. On our account, if a person does not comply with the general climate duty, they violate the correlative human rights. We generally recognise that if a person violates another person's human rights, they have a duty to rectify the wrong that they have done.[10] What does rectification require in the context of the general climate duty? Let us assume that rectification cannot take place until just institutions are in place and duties are specified and allocated. I would suggest that rectification requires that those who have not complied with the general climate duty should be allocated more burdensome duties, including, for example, lower limits on their future GHG emissions and a greater share of the monetary costs of adaptation measures. The minimum requirement should be that they are not advantaged over the course of their lifetime by their failure to comply with the general climate duty. Moreover, non-compliers might legitimately be required to accept a worse outcome if rectification (or compensation) of the situation of the victims of climate-related human rights violations requires it. In sum, the general climate duty implies a duty of rectification: under effective institutions, previous non-compliers must accept more burdensome duties that may make them worse off than they would have been if they had always complied with the general climate duty.

The second duty that follows from the general climate duty is the duty not to accept benefits that result from actions that violate someone's human rights. If there were full compliance with the general climate duty, we might plausibly assume that effective institutions, for specifying and allocating duties to protect the human right to development from the threat posed by anthropogenic climate change, would quickly be implemented. Let us assume that some people comply with the general climate duty but others do not and, as a result, just institutions are not implemented. Some of the compliers may benefit from the delayed implementation of just institutions if, for example, they have been enjoying a lifestyle dependent on a higher level of emissions than they would have been permitted under just institutions. We might reasonably say that they are benefiting from the actions of the non-compliers. In other words, they are benefiting from actions that violate human rights. It is, however, surely wrong for someone who takes human rights seriously to accept benefits that result from human rights violations. Therefore, I would suggest that the general climate duty also implies a duty not to accept benefits that result from the failure of other people to comply with the general duty.

What does this additional duty require? I would suggest that it requires each person (a) to reduce their GHG emissions to a level that they can reasonably believe would be consistent with the specification and allocation of duties by just institutions and (b) to accept that just institutions can legitimately take into account the historical emissions (and other relevant actions) of those who have complied with the general climate duty (as well as those who have not complied) during the period that just institutions were delayed by non-compliance. In other words, the duty not to accept benefits requires both individual action now, even in advance of just institutions, and compliance with institutions that (fairly and effectively) specify and allocate duties 'retrospectively'.

If this account of duties of rectification is plausible, the failure of Northern states and Northern citizens to comply with the general climate duty over (at least) the last 20 or 30 years has significant implications for their duties now and in the future. The North is guilty of a moral failure in recent times and should seek to rectify that failure. Northern citizens are not only required to comply with the general climate duty (that is, 'do their bit' to promote just institutions) but are also required to limit their own current and future emissions to a level that they can reasonably believe would be consistent with the specification and allocation of duties by just institutions. Moreover, Northern citizens should be seeking to promote just institutions that will demand a lot from them, including compensation for the excessive (unjust) emissions that they have emitted since they acquired the duty to promote just climate institutions in the late 20th century.

Conclusion

I began this chapter with two key principles that underpin the Chinese position on the allocation of the costs of climate change. In the first section, I offered an individualistic interpretation of the right to development as a human right. In the remainder of the chapter, I considered the implications of this starting point for an account of climate duties and, in particular, the principle of historic responsibility. I outlined three kinds of climate duty. First, we have a general climate duty to promote just institutions that will protect the human right to development from the threat posed by anthropogenic climate change. I suggested that a reasonable account of this duty undermines one important argument – the argument from 'moral failure' – for taking *all* historical emissions into account when we allocate climate duties. We cannot justifiably claim, as the Chinese government has done, that Northern citizens or Northern states should be held morally responsible for their historical emissions prior to the time when they can reasonably be said to have acquired the general climate duty. However, they can be held morally responsible for their failure to comply with that duty since they acquired it. If we assume that Northern citizens only acquired the general climate duty sometime in the last two decades of the 20th century, we should regard their pre-1980s emissions very differently from their emissions since that time.

Second, we have a duty to comply with effective institutions that fairly specify and allocate duties to protect the human right to development from the threat posed by climate change. I suggested that one common argument for taking historical emissions into account when allocating climate duties was based on the idea of a universal right to equal emissions. I offered two criticisms of this argument. First, it is unclear why we should be egalitarians about GHG emissions permits when we are not generally egalitarians about other resources. Second, I suggested that egalitarianism about emissions ignores the difference between luxury and subsistence emissions and, more generally, does not take into account the variation between the marginal costs of emissions reductions for different people in different places and at different times. Therefore, I suggested that a fair allocation of emissions (or emission permits) is not likely to be an equal allocation. Instead, I suggested that current citizens of the global North might be entitled to emit less than their predecessors. As a result, it may be that previous generations in the North have not exceeded their fair share of emissions by as much as some have suggested. However, current generations in the global North may be exceeding their fair share of emissions by even more than the principle of equal emissions suggests.

The third kind of climate duty that I have identified is duties of rectification. I suggested that most Northern citizens do have duties to rectify their failure to comply with the general climate duty (since they acquired it in the late 20th century). These duties include a duty to reduce their own emissions immediately to a level that they can reasonably believe is consistent with the allocation of climate duties under just institutions. In addition, Northern citizens should – to comply with the general climate duty and the duties of rectification – be seeking to promote a global climate regime and effective institutions that will make severe demands on them. In particular, most Northern citizens should expect to be required under just institutions to pay compensation for their unjust post-1980s emissions.

Climate change poses a very serious threat to human rights, including the human right to development, in the 21st century and beyond. We have a duty to protect the human right to development from the threat posed by anthropogenic climate change. In this chapter, I have offered the outline of a distinctive account of how we should understand our climate duties. In particular, I have explored the relevance and the role of historical emissions in the allocation of climate duties. The Chinese government, like many in the global South, has argued consistently that the global North should be held responsible for the costs of climate change because it is their historical emissions that have caused the problem. I have suggested that this claim should not be accepted without further consideration and refinement. Specifically, I have suggested that the citizens of the global North do have a duty to pay compensation for their excessive (unjust) emissions during the last 20 or 30 years.[11] However, I have also suggested that earlier emissions should not be treated in the same way. Earlier emissions may be relevant for the allocation of climate duties under just institutions, but they are not relevant in the straightforward way that often seems to be assumed by Chinese officials or in general debates about climate justice.

Notes

[1] I have developed a related but different account of climate duties in Bell (2010). The account developed in this chapter is intended as an exploration of the implications of starting from a human right to development.

[2] For a more detailed defence, see Bell (2011a: forthcoming). For related but different discussions of a human right not to suffer the ill-effects of climate change, see, for example, Caney (2006, p 263, 2008, p 539, 2009), Shue (1999, p 539) and Vanderheiden (2008, p 252). The threat posed by climate change to human rights has also been identified by the United Nations Office of the High Commissioner for Human Rights (2007).

[3] Hayward (2005, p 53) has argued that the problem of unspecified duties extends to all negative rights, including, for example, the right not to be tortured:'the circumstances under which a right not to be tortured is violated are not brought about simply by numbers of individuals failing to recognize their negative duty, but rather are a result of a systematic organization of power within which specific responsibilities are murkily dispersed'.

[4] For a fuller discussion of the role of 'standard threats' in an account of human rights and correlative duties, see Bell (2011a: forthcoming).

[5] We might also need principles to specify and allocate duties when some people do not comply with just (or fair and effective) institutions. However, for institutions to qualify as 'effective', and therefore as 'just', they must prevent large-scale non-compliance. I will not address the problem of non-compliance under just institutions in this chapter. Instead, I make the simplifying assumption that we can make fair institutions effective by designing appropriate penalties and punishments for non-compliance.

[6] Jonathan Symons' argument in Chapter Five offers one way of interpreting the implications of the general climate duty for states, including China.

[7] Shue (1999, p 535) has argued that the excusable ignorance objection 'rests upon a confusion between punishment and responsibility'. Shue's point is that developed states might be liable for the costs associated with their historical emissions without being morally culpable for those emissions. I have discussed Shue's argument and the problem of excusable ignorance in more detail in Bell (2011b: forthcoming). See also Chapter Four in this volume.

[8] I have discussed some of these problems in Bell (2008).

[9] We are, of course, violating human rights by not complying with the general duty to promote just institutions. However, the argument so far does not imply that we would be violating human rights by continuing to emit high levels of GHGs.

[10] There may also be reason to punish them for the wrong that they have done.

[11] Chapters Nine and Ten argue that affluent people in China may have similar obligations.

Acknowledgements

I would like to thank the UK Arts and Humanities Research Council for funding a research project, 'Global Justice and the Environment', and subsequently a period of research leave for me to work on 'Global Justice and Climate Change', during which many of the ideas presented here were developed. I would also like to thank my colleagues on the research project, especially Simon Caney, Pia Halme and Clare Heyward, for many helpful discussions of these issues.

References

Ashford, E. (2007) 'The duties imposed by the human right to basic necessities', in T. Pogge (ed) *Freedom from poverty as a human right: Who owes what to the very poor?*, Oxford: Oxford University Press.

Baer, P., Athanasiou, T. and Kartha, S. (2007) *The right to development in a climate constrained world: The Greenhouse Development Rights Framework*, Berlin: Heinrich Böll Foundation, Christian Aid, EcoEquity and the Stockholm Environment Institute, www.ecoequity.org/docs/TheGDRsFramework.pdf

Baer, P. with Athanasiou, T., Kartha, S. and Kemp-Benedict, E. (2009) 'Greenhouse Development Rights: a proposal for a fair global climate treaty', *Ethics, Place and Environment*, vol 12, no 3, pp 267-81.

Beckerman, W. and Pasek, J. (1995) 'The equitable international allocation of tradable carbon emission permits', *Global Environmental Change*, vol 5, no 5, pp 405-13.

Bell, D. (2008) 'Carbon justice? The case against a universal right to equal carbon emissions', in S. Wilkes (ed) *Seeking environmental justice*, Amsterdam: Rodopi.

Bell, D. (2010) 'Justice and the politics of climate change', in C. Lever-Tracy (ed) *Handbook of climate change and society*, London: Routledge.

Bell, D. (2011a: forthcoming) 'Does anthropogenic climate change violate human rights?', *Critical Review of International Social and Political Philosophy*, vol 14, no 2.

Bell, D. (2011b: forthcoming) 'Global climate justice, historic emissions and excusable ignorance', *The Monist*, vol 94, no 3.

Caney, S. (2006) 'Cosmopolitan justice, rights and global climate change', *Canadian Journal of Law and Jurisprudence*, vol 19, no 2, pp 255-78.

Caney, S. (2008) 'Human rights, climate change, and discounting', *Environmental Politics*, vol 17, no 4, pp 536-55.

Caney, S. (2009) 'Climate change, human rights and moral thresholds', in S. Humphreys (ed) *Human rights and climate change*, Cambridge: Cambridge University Press.

Feinberg, J. (1984) 'Environmental pollution and the threshold of harm', *The Hastings Center Report*, vol 14, no 3, pp 27-31.

Hayward, T. (2005) *Constitutional environmental rights*, Oxford: Oxford University Press.

IPCC (Intergovernmental Panel on Climate Change) (2007) *Climate change 2007: Synthesis report: Contribution of Working Groups I, II and III to the fourth assessment report of the Intergovernmental Panel on Climate Change* (Core Writing Team, R.K. Pachauri and A. Reisinger, A. [eds]), Geneva: IPCC.

NDRC (National Development and Reform Commission) (2010) 'Letter including autonomous domestic mitigation actions', http://unfccc.int/files/meetings/application/pdf/chinacpphaccord_app2.pdf

O'Neill, O. (1986) *Faces of hunger: An essay on poverty, justice and development*, London: Allen & Unwin.

O'Neill, O. (1996) *Towards justice and virtue: A constructive account of practical reasoning*, Cambridge: Cambridge University Press.

Raz, J. (1986) *The morality of freedom*, Oxford: Clarendon Press.

Shue, H. (1980) *Basic rights: Subsistence, affluence and US foreign policy*, Princeton, New Jersey: Princeton University Press.

Shue, H. (1993) 'Subsistence emissions and luxury emissions', *Law and Policy*, vol 15, no 1, pp 39-59.

Shue, H. (1999) 'Global environment and international inequality', *International Affairs*, vol 75, no 3, pp 531-45.

UNFCCC (United Nations Framework Convention on Climate Change) (2009) *Report of the Conference of the Parties on its fifteenth session, held in Copenhagen from 7 to 19 December 2009*, http://unfccc.int/resource/docs/2009/cop15/eng/11a01.pdf#page=4

United Nations Office of the High Commissioner for Human Rights (2007) 'The human rights impact of climate change', in United Nations joint press kit for Bali climate change conference, 3–14 December 2007, www.un.org/climatechange/pdfs/bali/ohchr-bali07-19.pdf

Vanderheiden, S. (2008) *Atmospheric justice: A political theory of climate change*, New York, NY: Oxford University Press.

THREE

Responsibility for emissions and aspirations for development

Olivia Bina

As diplomats and leaders met in Rio de Janeiro for the 1992 United Nations Conference on Environment and Development, the world had enough evidence to know that economic growth was taking its toll on the planet, and that the benefits of growth were very unevenly distributed. It also knew that dependence on fossil fuels to deliver most of those unevenly distributed benefits (registered as annual gross domestic product [GDP] growth) was resulting in dangerous concentrations of greenhouse gases (GHGs) in the atmosphere. Fast-forward almost two decades and little has changed. A staggering amount of information, reports, renewed commitments and a regularly rediscovered urgency with which environmental 'crises' ought to be addressed, characterised the 1990s and the first decade of this century like a relentless, yet muffled, beat. Climate change is emblematic of the extent of our impact, the urgent need for a response and the seemingly endless postponement of action. Although it is but the final symptom of a long chain of effects caused by humanity's 'continuing transformation of the earth' (Schellnhuber et al, 2005, p 13) in its pursuit of prosperity (see Nellemann and Corcoran, 2010), climate change stands out as the issue that best illustrates our interdependence, not just between nations but also among all species and habitats on whose services humans 'fundamentally depend' (MEA, 2005, p v).

Against this backdrop, China has rapidly taken centre stage, at once as 'victim' of historical transformation and pollution of the biosphere by developed nations, and as 'perpetrator' – as it steals the title of 'first polluter' from the United States (US) (Bina and Soromenho-Marques, 2008). By virtue of its sheer size and growth trajectory, China appears to have focused the minds of leaders across the world on the physical limits of our planet and on the challenge of having to share common resources with a growing population, in ways that predictions of the Earth's limitations, such as *The limits to growth* (Meadows et al, 1972), *Our common future* (WCED, 1987), *Agenda 21* (UNCED, 1992) and the Millennium Ecosystem Assessment (MEA, 2005), have frustratingly failed to do. Economic growth and the environment have never looked quite so in conflict as in the case of China. The contribution of its economic growth to climate change is raising alarm inside and beyond the country's borders, precisely as a result of the ecological interdependence so strenuously ignored thanks to the successful separation of the world of economics from that of the biosphere.

The climate change crisis is the ultimate expression of unsustainable patterns of growth. The tension surrounding climate change negotiations is therefore inextricably linked to the fundamental unresolved question of how to reconcile an increasingly widespread pursuit of growth with the finite nature of our planet. The use of energy, upon which modern patterns of growth depend, is illustrative. According to the International Energy Agency (IEA) (IEA, 2009, p 3), '[t]he scale and breadth of the energy challenge is enormous – far greater than many people realise', and China plays an especially important role. It overtook the US in 2009 to become the world's largest energy user (IEA, 2010), it has accounted for four fifths of the growth of industrial production and carbon dioxide (CO_2) emissions over the past 25 years, and the IEA (2007) predicts that, between 2004 and 2030, China and India will account for approximately 75% of global coal demand, 35% of oil demand and 35% of global power generation capacity. Three quarters of the 11–gigatonne increase in energy-related CO_2 emissions expected between 2007 and 2030 will come from China (IEA, 2009).

Based on a perspective that links climate change to the issue of growth, this chapter explores the theme of responsibility as traditionally focused around the need to limit emissions, but also in terms of the obligation to pursue development aspirations through a different path. It considers the argument that China's leadership has an opportunity to embark on a path that is consistent with the need to secure a 'common future' for everyone, and it highlights both the promise and contradictions of current Chinese policy. On balance, evidence suggests that this opportunity is still to be taken, while there is a risk of falling into 'undifferentiated irresponsibility' by all parties – rather than the 'common but differentiated responsibility' agreed in international climate negotiations. This risk threatened to become reality at the 15th Conference of the Parties (COP15) to the United Nations Framework Convention on Climate Change (UNFCCC) held in Copenhagen in December 2009, which ended with very limited results (Grubb, 2010; IEA, 2010). The conclusion of that meeting challenges the idea that there is a significant difference between the position of China's government and that of most developed nations, and it suggests that the promise of a new path for development might still be met if contradictions are finally acknowledged, and experimentation is adopted to pursue bold alternatives rather than efficient growth models.

Framing the issue of responsibility

The Chinese government does not deny the science or the importance of the climate change crisis (NDRC, 2007b). Ambassador Yu Qingtai (Yu, 2008), China's Special Representative for Climate Change Talks, acknowledges that climate change 'affects not only the development of the global economy and prosperity, but also the very existence of mankind', and confirms that his government actively supports 'the leadership role played by the United Nations in responding to climate change'. This position has been maintained throughout the period leading up to COP15 in Copenhagen. In his speech to the United Nations (UN) General Assembly in September 2009, President Hu Jintao (Hu, J., 2009) reiterated that '[g]lobal climate change has a profound impact on the survival and development of mankind. It is a major challenge facing all countries'.

Within the international framework of negotiations, three 'principles' seem crucial, and they have been repeated consistently by the Chinese government's highest representatives in the years leading up to COP16 in Cancún, Mexico, in late 2010 (Yu, 2008; Hu, J., 2009; Liu et al, 2010):

- adherence to the UNFCCC fundamental principle of 'common but differentiated responsibility' (CBDR) as the 'very foundation for international cooperation' (Yu, 2008);
- support for developing countries in tackling climate change through adaptation, technology transfer and financial resources from developed countries; and
- promotion of 'common development' – and hence 'substantive actions on financial and technological assistance … and capacity building, *to facilitate their achievement of sustainable development*' (Yu, 2008, emphasis added) as a way to ensure the effective participation by developing countries in international effort to address climate change

Together, these principles define the strengths as well as the contradictions in the approach of China's leadership to responsibility. They are discussed in detail throughout the remainder of this section.

The first reference to CBDR refers to the need to limit emissions and is central to the debate and the impasse in international negotiations. While this is not the interpretation of responsibility used in this chapter, it is the starting point for the argument whereby responsibility ought to relate to *how development is conceived* rather than to *how to responsibly clean up after development* (or at least after a certain level of development) has been achieved. In the case of China, as discussed below, this level is likely to be the 'moderately prosperous society' (Fewsmith, 2004) of approximately US$4,000 per capita. Among the arguments used by the Chinese government to resist adopting emission targets is an appeal to the concept of historical responsibility and to the need for 'developed nations to significantly raise their targets for cutting emissions and take into account a developing country's right to reduce poverty and improve living standards' (Su Wei, China's chief climate change negotiator in 2010, cited in Liu et al, 2010). Quite apart from the intrinsic weaknesses of the concept (Miller, 2008; see also Chapters Two and Three), reference to the presumed irresponsibility of Britain, Germany and the US – followed by the rest of the developed nations – seems hardly a justification for the Chinese government's insistence that it need focus only improving energy and carbon efficiency per unit of GDP (Pan, 2010), rather than limiting China's total CO_2 emissions.

To be sure, the richest 20% of the world use over 75% of global resources and emit 51% of CO_2 to maintain their way of life.[1] Undoubtedly, developed nations contributed to a significant part of current concentrations of GHGs in their quest for development, and while the benefits (that is, development and lifestyle) are confined to political borders, the price of those benefits is being shared by humanity as a whole, with particularly negative effects in developing countries (UNDP, 2007). The latter developing countries see the current crisis as the price for the development path chosen by rich countries to reach current levels of wealth. The perceived injustice explains the appeal to notions of responsibility, notably responsibility in relation to choices of development paths. However, objections to those past choices cannot be raised without implying that current and future development paths ought to avoid irresponsible choices. This has important implications for the choices made by China's leaders (see Chapter Eight).

The pressure on China's government rose in 2006 when it attained the dubious honour of 'first polluter' for energy-related CO_2 emissions (Levine and Aden, 2008), and largest energy consumer in 2010 (IEA, 2010). Its response has been to counter charges of environmental irresponsibility by reframing the climate debate as a problem of 'development', essentially appealing for the right to develop (NDRC, 2007b). The right is rooted in provisions of the Charter of the United Nations (UN, 1945, preamble) promoting 'social progress and better standards of life in larger freedom'. During the last 75 years, the number of commitments to this right have multiplied, and its articulations have explored the link with nature (for example the United Nations Conference on Human Environment, held in Stockholm in 1972) and subsequently found expression in the notion of 'human development' by Mahbub ul Haq (UNDP, 1990) and Amartya Sen (Sen, 1999), which was popularised in the UN's *Human development reports* (for example, UNDP, 2007). Thus, President Hu Jintao (Hu, J., 2009) has argued that 'promoting common development should be the basis of our effort. We should and can only advise our efforts to tackle climate change in the course of development'. An almost identical statement was delivered in 2007 (Feng, 2007) and – in line with international trends – one with a green development angle characterised the Chinese position at the 2010 UN climate change meeting in Tianjin (Liu et al, 2010). China's leaders take every opportunity to remind the rest of the world that they must still battle with poverty reduction and that, in per-capita terms, the country's energy emissions and overall resource consumption levels are well below the average for developed nations (see, for example, CCICED and WWF, 2008). They also point out that the 'ownership' of those emissions, and related responsibility, is a matter for discussion, since approximately 33% of China's domestic CO_2 emissions were due to production for export in 2005 (Weber et al, 2008).

The link between the risk of climate change and development is indeed at the heart of the problem, and the binding factor is energy. The use of energy plays a major role in shaping the interaction between the various parts of human society and the rest of the ecosystem. Societies grow in size and complexity thanks to ever-increasing use of energy, and to date almost 80% of the world's primary sources are fossil fuels (IEA, 2009). Development depends on energy, all the more so in a country that has grown at an average of 9-9.5% over five decades (with only a small pause between the 2008-09 financial crisis), primarily thanks to industrialisation and, since 2002, energy-intensive industries. Even if all of China's efforts to promote clean(er) and more efficient use of energy were to bear their fruit (NDRC, 2007a, 2007b; Pan, 2010), the main source of energy will remain coal for decades to come (IEA, 2007, 2010). This, combined with the growth projections for China, is bound to wipe out most benefits. By linking its right to develop with the need to remain free of any binding commitments (that is, emission-reduction targets) – as it did during COP15 in Copenhagen – the Chinese government is effectively expecting to take its turn on the *irresponsible* path, which is the same path tread by European and North American societies.

Is the appeal to historical responsibility combined with the right to pursue development the equivalent of wanting to extend a right to irresponsibility for all nations, albeit at different times in history? The Chinese government's aim for persistently high rates of growth until the country reaches the level of development of a moderately prosperous society is not only justified on grounds of poverty reduction, but also as a way of legitimising the ruling party and maintaining social stability: '[t]aking economic development as the central task is vital to invigorating our nation and is the fundamental requirement for the robust growth and lasting stability of the Party and the nation' (Hu, 2007).

Since the reform era began in the 1970s, China's remarkable growth has meant an equally remarkable – although less admirable – increase in its ecological deficit. Since the mid-1970s, it has been demanding more capacity than its own ecosystems could provide, and it now requires 'the equivalent of two Chinas' worth of bio-capacity (CCICED and WWF, 2008, p 13). Given the record of environmental pollution linked to its development, which is affecting the lives of its people as well as contributing to the climate change crisis, the leadership's appeal to notions of historical responsibility could result in denial of the whole concept of responsibility, both within and beyond its country's borders (Liu and Diamond, 2005; Pan and Zhou, 2006).

The second and third principles mentioned at the beginning of this section and central to the government's position (Yu, 2008; Hu, 2009), complete the link between (ir)responsibility, pollution and development. There is a lot, such as funds and technology, that developed nations ought to offer to enable developing countries to catch up in the general rush to 'develop' before the latter is willing to engage in greater levels of responsibility. This is even more true when engaging with undifferentiated levels of responsibility, which would result from calls to reduce the responsibility gap between 'developed' and 'developing' nations that achieved high levels of growth. China's diplomats reveal an uncompromising stance on this issue, as it allows them to maintain differentiated, low levels of responsibility, but also to claim a higher moral ground by depicting their efforts as significant: 'China is making huge efforts to combat climate change despite the fact that it remains a low-income developing county' (Xie, 2009; see also Hu, A., 2009; and Liu et al, 2010). In addition, the general failure to comply with commitments and promises by rich nations within the context of the Kyoto Protocol and subsequent negotiations has been noted by China: 'It is a pity that developed countries have shown insufficient sincerity and made inadequate efforts to fulfil ... obligations' in terms of financial resources and transfer of technology (Feng, 2007; see also Pan, 2010). This gives developing nations an additional argument in support of their claims.[2]

Furthermore, the weakness of developed nations' commitments presented at COP15, combined with weak implementation records, reveals a failure to grasp the significance of the challenge posed by a development (growth) model that they conceived and have benefited from (Homer-Dixon, 2006). Nevertheless, failure to deliver by developed countries cannot justify the pursuit of *undifferentiated irresponsibility*. Such a path would contradict the Chinese government's message to the world (NDRC, 2007b), exemplified by an article in Britain's *The Guardian* newspaper attributed to Xie Zhenhua, Hu Jintao's Special Representative on Climate Change: '[w]ith a deep sense of responsibility for its own people and the entire human race, China will continue to implement proactive policies and measures to address climate change and make unremitting efforts to protect Earth' (Xie, 2009).

Opportunity and expectation: a promised new path

How can one reconcile a claim to differentiated, essentially limited, responsibility with the proclaimed objective to achieve 'sustainable development' and 'protect Earth'? The Chinese government claims that it wants to pursue a new development path that would make it responsible to its people by improving the state of the environment at home, and to humanity as a whole by improving the efficiency with which it uses energy and other resources (*Xinhua*, 2006). It is this promise, encapsulated in the political programme of 'scientific outlook on development' (*kexue fazhan guan*) and 'ecological civilisation' (*shengtai wenming*), that suggests that China's rise might be an opportunity for its people and for a common future. The pursuit of a new path acknowledges that economic growth is being 'realized at an excessively high cost of resources and the environment' (Hu, 2007). The cost, depending on whose calculation is considered, varies between 2 and 20% of China's GDP (Liu and Diamond, 2005; *China Daily*, 2006). As a result, the 2006 Economic Work Conference of the Communist Party Leadership marked a departure from the uncompromising pursuit of rapid growth that has characterised the last five decades, concluding that the country must 're-engineer the economy' and search for 'a new growth pattern that is energy-saving, environmentally friendly and sustainable' (*Xinhua*, 2006). A year later, the change was enshrined in Hu Jintao's *Report to the Seventeenth National Congress of the Communist*

Party of China as 'scientific outlook on development' (Hu, 2007), and since then the discourse of change remains central: China's Deputy Prime Minister, Li Keqiang, recently emphasised the urgent need to adjust the pattern of development, away from 'inefficient growth' and excessive reliance on investment and exports (Bennhold, 2010).

The programme for a scientific outlook on development encompasses a range of ideas on and around the sustainability of development. It emphasises the pursuit of 'a better life and sound ecological and environmental conditions' and embraces principles of efficiency, resource (primarily energy) saving and decoupling of economic growth from pollution – all of which occupy a special place in driving the modernisation of the state (Yao et al, 2005). The scientific outlook on development is also seen as a driver for a new, people-oriented, more compassionate direction of China's development that responds to increasing social disparity (Liu, 2007). However, to date this new path is primarily one based on technological fixes, notably through improved efficiency as the principal delivery mechanism of 'a resource-conserving and environment-friendly society' (Hu, 2007), which has found expression in concepts of a circular economy (that is, reduce, reuse, recycle) (NDRC, 2007a; Jin, 2008). It is efficiency and the pursuit of a circular economy that the government believes will enable a quadrupling of GDP by 2020 while ensuring 'sound ecological and environmental conditions' (Hu, 2007). The government's ongoing stimulus package of 400 trillion RMB (approximately 37 trillion GBP) is testament to this focus: several investments within its Ten-Point Plan include an energy-efficiency element, and 210 billion RMB (approximately 19.7 trillion GBP) are specifically earmarked for energy and the environment, including upgrading refineries (World Bank, 2009). In a country with 20% of the world's population, and 7% of the world's land and water, efficiency in the use of resources makes eminent sense. The significant role of heavy- and energy-intensive industry over the last decade has meant that a reduction of energy intensity by 20% per unit of GDP by 2010 (against 2005 levels) is now a national priority (NDRC, 2007a), combining with the recent pledge to reduce carbon intensity by 40 to 45% over a 15-year period to 2020 (Pan, 2010).

Similarly, great effort and resources are being devoted to the more efficient use of water and scarce land, especially agricultural land. Beyond the generic statements of intention there is a very significant body of practical and administrative measures that, especially since the approval of the 11th Five-Year Plan (2006–10), have been attempting to balance the pursuit of economic growth with greater attention to the needs of the environment and of the less fortunate sections of China's rural society that are more closely in contact with the devastating effects of environmental degradation (Pan and Zhou, 2006; NDRC, 2007a; Song et al, 2008). However, it is worth noting that the updated version of the stimulus plan (from November 2008 to March 2009) witnessed a significant contraction of the amount devoted to 'sustainable environment' in favour of 'technology and industry' and 'housing' (*The Economist*, 2009), with investment in energy-intensive industries (including cement, glass and steel) increased despite high-level commitment to move away from them (Huang, 2010). This suggests that the pressure of the 2007 financial and economic crisis justifies a (partial) return to the grow-now, clean-up-later approach.

'Ecological civilisation' was officially introduced together with scientific development at the Seventeenth National Congress of the Communist Party of China. Official discourse refers to both the scientific outlook on development and ecological civilisation, often with no clear distinction, as illustrated by Jia (2009), director of the State Forestry Administration, who links the scientific outlook of development with ecological civilisation and the need to 'protect ... global ecological security and sustain ... human culture', acknowledging climate change as 'a prominent threat to the progress of civilization'. However, it is suggested here that the scientific outlook and ecological civilisation are not two dimensions of the government's promised new path, but rather the former might be usefully considered as the means to the latter. The means focus on efficiency; the end questions the development paradigm and aspires to a new era for humanity. Ecological civilisation represents a wider mission statement in response to the ecological crisis that is affecting the country. It is an acknowledgement of the need to rethink traditional models of growth in a country with limited bio-capacity and limited options to export waste and pollution beyond its borders. The idea is to provide a cultural basis from which to transcend industrial civilisation and capitalism, advocating the pursuit of material and spiritual wealth through an ecological harmony rooted in traditional Chinese cultural ethics that recognises value in both humankind and nature (*Beijing Review*, 2006). In the words of Pan Yue (Pan, 2004, pp 47-56), it represents a 'historical mission' for China to promote an 'advanced culture' that recognises humankind as 'inseparable from other forms of life in nature' and which can only coexist through mutual restraint: 'all advanced cultures exist in nature.... Man has the right ... to enjoy material lives and seek freedom and happiness. However, such rights must be limited by the scale [of] environmental capacity'.

This interpretation is in line with the idea of interdependence and necessary limits introduced in the late 1960s and rediscovered with renewed urgency ever since. It reflects the leadership's concern with 'the future of global civilisation' given global constraints as well as global ecological problems epitomised by dangerous climate change (Ma, 2007). Ecological civilisation subscribes to the idea that the right to human development must be accompanied with the obligation to pursue a different development path. This is of course as true for China as it is for the rest of the world, since limits and restraint can only make sense when national perspectives are transcended and consideration is given to the Earth system (discussed further below).

Chinese official discourse on the need for a new development path has thus witnessed interesting developments since the Sixteenth National Congress of the Communist Party of China. It suggests that the government intends to take a responsible approach both towards its people and towards the rest of the planet. This represents an opportunity to avoid dangerous climate change. Whether such opportunity materialises will depend on the further articulation of both the means (scientific outlook on development) and the end (ecological civilisation), as well as the capacity of government to deliver on its promises. It is worth noting that the promise has been matched by expectations across the world. Internationally renowned scholars, including Jeffrey Sachs and Joseph Stiglitz, as well as noted commentators, including Sir Crispin Tickell, Lester Brown and Jonathon Porritt, have in recent years expressed the hope that China might lead the world to a new era of sustainable development. China is 'a relatively late comer to the industrial world [and] has the opportunity to leapfrog over the mistakes of others' (Tickell, 2007). Technology will play a crucial part in delivering more sustainable development (Brown, 2006; Sachs, 2007), and there is 'no reason why China shouldn't become the world's number one nation in terms of eco-efficiency', according to Porritt – who defines the situation in China as 'an ecological apocalypse' (Green Futures, 2006, p 3).

It seems that there is almost 'a *desire* for hope' that makes most commentators tread the uneasy path between hope and despair, as if afraid to contemplate the wider consequences of China's possible demise (Bina, 2007). A substantial part of this hope is supported by faith in technology and efficiency gains as the foundations of a sustainable future. This faith is shared by the developing discourse of scientific outlook on development, and the related notion of circular economy. However, based on the Chinese government's current policies and funding priorities, a number of contradictions can be identified, suggesting that the solutions devised by the scientific development programme (the means) may not lead to the radical changes needed to shift to the new development paradigm of ecological civilisation (the end). The result could be a failure to address the underlying causes of China's environmental crisis, and thus a failure to avert dangerous climate change.

The contradiction in the promise

Considering China's most recent policies, economic plans and funding priorities, the opportunity for containing the risk of dangerous climate change that might have come from a new development path may be significantly weaker than expected. The primary contradiction is perhaps the simplest and one, which remains unresolved in many parts of the world, not only in China: that between environmental protection and development. While Hu Jintao's speech delivered at the opening ceremony of the Boao Forum for Asia Annual Conference in 2008 (Boao, Hainan, 12 April 2008) suggested that there is still a desire to 'explore and improve our development path and model in keeping with China's national conditions', he also confirmed a 'commit[ment] to promoting the sustained and steady growth of the world economy' (Hu, 2008). An echo of the wave of 'green growth' and 'green new deals' that has characterised international agencies' responses to the financial crisis begun in 2007 (for example, UNEP, 2009; UNESCAP, 2009). Thus, the contradiction between improving the quality of development and the need for rapid growth persists. The government advocates 'sound and rapid economic growth' through the quadrupling of per-capita GDP between 2000 and 2020, and it expects this growth to deliver 'balanced development' by 'reducing consumption of resources and protecting the environment' (Hu, 2007). China's 11th Five-Year Plan was meant to promote this balanced outcome, yet a mid-term evaluation suggests that it failed to live up to the promise: 'insufficient progress on macroeconomic rebalancing and changing the economic and industrial structure has [meant] limited progress on energy and water intensity, and environmental quality' (World Bank, 2008, p 11). Analysis explains how the country's growth continues to be a key driver of economic and social imbalances:

> First, the capital–intensive, industry–led growth had been particularly intensive in energy, natural resources, and environmental degradation, thus accentuating the associated imbalances noted above. While energy and natural resource

intensity was declining in several sectors, the relatively rapid growth of industry increased the weight in GDP of the most energy and resource intensive sectors. Second, capital-intensive growth created fewer jobs than a services-led growth pattern, limiting the absorption of surplus agricultural labor and contributing to the rising rural–urban income inequality and rural poverty. (World Bank, 2008, p 3)

China's development path remains inspired by a traditional model of industrial growth and a market economy that depends on global exports. Plans for the 12th Five-Year Plan suggest that little change is to be expected until 2020. The new plan's four key stages of economic growth were summarised by Wu Shunze, Deputy Director General of the China Academy of Environmental Planning, as:

- industrialisation to be completed by 2030;
- a peak in the use of resources and energy between 2020 and 2030;
- modernisation, including growth of the service industries and a reduction in pressure on the environment, to be attained between 2030 and 2050; and
- mature urbanisation, high–income status and the largest world economy by 2050 (China Environmental Law, 2009).

The new plan will include 'goals for cuts in greenhouse-gas emissions, with binding targets set for both provinces and industries in order to strengthen implementation' (Pan, 2010).[3] However, overall, the environmental chapter of the national plan is being drafted not in order to address the ecological crisis, but rather to support the imperatives of economic growth and social stability through the achievement of a moderately prosperous society by 2020. Initial proposals suggest that 'the pre-ordained economic development model determines environmental progress' and that until 2020 China can expect the relationship between the economy and the environment to be in 'contradiction' and only 'preliminarily harmonious' by 2030 (China Environmental Law, 2009; for an overview of these challenges, see Bina, 2010).

Despite calls for significant structural changes in the economic model (Greenwood, 2010), a move away from heavy, energy-intensive and polluting industries appears increasingly unlikely – partly as a result of the global economic crisis. The implementation of the much-praised 'green' stimulus package of 400 trillion RMB is also revealing its contradictions as environment and social concerns are sidelined in favour of economic priorities, mainly expressed in terms of infrastructure investment (Tan, 2009; *The Economist*, 2009). In the words of Environment Minister Zhou Shengxian: 'environmental protection [is] not being highlighted in the overall plan' and recent reviews show a relaxation of the already bland implementation of pollution controls, and new environmental problems arising from many of the industrial plans in the Centre and West regions (Li, 2009b).

The overall approach that transpires from the last decade of planned economic growth suggests that China's leaders are waiting to reach the theoretical point in the environmental Kuznets Curve of industrialisation and per-capita income where pollution levels begin to drop. Quite apart from the critiques of the curve's assumptions (for example, Caviglia-Harris et al, 2009), this approach offers nothing that can be defined as a new, more responsible path of development. Instead, the plan seems to be business as usual for at least a few decades to come. Given the efforts by the government to redefine China's path to development, these results might seem surprising, were it not for a deeper contradiction within the overall promise: a contradiction between the ultimate need for restraint that is intrinsic to ecological civilisation (the end), and the unquestioned pursuit of growth, albeit efficient growth, central to the programme for a scientific outlook on development (the means). The latter is arguably aimed at 'putting people first' (Hu, 2007), but its foundations in greater efficiency of resource use, primarily energy resources, seem to have sidelined the social dimension and the need to work within the country's bio-capacity limits.

Because of the efficiency credentials in the scientific outlook approach, it is being considered a contribution towards climate change policies (NDRC, 2007b). This appeal, almost fascination, with the potential of efficiency to deliver sustainable development can be linked to a desire to rationalise, control and shape nature (uprooting forests, redirecting rivers), which has characterised China's leaders for millennia (Elvin, 2004). Indeed, the relationship with nature is also characterised by contradiction as successive governments have sought to control key resources for political and military reasons, all the while demonstrating a remarkable sensitivity and respect for nature's beauty and spiritual dimension: 'classical Chinese culture was as hostile to forests as it was fond of individual trees' (Elvin, 2004, p xvii; see *Beijing Review*, 2006).

But China is not alone in pursuing the efficiency promise. The global financial crisis has coincided in time with the growing awareness of the climate change problematique, primarily because of the media attention around the geopolitical tensions that characterised the build-up to, and limited results of, the Copenhagen summit (COP15). This 'combination' has helped trigger a new wave of policies and measures linked to concepts of green growth, efficient growth and low-carbon growth (OECD, 2009; UNEP, 2009; UNESCAP, 2009). One of the key drivers of this renaissance of 'green economy' ideas (see Ekins et al, 1992) seems to be the promise of 'win-win' solutions, especially in terms of the potential creation of much-needed new jobs (UNEP, 2009). It is therefore not surprising that draft climate change legislation, endorsed by China's National People's Congress, again combines the climate agenda with that of economic growth, calling for a 'green economy' that can promote green investment and consumption patterns, and a shift towards a low-carbon economy (Li, 2009a).

As a crucial strategy for the future, the leadership's emphasis on efficiency seems to ignore a fundamental weakness. The inefficiency of China's industry is well known and certainly will benefit from greater efficiencies, but historical evidence shows that higher efficiency of energy conversion leads eventually to higher, rather than lower, energy use, ultimately negating the initial benefits (Smil, 2005). The emphasis on energy efficiency so as to 'produce more with less', has well-known limits and even risks, as well as obvious immediate and short-term benefits. The Jevons Paradox and the Khazzoom-Brookes postulate warn of rebound effects whereby savings accruing from more efficient use of energy lead to lower prices and eventually to increased consumption (see House of Lords, 2005; Smil, 2005; York, 2006). This is especially true for a country that is planning rapid and sustained economic growth, as well as unprecedented urbanisation by 2050, with the government consequently concerned about its ability to meet efficiency targets: 'the task will be difficult', admits Xie Zhenhua, the vice chairman of the National Development and Reform Commission (*AFP*, 2010). Indeed, results to date have been disappointing (Pan, 2010). There is therefore a second contradiction in the promise of China's leaders: it can be expressed as faith in *efficient growth*.

In spite of the rhetoric invoking a different, more responsible development path, there is enough evidence to suggest that the Chinese leadership is pursuing the same path and committing the same mistakes that today's richest countries experienced. Both sides seek to mediate their responsibilities towards emission reductions through the seemingly unquestionable right to growth and to the pursuit of ever-higher standards of living. The result is likely to be one more step towards undifferentiated irresponsibility. Efficiency per se ensures no harmony between humans and nature. It acknowledges their interdependence, but without reference to limits and the need for restraint, it cannot lead to lasting harmony. This is, of course the problem with the 'limited' responsibility at the heart of the Chinese government's position in the climate change negotiations. Many of the arguments explored above will support limited responsibility on the grounds of equity. In practice, however, the government is confronted with the simple fact that by virtue of having the largest population in the world, and being one of its largest economies, it is also one of the largest and fastest-growing pressures on the planet. Being a responsible player both at home and abroad will take more than efficient growth, and the shortcomings of recent plans confirm this.

Conclusion

The analysis of the contradictions and limitations of current proposals echoes with that of O'Riordan (1983), who reminds us that contradictions lie at the heart of modern environmentalism. Environmentalism has its origins in divergent ideological modes of interpreting the environmental question: the ecocentric mode that assumes a natural order that humankind has the power to disturb, potentially leading to the destruction of the biosphere, and the technocentric mode that focuses on rational, value-free scientific managerial techniques to shape the natural environment and humankind's destiny (O'Riordan, 1983). The first mode is concerned with 'ends', and the moral and spiritual dimension of choices, while the latter is primarily interested in the potential of science to develop the necessary 'means' of human progress. In many ways, technocentrism has succeeded in defining both the problem (be it climate change or development) and the solution (efficient growth, green economy). Ecocentrism instead struggled to translate generic consensual objectives into concrete policies and actions. The divide between ecocentrism and technocentrism echoes the divide between the idea of ecological civilisation and the scientific outlook on development (although the former is not the same as ecocentrism). If the Chinese leadership is to live up to its promise, and to the hope and growing expectations that it has contributed to creating around the world, it will have to address the contradictions in its scientific outlook on development and invest greater effort in defining more clearly the nature of an ecological civilisation – its end – before choosing the means to achieve it. Taking responsible action to avert dangerous climate change will require much more bold proposals than those tabled to date, which subscribe more to a *responsibility for cleaning up after development*, than *for redefining development* in ways that openly addresses the environmental limits we face.

As Harvey (1996) notes, globalisation is characterised by a time–space compression. The turn of the century has been marked by a renewed awareness of the Earth as a closed system, with clear limits in terms of capacity and resources. These limits are made more tangible thanks to the projected population growth in China, India and Africa, and the sheer impossibility of extending the current lifestyle of rich countries to the 'newcomers' (see Brown, 2006; Harris, 2010). The Chinese leadership seems fully aware of this: 'I cannot accept the argument that I, as a Chinese, am only entitled legally to one quarter of what you are entitled to.... But ... being equal to an American when it comes to per-capita emissions would be a nightmare for the Chinese' (Ambassador Yu Qingtai, cited in Heilprin, 2008).

Responsibility must therefore include limits and mutual restraint for the benefit of the commons and thus for our common future. This is as true for China's representatives as for those of all countries. Indeed, a question inevitably arises from this analysis: can any country be reasonably expected to define a new development path in an interdependent and globalised world? Given the current state of the global commons and the implications for dangerous climate change, the time for limited responsibility, whether by developed or developing countries, no matter how poor, seems to be over, and a new development path may have to be a global obligation.

The acknowledgement and analysis of contradiction is a distinctive characteristic of Chinese political thought, as much as experimentation is a unique trait derived from its revolutionary past (see Dirlik, 2009). Perhaps the greatest contribution from China towards finding a solution to the multiple crises the world is facing could be to put on the global agenda the contradiction between environment and development that is the legacy of Euro-American capitalism, forcing heads of state across the world to acknowledge that 'win–win' situations are rare and their pursuit is encouraged only thanks to the vagueness of sustainable development concepts. The climate change crisis is the ultimate expression of such contradiction. Chinese leaders have an opportunity to show a different path, living up to the promise of an ecological civilisation that is not simply a rehearsal of technocentric beliefs and efficiency-driven solutions. There is a need for radically different ways of thinking about the medium term – for long term is now a luxury of the past if the conclusions of climate scientists are to be taken at face value – and there is a need to experiment now with models that will have to be in place in a matter of decades, not centuries.

This book illustrates the complexity of the debate on the extent of China's responsibility for climate change and this chapter has argued that, independently of the merits (or demerits) of the historical responsibility claims, Chinese leaders risk leading the world, by virtue of sheer scale and growth trends of its emissions, down a route of undifferentiated irresponsibility. Failure of developed nations to act responsibly is not, in and of itself, a justification for additional irresponsibility. Least of all if, as is the case with Chinese leaders, a pledge to protect the Earth and pursue a new path to development underpins their official position.

Only if all world leaders, including the Chinese government, are prepared to see the contradiction inherent in simple numbers, such as the energy figures from the IEA, will they take steps towards addressing – rather than merely discussing – the dangers of climate change. Only then will they show the long-awaited responsibility and leadership they owe to the world's common future, averting decline and a fall into a pattern of undifferentiated irresponsibility. In the words of a 12-year-old: 'do not forget why you are attending these conferences, who you are doing this for. We are your own children, you are deciding what kind of world we are growing up in ... I challenge you, please make your actions reflect your words' (Severn Suzuki, 1992, speaking at the UN Earth Summit).

Notes

[1] This figure represents million metric tons of CO_2 emitted by all 'high-income countries' in 2003; the figure for all 'developed countries' is 61% (IEA in EarthTrends – http://earthtrends.wri.org – searchable database results).

[2] See Chapter Seven for an interesting argument in favour of available and cost-effective technological solutions.

[3] See Chapter Six for a discussion of governance issues.

Acknowledgements

I wish to thank Arif Dirlik for a challenge that has been the greatest encouragement, and Andrea Ricci for his many questions.

References

AFP (2010) 'China environment worsening, may miss energy goals', *AFP*, 13 March, www.google.com/hostednews/afp/article/ALeqM5hCjnpTJ1q3S1HPTkGnTCuVyCttLg

Beijing Review (2006) 'Evolution of an ecological civilization', *Beijing Review*, no 45, updated 15 December, www.bjreview.com.cn/expert/txt/2006-12/15/content_50890.htm

Bennhold, K. (2010) 'China's next leader offers a glimpse of the future', *New York Times*, 28 January, www.nytimes.com/2010/01/29/business/global/29yuan.html?partner=rssnyt&emc=rss

Bina, O. (2007) 'Despair or hope? China's choice between ecological crisis and sustainable futures', in *2007 Beijing International Conference on Environmental Sociology – collection part I* (pp 69-100), Beijing: Centre for Studies of Sociological Theory and Method, Renmin University of China.

Bina, O. (2010) 'Environmental governance in China: weakness and potential from an environmental policy integration perspective', *The China Review*, vol 10, pp 207-40.

Bina, O. and Soromenho-Marques, V. (2008) 'Inequality, trust and opportunity', in *Chinadialogue*, 5 November, www.chinadialogue.net/article/show/single/en/2535-Inequality-trust-and-opportunity

Brown, A.L. (2006) *Plan B 2.0: Rescuing a planet under stress and a civilization in trouble*, New York, NY: W. W. Norton, www.earth-policy.org/Books/PB2/index.htm

Caviglia-Harris, J.L., Chambers, D. and Kahn, J.R. (2009) 'Taking the 'U' out of Kuznets: a comprehensive analysis of the EKC and environmental degradation', *Ecological Economics*, vol 68, pp 1149-59.

CCICED (China Council for International Cooperation on Environment and Development) and WWF (World Wide Fund for Nature) (2008) *Report on ecological footprint in China*, Beijing: CCICED and WWF, www.footprintnetwork.org/download.php?id=503

China Daily (2006) 'Water pollution study keeps innovation in mind', *People's Daily*, 21 August, http://english.people.com.cn/200608/21/eng20060821_295230.html

China Environmental Law (2009) *China's 12th Environmental Five-Year-Plan: National preparation efforts*, China Environmental Law – a discussion of China's Environmental and Energy laws, regulations and policies, www.chinaenvironmentallaw.com/2009/05/15/chinas-12th-environmental-five-year-plan-national-preparation-efforts/

Dirlik, A. (2009) 'Post-socialism revisited: reflections on 'Socialism with Chinese characteristics,' its past, present and future', *Marxism and Reality*, October.

Ekins, P., Hutchinson, R. and Hillman, M. (1992) *The Gaia atlas of green economics*, New York, NY: Anchor Books.

Elvin, M. (2004) *The retreat of the elephants: An environmental history of China*, New Haven, CT: Yale University Press.

Feng, Q.(2007) 'Climate change and the right to develop', *China Daily*, 31 October, www.chinadaily.com.cn/opinion/2007-10/31/content_6218475.htm

Fewsmith, J. (2004) *Promoting the scientific development concept*, China Leadership Monitor no 11, Stanford, CA: Hoover Institution, www.hoover.org/publications/clm/issues/2904171.html

Greenwood, C.L., Jr (2010) 'Rebalancing economic, environmental, and social performance during China's 12th Five-Year Plan', Speech by ADB Vice President at the International Seminar on the Direction and Policy Orientation of the 12th Five Year Plan, Beijing, 19 January, www.adb.org/Documents/Speeches/2010/ms2010005.asp

Grubb, M. (2010) 'Copenhagen: back to the future?', *Climate Policy*, vol 10, pp 127-30, doi:10.3763/cpol.2010.ED83.

Harris, P.G. (2010) *World ethics and climate change: From international to global justice*, Edinburgh: Edinburgh University Press.

Harvey, D. (1996) *Justice, nature and the geography of difference*, Oxford: Blackwell.

Heilprin, J. (2008) 'UN debate keys on rich nation emissions', *Associated Press*, 15 February, http://ap.google.com/article/ALeqM5iQmBUlYskvnKT0CLHBucXxY5_wKAD8UPOK0G3

Homer-Dixon, T. (2006) *The upside of down: Catastrophe, creativity, and the renewal of civilization*, Washington, DC: Island Press.

House of Lords (2005) 'The economics of energy efficiency', in Science and Technology Committee, *Second report* (chapter 3), Report of Session 2005-2006, London: House of Lords, www.publications.parliament.uk/pa/ld200506/ldselect/ldsctech/21/2106.htm

Hu, A. (2009) 'A new approach at Copenhagen (three parts)', *China dialogue*, 6 April, www.chinadialogue.net/article/show/single/en/2892

Hu, J.(2007) 'Hold high the great banner of socialism with Chinese characteristics and strive for new victories in building a moderately prosperous society in all respects', *China Daily*, Report to the Seventeenth National Congress of the Communist Party of China, 15 October, www.chinadaily.com.cn/china/2007-10/25/content_6204663.htm

Hu, J. (2008) 'Full text of Hu Jintao's speech at the opening ceremony of the Boao Forum for Asia Annual Conference 2008', *Xinhua Online*, 12 April, http://news.xinhuanet.com/english/2008-04/12/content_7966431.htm

Hu, J.(2009) 'Hu Jintao's speech on climate change', *The New York Times*, 22 September, A transcript of a speech given by President Hu Jintao of China to the United Nations General Assembly, as provided by the Federal News Service, www.nytimes.com/2009/09/23/world/asia/23hu.text.html?_r=1

Huang, C. (2010) 'Hu ramps up pressure for shift to smart economy', *South China Morning Post*, 8 February, p 6.

IEA (2009) *World energy outlook: Executive summary*, Paris: OECD/IEA.

IEA (2010) *World energy outlook: Executive summary*, Paris: OECD/IEA.

IEA (International Energy Agency) (2007) *World energy outlook 2007: China and India Insights*, Paris: IEA, www.worldenergyoutlook.org/

Jia, Z. (2009) 'Creating harmony between people and nature', *Beijing's Review*, no 52, pp 24-4, www.bjreview.com.cn/nation/txt/2009-05/26/content_197521.htm

Jin, Y. (2008) 'Ecological civilization: from conception to practice in China', *Clean Technologies and Environmental Policy*, vol 10, no 2, pp 111-12, DOI 10.1007/s10098-008-0147-6.

Levine, M.D. and Aden, N.T. (2008) 'Global carbon emissions in the coming decades: the case of China', *Annual Review of Environment and Resources*, vol 33, pp 19-38.

Li, J.(2009a) 'Climate change law to bring teeth to emissions mandates', *China Daily*, 26 August, www.chinadaily.com.cn/bizchina/2009-08/26/content_8618043.htm

Li, J. (2009b) 'Minister makes call to go green', *China Daily*, 5 June, www.chinadaily.com.cn/china/2009-06/05/content_8250385.htm

Liu, G. (2007) 'The challenges of China's peaceful development', in J.Y.S. Cheng (ed) *Challenges and policy programmes of China's new leadership* (pp 245-72), Hong Kong: City University of Hong Kong Press

Liu, J. and Diamond, J. (2005) 'China's environment in a globalizing world', *Nature*, vol 435, no 4076, pp 1179-86.

Liu, J., Xiong, P. and Fu S.(2010) 'Concrete actions matter for climate change talks: backgrounder: key facts of UN Framework Convention on Climate Change', *Xinhua*, 6 October, http://news.xinhuanet.com/english2010/china/2010-10/06/c_13544344.htm

Ma, J. (2007) 'Ecological civilisation is the way forward', *Chinadialogue*, 31 October, www.chinadialogue.net/article/show/single/en/1440-Ecological-civilisation-is-the-way-forward

MEA (Millennium Ecosystem Assessment) (2005) *Ecosystems and human well-being: Synthesis*, Washington, DC: Island Press.

Meadows, D.H., Meadows, D.l., Randers, J. and III, W.W.B. (1972) *The limits to growth: A report for the Club of Rome's project on the predicament of mankind*, New York, NY: Universe Books.

Miller, D. (2008) 'Global justice and climate change: how should responsibilities be distributed? Parts I and II', in *Tanner lectures on human values*, Beijing: Tsinghua University.

NDRC (National Development and Reform Commission) (2007a) *China sustainable development strategy report*, Beijing: NDRC.

NDRC (2007b) *China's National Climate Change Programme*, Beijing: NDRC, www.wilsoncenter.org/index.cfm?topic_id=1421&fuseaction=topics. item&news_id=239678

Nellemann, C. and Corcoran, E. (eds) (2010) *Dead planet, living planet: Biodiversity and ecosystem restoration for sustainable development: A rapid response assessment*, United Nations Environment Programme, Arendal, Norway: GRID-Arendal, www.grida.no/publications/rr/dead-planet/

OECD (Organisation for Economic Co-operation and Development) (2009) *Declaration on green growth, adopted at the council meeting at ministerial level on 24 June 2009*, C/MIN(2009)5/ADD1/FINAL, Paris: OECD.

O'Riordan, T. (1983) *Environmentalism*, London: Pion Press.

Pan, J. (2010) 'Low-carbon logic', *Chinadialogue*, 8 November, www. chinadialogue.net/article/show/single/en/3927-Low-carbon-logic?

Pan, Y. (2004) 'Environmental culture and national renaissance', in *Untitled*, Beijing: State Environmental Protection Administration/PRC, distributed at the Forum on Environmental Impact Assessment, BoAo, Hainan Island, PRC, 13–15 December.

Pan, Y. and Zhou, J. (2006) 'The rich consume and the poor suffer the pollution', *Chinadialogue*, 27 October, www.chinadialogue.net/article/show/single/en/493--The rich-consume-and-the-poor-suffer-the-pollution-

Sachs, J. (2007) *Survival in the Anthropocene*, Reith Lectures 2007, transcript of Lecture 2, delivered on Wednesday 18 April, 8pm, at the China Centre for Economic Research at Peking University, www. bbc.co.uk/radio4/reith2007/lecture2.shtml#lecture2 (accessed: 19/4/07).

Schellnhuber, H.J., Crutzen, P.J., Clark, W.C. and Hunt, J. (2005) 'Earth system analysis for sustainability', *Environment*, vol 47, no 8, pp 11-25.

Sen, A. (1999) *Development as freedom*, Oxford: Oxford University Press.

Smil, V. (2005) *Energy at the crossroads*, Cambridge, MA: MIT Press (first published 2003).

Song, G., Xu, S., Jin, S., Fu, Y., Li, P., He, Y., Wang, C. and Zhu, X. (2008) *China's environmental policy analysis*, Beijing: Chemical Industry Press (in Mandarin: *Huanjing Zhengce Fenxi*).

Suzuki, S. (1992) Severn Suzuki speaking at UN Earth Summit 1992, www.youtube.com/watch?v=5g8cmWZOX8Q

Tan, Y. (2009) 'Experts urge stimulous package on social welfare', *China Daily*, 24 June, www.chinadaily.com.cn/china/2009-06/24/content_8315710.htm

The Economist (2009) 'A time for muscle-flexing', *The Economist*, 21 March, pp 29-31.

Tickell, C. (2007) *China's environment: Prospects and hazards*, chinadialogue.net, www.chinadialogue.net/article/show/single/en/896-China-s-environment-prospects-and-hazards (accessed: 11/94/07).

UN (United Nations) (1945) *Charter of the United Nations*, New York, NY: UN.

UNCED (United Nations Conference on Environment and Development (1992) *Agenda 21*, New York, NY: United Nations General Assembly, wwwunorg/esa/sustdev/agenda21texthtm

UNDP (United Nations Development Programme) (1990) *Human Development Report 1990*, United Nations Development Programme, New York, http://hdr.undp.org/en/reports/global/hdr1990/chapters/ (accessed: 22/9/09).

UNDP) (2007) *Human development report 2007/2008: Fighting climate change: Human solidarity in a divided world*, Summary version, New York, NY: UNDP, http://hdr.undp.org/en/reports/global/hdr2007-2008/

UNEP (United Nations Environment Programme) (2009) *Global green new deal: Policy brief, March 2009*, Geneva: UNEP, http://unep.org/pdf/A_Global_Green_New_Deal_Policy_Brief.pdf

UNESCAP (United Nations Economic and Social Commission for Asia and the Pacific) (2009) *Greening growth in Asia and the Pacific*, Bangkok: UNESCAP, http://climate-l.org/2009/10/19/unescap-releases-report-on-greening-growth-in-asia-and-the-pacific/

WCED (World Commission on Environment and Development) (1987) *Our common future*, Oxford: Oxford University Press.

Weber, C.L., Peters, G.P., Guan, D. and Hubacek, K. (2008) 'The contribution of Chinese exports to climate change', *Energy Policy*, vol 36, pp 3572-7, doi: 10.1016/j.enpol.2008.06.009.

World Bank (2008) *Executive summary: Mid-term evaluation of China's 11th Five Year Plan*, Beijing: World Bank, http://siteresources.worldbank.org/CHINAEXTN/Resources/318949-1121421890573/China_11th_Five_Year_Plan_overview_en.pdf?cid=EXTEAPMonth1

World Bank (2009) *Quarterly update: March 2009*, Washington, DC: World Bank, http://siteresources.worldbank.org/INTCHINA/Resources/318862-1237238982080/CQU_March2009_fullreport.pdf

Xie, Z. (2009) 'China has no other choice thank to pursue sustainable development', *The Guardian*, 27 May, www.guardian.co.uk/environment/cif-green/2009/may/27/china-climate-change

Xinhua (2006) 'Efficiency overtakes speed as primary goal', *Xinhua Online*, 3 December, http://news.xinhuanet.com/english/2006-12/03/content_5428169.htm

Yao, R., Li, B. and Steemers, K. (2005) 'Energy policy and standard for built environment in China', *Renewable Energy*, vol 30, pp 1973-88.

York, R. (2006) 'Ecological paradoxes: William Stanley Jevons and the paperless office', *Human Ecology Review*, vol 13, pp 143-7.

Yu, Q.(2008) 'Statement by H.E. Ambassador Yu Qingtai, China's Special Representative for Climate Change Talks, at the thematic debate of the United Nations General Assembly on Climate Change', New York, 12 February, www.fmprc.gov.cn/eng/wjb/zwjg/zwbd/t406936.htm

FOUR

Differentiating historical responsibilities for climate change

Christian Ellermann, Niklas Höhne and Benito Müller

Climate change has strong ethical dimensions, and global solutions to this problem are unlikely to be crafted, or to be stable, without some broad conception of what is fair (see IPCC, 1996; Stern, 2006). There is a burgeoning literature on these dimensions (Müller, 2001; Gardiner, 2004; Brown et al, 2006; Klinsky and Dowlatabadi, 2009; Harris, 2010; see also Chapter Six), with part of this work focusing on historical responsibility for climate change (Botzen et al, 2008; Friman and Linnér, 2008; Klinsky and Dowlatabadi, 2009). The notion of historical responsibility for climate change of 'Annex I' (that is, developed country) parties to the United Nations Framework Convention on Climate Change (UNFCCC) has been regularly invoked by developing-country governments. Historical responsibility is also one of the main lines of argument underlying the principle of common but differentiated responsibility for climate change, and the polluter pays principle more generally. Discussion on equity – a political-economic approach to historical responsibility (Friman, 2007) – has been widely present in the Chinese debate on climate change. It is indeed one of the main discursive elements in China's official position (Ellermann and Mayer, 2010), framing understanding of the country's ethical position vis-à-vis developed countries and the rest of the world.

In this chapter, we examine the Chinese position on responsibility for climate change by drawing on the results of the Ad-hoc Group for the Modelling and Assessment of Contributions of Climate Change (MATCH), a group that was created in 1997 following a proposal from Brazil (UNFCCC, 1997). The MATCH group has concentrated on the causal attribution of historical greenhouse gas (GHG) emissions to countries (see Ito et al, 2008; Prather et al, 2009; Höhne et al, submitted).[1]

Contributions versus responsibility

Climate impacts, whether anthropogenic or due to natural variability, will inevitably have a multitude of causes. The moral responsibility for climate impacts will typically be shared by a number of actors. There is a link between a moral agent causally contributing to an impact and being (partly) morally responsible for it, but that does not mean that the two are the same. The MATCH project modelling focused on determining the *causal contribution* of GHGs covered under the UNFCCC to certain climatic impacts, in particular to changes in mean global temperature. The message from the project is that we cannot accurately discuss causal contributions to climate change per se, at least not if one is intent only on specifying numerical shares thereof, because such calculations require making normative decisions. One of the key normative decisions is the way in which emissions are associated with particular countries. It is one thing to say that a series of emissions has contributed a certain percentage to the increase in global mean temperature over the 20th century, for example, and quite another to say that China has done so. The former is purely scientific, whereas the latter involves a normative decision of how to identify 'the emissions of China' at a given time.

The implicit assumption of the MATCH team was that anthropogenic emissions associated with a particular country for a given period of time are those emitted from within its sovereign territory, and that the sovereign territory is changing over time. There are a number of problems with this traditional conception, not least that it does not lend itself easily to accommodate 'bunker fuel' emissions from international travel and transport. Another, lesser-known problem with this sort of traditional sovereignty-based definition is that it does not lend itself to take account of joint contributions and responsibilities, short of pooling the sovereignty of the territories in question. This shortcoming shall be discussed briefly in the context of Article 4 of the UNFCCC, which can be interpreted as implying joint North–South responsibility for the increments in emissions in developing countries since the convention was signed in 1992.[2]

The normative issue of identifying the sovereign emissions of China is not completely straightforward because the sovereign territory of the People's Republic of China has changed through history. In this chapter, we rely on the decisions regarding the attribution of the emissions made by the MATCH team. The data recorded for China are largely dominated by emissions from fossil-fuel combustion, as recorded in Marland et al (2005), for 'mainland China' (that is, excluding Hong

Kong, Macau and Taiwan). Figure 4.1 displays emissions during different historical periods. Until 1911, China was under the rule of the Qing Dynasty, but during some of this period, parts of the country were occupied by foreign powers. However, there was no major colonial rule over China that would warrant a deep discussion of the attribution of emissions during that time, which amounted to 6% of total emissions between 1890 and 2005. The period from 1912 to 1937 saw major domestic conflict, with warlords fighting over regional rule in the Republic of China. There should be little question over the attribution of emissions during this time, which amounted to 10% of China's emissions from 1890 to 2005. In contrast, major parts of China were occupied by Japan from 1937 to 1945. Marland attributes all emissions during this period to China (mirroring similar decisions about other countries, such as the attribution of pre-independence emissions throughout current Indian territory to India, rather than to the colonial power, the United Kingdom). In spite of the rapid industrialisation and deforestation during this time, the share of these nine years amounted to only 4% of total Chinese emissions.

Figure 4.1: China's emissions of GHGs during different historical periods

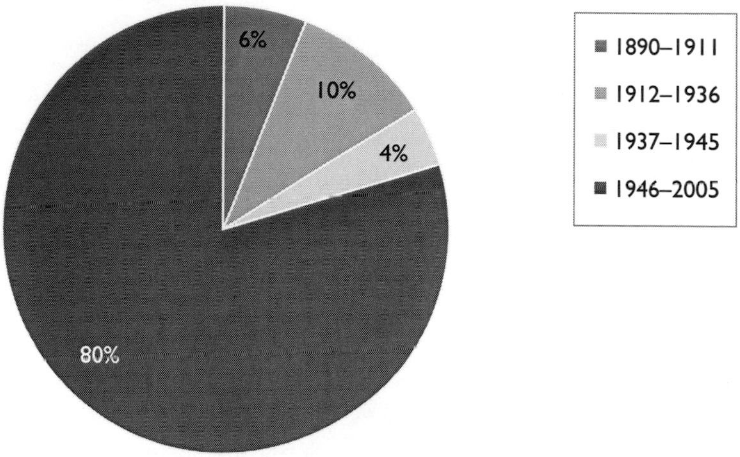

Source: Authors' calculation based on MATCH dataset

From 1946 on, sovereign rule over all of mainland China again became clearly Chinese. This historical period contributed 80% of the emissions from 1890 to 2005. While the question of Chinese sovereign emissions is not absolutely straightforward, the contribution during historical periods that could be contentious (1890-1911 and 1937-1945) make up only 10% of total Chinese emissions. In practice, therefore, the relevance of the normative debate surrounding this issue is limited. It may be safe to assume that this applies to most countries that have not seen major changes in territory since 1945.

Types of responsibility

To be responsible for something harmful is to be worthy of blame for it.[3] Aristotle (1908: III.1-5, 1110a-1111b4) contended that blame and praise are bestowed on *voluntary* actions, while involuntary ones are pardoned. The key to responsibility for actions is thus their voluntary status, for which he gives two necessary conditions:

> First, there is a control condition: the action or trait must have its origin in the agent. That is, it must be up to the agent whether to perform that action or possess the trait — it cannot be compelled externally.

> Second, Aristotle proposes an epistemic condition: the agent must be aware of what it is she is doing or bringing about. (Eshleman, 2004)

However, ignorance per se seems to be slightly too easy for pardoning, which is why the condition is usually strengthened in so far as the agent *could have reasonably been expected to know*.

Aristotle's conception of 'responsibility' is based in his theory of virtue, which concerns 'passions and actions'. But there are other theories which see the concept in the context of duties, in particular in derelictions of duty, which are not (necessarily) actions but equally liable to give rise to blame. Figure 4.2 is an attempt at representing the interplay between the distinctions of voluntary/involuntary, harmful/ harmless, agency/duty based and type/level of blameworthiness (responsibility). Aristotle's conditions on assigning blame to actions (and to agents) are about whether they are carried out voluntarily or involuntarily. However, as illustrated in Figure 4.2, blame can also be assigned or withheld regardless of this distinction. If, for example, the effects of an action are *harmless* (category I), then clearly no blame should be attached to it, even if it was voluntary. Moreover, there are situations where, contrary to Aristotle's conditions, 'strict' blame (responsibility) is handed out simply because the effects are harmful, regardless of whether the harm was done voluntarily or involuntarily (category III.b).

Figure 4.2: Categories of blame/responsibility

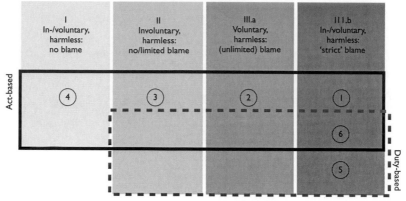

In the context of climate change, blame/responsibility is usually seen as applying to certain acts, namely the emissions of GHGs; thus, blame is act based. For example, if someone drives a car, and if the emissions resulting from this act are deemed to be harmful, then they may be judged to deserve unreserved blame just because the emissions are harmful (strict blame, ① in Figure 4.2), or because they drove voluntarily, in the full knowledge of the harmfulness of the emissions and without coercion (unlimited blame, ②). If, however, they can plead reasonable ignorance or coercion, then they may get a (limited) pardon (no/limited blame, ③). Finally, if the emissions in question are classified as harmless, then no one can justly be blamed (no blame, ④).

What is not usual is to consider blaming someone for certain harmful emissions, not because they were actively engaged in emitting them but because they had a duty to prevent them. Thus, if two individuals, say Jane and John, enter a contract stating that Jane is to reduce her emissions and that John is to bear her additional costs, then it can be argued that they both have a joint duty to reduce Jane's emissions, and that if the reduction does not occur they could be jointly blamed. The blame may, of course, not lie equally. Jane may have wished to reduce emissions but did not receive the money to do so, or John may have wished to pay for Jane's emissions reduction but Jane had no inclination to undertake that reduction. The point is that John might have to take responsibility for a certain amount of emissions even though those emissions were not actually emitted by him (⑤), while Jane may not have to take responsibility for the whole of the emissions increment she failed to reduce because there was a joint dereliction of duty (⑥).

Differentiating contributions and responsibilities

The methodology of the MATCH project was designed to establish the relative causal contributions by countries to changes in global average temperature. The MATCH percentage figures for countries' shares in contributing to these changes are determined by the anthropogenic emissions that have historically been emitted from their sovereign territory. These percentage shares are themselves relative to the type of impact, and they depend on the sequential order of the emissions series in question. However, to simplify calculations for this chapter, it is possible to use the sum of historical emissions (or their relative size) as a reasonable approximation for relative causal contributions (den Elzen et al, 2005; Hope, 2008). Here we use aggregate historical country emissions emitted between 1890 and the present (2005) – using 1995 Global Warming Potentials (GWPs) for different gases consistent with the Kyoto Protocol – as determinants of responsibility.[4] Using GWP factors can only be considered an approximation; they ignore the feedbacks and long-term changes in global warming potentials. Marginal damage from a unit of emissions is smaller today than it was at the beginning of industrialisation. For simplicity, we assume that emissions at all times are weighted equally by using constant GWPs (see Höhne and Blok, 2005).

The problem with either aggregate (that is, country-wide) or per-capita emissions measures is that, while they may capture some facet of the relevant notion of 'responsibility', they both fail in capturing other facets. The percentage shares derived from the aggregate figures clearly capture the causal-contribution aspect of responsibilities, but they cannot, by definition, reflect other potentially relevant country aspects, such as population size. Per-capita emissions figures, on the other hand, do reflect population size, but they are unable to reflect causal contributions. For example, they would assign the same responsibility to both China and Latvia, with 0.8tC/cap in each country, despite there being a 500-fold difference in aggregate emissions (WRI, 2009).

There is no general answer to whether responsibility should be measured in absolute (single-parameter) or in relative (multi-parameter) terms. There are cases of emissions-based responsibilities, which should be quantified in absolute terms (that is, in terms involving only one parameter, namely physical emissions). In other cases, it may be necessary to 'relativise' these figures in terms of other relevant parameters, such as population sizes (when talking about group/country responsibilities) or wealth and economic production. Traditionally, these relativisations have been operationalised by simple parameter divisions, such as per-capita and per-unit-of-economic-output (gross domestic product [GDP]) measures. For example, Baer et al (2008) name 'cumulative per-capita CO_2 [carbon dioxide] emissions from fossil fuel consumption since 1990' as a 'reasonable' definition of responsibility. Research institutes close to the Chinese government have in recent years undertaken significant work in a similar direction; they promote 'cumulative per capita emissions … as an indicator for equity' (Pan et al, 2009).[5]

Aggregate country or regional responsibility for climate change (impacts) should be relativised in the sense that it has to be measured in multi-parameter terms, including – apart from emissions – the size of (certain) populations. The traditional operationalisation in per-capita terms oversimplifies the situation. Instead, in this chapter, we use a bottom-up, allowance-based methodology. This generalises both the traditional absolute and per-capita measures. The idea is that allowances may be allocated to emitters, which they can use against their emissions in calculating their level of responsibility. It is, in general terms, analogous to the system of tax allowances used in most countries in differentiating tax burdens. There can be different kinds of 'climate change responsibility allowances' depending on the (moral) justification for why they should be allocated. For example, if a certain level of GHG emissions is deemed to be harmless, then one would have to allocate what we call 'basic allowances' to cover these harmless emissions, on the grounds that no person should be held responsible (blamed) for a harmless activity.

Other allowances could be allocated on the basis of basic needs, in turn justified by way of the Aristotelian 'control condition' that one cannot be held responsible for what is not in one's control. This kind of allowance has been implemented by looking at 'subsistence allowances', based on the assumption that poverty eradication is an overriding moral aim, and that in present circumstances it can only be achieved through activities that generate GHG emissions. There may be other basic needs-based allowances that might have to be considered, such as the need to keep temperatures within certain boundaries in order to ensure people's survival. The Aristotelian epistemic condition that one should not be held responsible for actions that one could not have reasonably been expected to know were harmful – mere ignorance is not sufficient – could also be used to justify the introduction of what might be called 'epistemic allowances'. The main difference between these Aristotle-based allowances and the above-mentioned basic kind is that while the latter can be seen as 'certificates of harmlessness', the former are merely 'responsibility wavers' applied to emissions that would otherwise have been counted as harmful and blameworthy. The main consequences of this is that, while basic emissions should be transferable, these 'responsibility wavers' should not. The latter ought to be used only as a 'back-up' to the former, should both be issued, and not as a complement.

Apart from the question of what sort of allowances should be counted against one's responsibility for climate change, a key issue with this sort of methodology is how to allocate them. In the case of basic and subsistence allowances, we believe that a 'bottom-up' approach to country allocations – a definition of country allocations in terms of personal ones – is most appropriate. In the case of epistemic allowances for operationalising Aristotle's epistemic condition, there is no need to take recourse to such a bottom-up approach to country allocations, particularly if one adheres to the traditional definition of country emissions. All that is necessary, on either the personal or the country level, is to ensure that all emissions occurring in justifiable ignorance of their harmfulness be covered by allowances. Personal basic allocations should be allocated on an egalitarian principle for the same reasons that support the per-capita allocation of global emission permits.[6] The bottom-up methodology, then, implies that countries can disregard some of their emissions in responsibility calculations, using the following formula:

$$b \times p_i \text{ (where } b \text{ is the global per-capita figure of harmless emissions, and } p \text{ is the population of country/region } i)$$

Population figures enter allocation-based country responsibility measures, which is quite different from traditional per-capita measures.[7]

The difference becomes even more marked if other population-related allowances are considered. While there are arguments for a differentiated allocation (according to particular needs) in the case of subsistence allowances, it is clear that if emissions are equally allocated they would normally not be allocated to the whole population of a country, but rather to those who are living below a set poverty line. In other words, it is possible that the allocation of subsistence allowances to a country is dependent on population size, thus generating a population-relative responsibility measure. However, unlike in the traditional per-capita methodology, the populations in question are not *all* inhabitants but rather only special-needs groups, for example the country's poor. The proposed allowance-based methodology thus manages to reflect certain population sizes in establishing country/ regional climate change responsibilities without the danger of unjustifiably diminishing in-country responsibility differences – by letting the responsible, 'carbon-rich' people hide behind their carbon-poor compatriots – as can happen in the case of the traditional per-capita methodology.[8]

Chinese discourse on historical responsibility

Historical responsibility for climate change has been discussed in Chinese publications, with authors concentrating mainly on direct historical contribution of countries' CO_2 emissions from energy use (He et al, 2000; Zhao, 2007; Xu and Yu, 2008). According to a number of Chinese authors, developed countries bear responsibility for climate change because they have emitted 77% of CO_2 emissions from fossil-fuel use from 1950 to 2000.[9] He et al (2000, p 2) argue for actively using the notion of developed-country historical responsibility to 'protect China's interests'. To corroborate their point and 'refute arguments of "common responsibility" and the like', they calculate that developing-country annual emissions will surpass Annex I emissions only in 2037, and cumulative emissions only in 2147.[10] An analysis that goes beyond directly equating contribution shares to historical responsibility is lacking from these analyses, and it is usually restricted to the developed–developing country divide. However, Chen et al (1999) analyse the topic starting with the 'Brazilian proposal' of 1997 (UNFCCC, 1997), using that proposal's underlying concepts and calculations of national contributions to climate change. Comparing current (1990-2010) with historical contribution shares, Chen et al (1999) conclude that China's interests would not be served if it was singled out from the group of developing countries in analysing historical responsibility.

What is China's official view on responsibility for GHG emissions? The Chinese government first put forward a coherent climate policy in 2007. Its views on the application of historical responsibility for climate change have become manifest in various official documents. For example, government ministries have declared that:

> Both developed and developing countries are obligated to adopt measures to decelerate and adapt to climate change. But the level of their historical responsibilities, level and stage of development, and capabilities and ways of contribution vary. Developed countries should be responsible for their accumulative emissions and current

high per-capita emissions, and take the lead in reducing emissions. (NDRC, 2008)

According to the principle of 'common but differentiated responsibilities' of the UNFCCC, the Parties included in Annex I to the Convention [developed countries] should take the lead in reducing greenhouse gas emissions. For developing countries with less historical emissions and current low per capita emissions, their priority is to achieve sustainable development. As a developing country, China will stick to its sustainable development strategy ... and make further contribution to the protection of [the] global climate system. (NDRC, 2007)

Developed countries shall take responsibility for their historical cumulative emissions and current high per capita emissions to change their unsustainable way of life and to substantially reduce their emissions and, at the same time, to provide financial support and transfer technology to developing countries.... Given their historical responsibility and development level and based on the principle of equality, developed countries shall reduce their GHG emissions in aggregate by at least 40% below their 1990 levels by 2020 and take corresponding policies, measures and actions. (NDRC, 2009)

Climate change is primarily caused by developed countries' historical emissions over many years. (MOFA, 2008)

Similar to the Chinese academic views, the official line is that, first, China is a developing country, and second, developing countries have little responsibility for climate change. While low per-capita emissions are discussed directly for the case of China, in the case of historical responsibility, China is not mentioned individually but generally as a member of the group of developing countries with little responsibility overall.

The Chinese position on historical responsibility has become more clearly defined over time. A main purpose now seems to be to develop an effort-sharing scheme based on ideas of historical contributions to climate change. For some time, China subscribed to a position, shared by some other developing countries, that does not allow for global reduction commitments, but instead differentiates reduction targets for

Annex I countries by historical responsibility. More recently, however, China has started to formulate its own position, a 'cumulative per-capita emissions convergence' approach. It does not focus on historical responsibility shares as we do here, but instead bases responsibility on egalitarian grounds that require equality of cumulative historical and future country emissions divided by the population at the time of the target year (2100 in a Chinese proposal).[11] Figure 4.3 shows this calculation based on MATCH data. A more recent refined version of this approach works with 'per-capita emissions entitlements' (which only at first sight appears to be similar to our allocations) that would lead the world towards a global atmospheric concentration of 470ppmv CO_2 in 2050. Emissions budgets are then used that run either a surplus or a deficit in 2005, depending on the sum of a country's emissions above or below its population's 'entitlement' each year; equal cumulative per-capita emissions over time (operationalised as a budget of zero) are required in 2050.[12]

Figure 4.3: Cumulative emissions per capita in 2100 using MATCH data

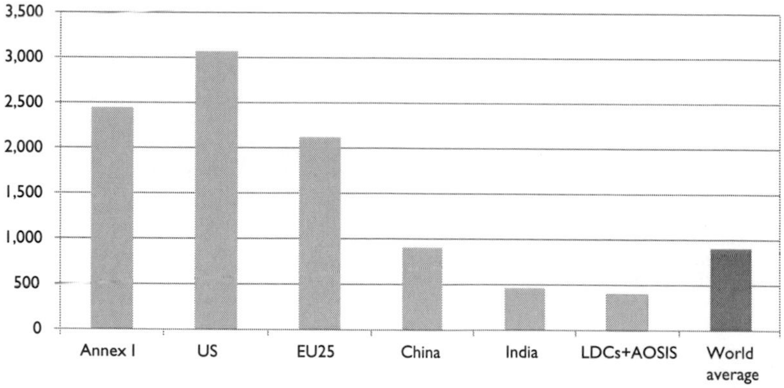

Note: LDCs = Group of Least Developed Countries; AOSIS = Alliance of Small Island States.

Source: Authors' calculations based on MATCH dataset.

Context

For this chapter, causal contributions to climate change were calculated for all countries, but in the remainder of the chapter we will focus on three individual countries – the United States (US), India and of course China – and three groups of countries – the group of industrialised countries listed in Annex I of the UNFCCC, the European Union

(EU) after the 2004 enlargement (the so-called 'EU25' countries), and the Group of Least Developed Countries combined with the Alliance of Small Island States (LDCs+AOSIS, totalling 76 countries).

Figure 4.4 depicts three non-emission parameters for the year 2005 (the last year of observed emissions in the MATCH dataset) that are of interest in discussing of the contribution to, and responsibility for, climate change by these countries and country groupings, in particular their share of:

- global wealth (defined in terms of current GDP purchasing power parity [PPP]);
- global population; and
- global poverty (measured in terms of the number of people living on US$1 or less per day).

Not surprisingly, the developed and developing worlds (Annex I/ non-Annex I; North/South) are not the same with respect to these three dimensions: While the 20% of the world population who live in Annex I countries produce 56% of global wealth, the non-Annex I countries are home to 99.2% of the world's very poor people. These proportions have some impact in our responsibility calculations. For example, consider the fact that in 2005 China's global share in abject poverty of 12% translated into 129 million people, and India's 35% into 377 million, while the population of those living below US$2 (PPP)/ day was 454 million in China, and a staggering 881 million in India.

Figure 4.4: Economic and demographic context (2005) (%)

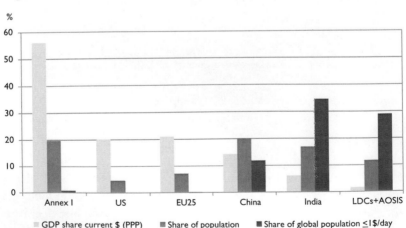

Source: Authors' calculations based on MATCH dataset.

According to our simplified methodology, the share of a country's (or a group of countries') contribution to climate change is determined by their share in the global warming potential of their historical GHG emissions. However, to be able to calculate these shares, some further parameters need to be specified, such as the timeframe, the types of emissions and the countries or groups of countries to be considered. For the purposes of this chapter, the chosen time horizon begins in 1890 and the emissions are those considered under the Kyoto Protocol.[13] Historically, industrialised countries (as listed in Annex I of the UNFCCC) have contributed the majority of GHGs to the atmosphere, namely 54.5%, a figure that in the present simplified methodology represents their share in the causal contribution to the climate change problem. The causal contribution shares in detail, as represented in Figure 4.5, are (in descending order of magnitude) the US (19.7%), EU25 (17.8%), China (10.8%), LDCs+AOSIS (5.7%) and India (3.9%). These proportions can vary significantly depending on the sorts of gases and sources/sinks that are taken into consideration. For example, if emissions from land use, land-use change and forestry (LULUCF), which are relatively uncertain, are excluded, Annex I contributions increase by almost a fifth (+10.2 percentage points), most of it absorbed by the US (+5.2 percentage points) and the EU (+4.3 percentage points), with chief beneficiaries Brazil (−2.3 percentage points, not shown here), Indonesia (−2.9 percentage points, not shown here) and LDCs+AOSIS (−2.3 percentage points). The Chinese contribution does not change drastically (−0.4 percentage points), meaning that China's

Figure 4.5: Causal contribution to climate change

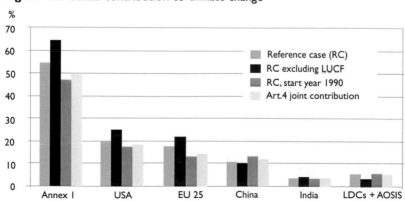

Note: LUCF = land-use change and forestry
Source: Authors' calculations based on MATCH dataset.

share of emissions from LULUCF in total emissions is not very far from the global average.

Differentiating causal contributions

Certain emissions, even when emitted over the sovereign territory of one country, should result in joint responsibility among more than one country. An example can be found in impact of China's exports:

> [T]he extent of 'exported carbon' from China should lead to some rethinking by government negotiators as they work towards a new climate change agreement. It suggests that a focus on emissions within national borders may miss the point. Whilst the nation state is at the heart of most international negotiations and treaties, global trade means that a country's carbon footprint is international. Should countries be concerned with emissions within their borders (as is currently the case), or should they also be responsible for emissions due to the production of goods and services they consume? (Wang and Watson, 2007)

In this chapter we accommodate this shared responsibility by introducing 'joint contributions'. Figure 4.6 depicts the joint contributions of China and other developing countries.

In order to have any significant variance from the sovereign country measures at all, the time horizon has also been limited to start in 1990. For the industrialised world, the switch to this sort of 50:50 joint

Figure 4.6: China's joint contribution with Annex II countries

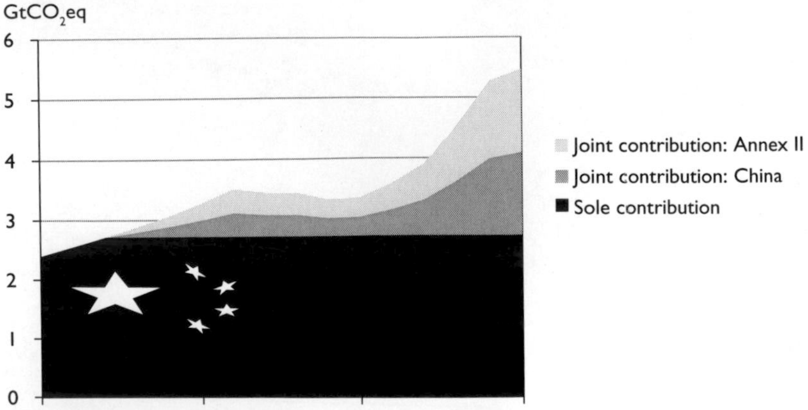

$GtCO_2eq$

Joint contribution: Annex II
Joint contribution: China
Sole contribution

Source: Authors' calculations based on MATCH dataset.

contribution would mean an increase of 3 percentage points since 1990, most of it going in roughly equal measure to the US and the EU (+1 percentage point each), and benefiting mostly China (−1.3 percentage points). Given these differences would practically disappear if one were to use the reference case (beginning in 1890) it was decided not to proceed along these lines for the moment.

Differentiating moral responsibilities

Strict responsibility

Strict responsibilities are determined by the level of aggregate historical emissions − representing causal contributions − and a per-capita allocation of the global total of harmless emissions according to the allowance-based approach outlined above. There has been some debate in the literature as to how much could be globally emitted without imposing harm, particularly in the context of defining what has become known as 'ecological space'. Commonly used values range between 2 GtC (gigatons of carbon) (7.3 $GtCO_2$) per year for oceanic sinks alone (Agarwal et al, 1999) and 4 GtCeq (gigatonnes of carbon equivalent) (14.7 $GtCO_2$eq) that also include terrestrial sinks (Retallack, 2005; MacGregor, 2006; Monbiot, 2007). Seven $GtCO_2$ as the global total of basic allowances has been adopted here, for the present purposes to be allocated on a per-capita basis.[14]

As can be seen in Figure 4.7, numerically, this choice implies an overall industrialised country (historical) climate change responsibility of 64%. The largest single country share is that of the US with 25.6%, followed by the EU (19.1%), China (6.4%) and finally a number of countries with low if not negligible responsibility: LDCs+AOSIS (4.1%) and India (0.3%). While it will not be surprising that individual AOSIS (Alliance of Small Island States) and LDCs have really no historical responsibility for the climate change problem (on average 0.05%), what may be less expected is to find India at the very end of our responsibility spectrum. The reasons for the extremely low Indian responsibility share are its relatively modest causal contribution share of around 4%, and its rather large global population share (16.9%), which determines the allocation of allowances.[15]

Figure 4.7: Moral responsibilities for climate change (%)

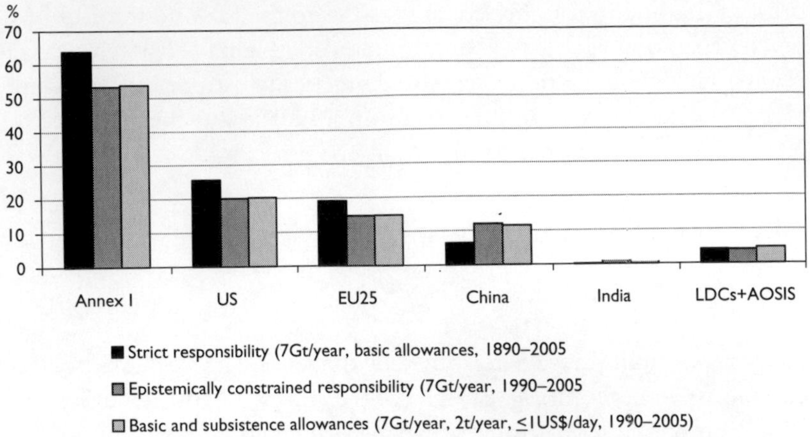

■ Strict responsibility (7Gt/year, basic allowances, 1890–2005)

▨ Epistemically constrained responsibility (7Gt/year, 1990–2005)

☐ Basic and subsistence allowances (7Gt/year, 2t/year, ≤1US$/day, 1990–2005)

Source: Authors' calculations based on MATCH dataset.

Limited responsibility I: epistemic constraints

There has been a robust difference of opinion – mostly along the developed–developing country divide – as to whether it is fair to use strict historical responsibility, or whether countries should be granted mitigating circumstances, such as ignorance of the effect of one's actions. This epistemic constraint of full responsibility has been implemented here by excluding emissions before 1990 from the calculations, on the grounds that after that year, which saw the beginning of the UNFCCC negotiations and the publication of the first reports by the Intergovernmental Panel on Climate Change (IPCC), no government could reasonably plead ignorance of the problem.

This implementation of ignorance as a mitigating circumstance does shift the burden of responsibility significantly from industrialised to developing countries, with Annex I as a whole losing 10 percentage points. The US (20.1%) and the EU (12.3%) both lose over a fifth of their responsibility relative to their historical strict responsibility shares, while China (12%) picks up about the same number of percentage points. For China this means almost a doubling of responsibility relative to the strict measure. This is certainly due to the much later onset of large GHG emission quantities, following the rapid economic development in the past two to three decades. On the whole, a limitation of responsibility by considering only post-1990 contributions benefits industrialised countries.

Limited responsibility II: epistemic constraints with subsistence allowances

One may argue for a certain dispensation of allowances for subsistence emissions, or rather emissions needed to overcome (abject levels of) poverty. For the purposes of this chapter, pre-1990 contributions continue to be disregarded in this context. This leaves two parameters to be determined: who should be eligible for the subsistence allowances, and how much should they be? The most readily available data are listed in the World Bank Development Indicators, which contain figures for people living on less than US$1 and US$2 per day. Our decision was to allocate 2 tCO_2 (total CO_2) per poor inhabitant per annum − equivalent to current non-forestry per-capita emissions of the developing world − to be subtracted from the aggregate historical emissions (instead of the basic allowance). In this case of US$1/day as the 'poverty threshold', the annual subsistence allowance of 2 tCO_2eq (which is larger than basic allowance per-capita level) is therefore used instead of the basic one for each inhabitant with an income of less than US$1 per day, for example 129 million people in China in 2005.

The results benefit developing countries more than developed ones. The shift of half a percentage point in responsibility towards Annex I (53.8%) does not, however, make up for the shift in the other direction due to ignoring pre-1990 emissions. The US gains 0.2 percentage points relative to the epistemologically constrained case, while India and China jointly loose nearly 1. And the situation does not differ significantly if one moves the poverty threshold to US$2/day. In other words, the choice of poverty threshold is not a particularly sensitive one, especially not in comparison to the effects of the chosen epistemic constraint, or the overall level of basic allowances.[16]

Mitigation through population control?

Since the end of the 1970s, China has taken extraordinary measures to curb the growth of its population. Based on the undoubted achievements of the policies that were implemented, Chinese politicians have repeatedly argued that population control is one of the most successful strategies to curb emissions and they coin it as one of the key mitigation efforts of China. The underlying assumption is that the increase in emissions would have been faster with higher population growth.[17] Estimates on the size of the current population in the absence of the policies that were implemented vary, and there is not any single number that is more correct than any other when looking at this hypothetical case. To simplify, we extrapolate 1978 population figures to 2005 at the growth rate of the population from the founding of the People's Republic in 1949 to 1978, leading to a hypothetical population of 1.62 billion instead of the official 1.3 billion in 2005. We then calculate the hypothetical emissions for the years 1978 to 2005 by multiplying actual emission with the factor of actual to hypothetical population of each year, which results in hypothetical Chinese emissions of 8.7 $GtCO_2$eq instead of 7 $GtCO_2$eq in 2005.

Figure 4.8 shows the new responsibility shares for a higher Chinese population and emissions growth under the assumptions outlined above. Note that the increase in the allocated share of basic allowances for the hypothetical population offsets part of the increase in responsibility for China. Shares in strict responsibility and epistemically constrained responsibility for Annex I countries (−0.5/−1.1 percentage points), the USA (−0.2/−0.4 percentage points) and EU25 (−0.2/−0.3 percentage points) are lower in this hypothetical case. Interestingly, the responsibility shares of India increase by roughly one 10th (but still less than 0.1 percentage point) because in relation to its low emissions the country profits most from the allocation of basic allowances, part of which are diverted to China due to a higher share in world population. The share of China's strict responsibility increases to 7.1% from 6.4% and for epistemically constrained responsibility (emissions from 1990

Figure 4.8: Hypothetical responsibility with faster Chinese population growth

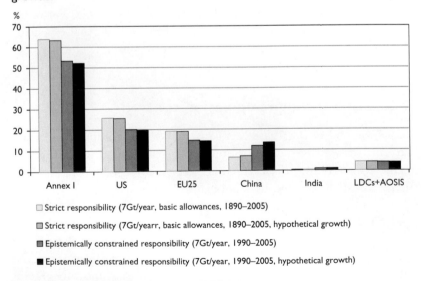

☐ Strict responsibility (7Gt/year, basic allowances, 1890–2005)

☐ Strict responsibility (7Gt/yearr, basic allowances, 1890–2005, hypothetical growth)

■ Epistemically constrained responsibility (7Gt/year, 1990–2005)

■ Epistemically constrained responsibility (7Gt/year, 1990–2005, hypothetical growth)

Source: Authors' calculations based on MATCH dataset.

only) to 13.6% from 12%. With all the caveats noted regarding the assumptions underlying this calculation, it can be claimed that China hypothetically reduced its responsibility for climate change by 10% and 13.5%[18] respectively by means of population control.

Projecting responsibility into the future

China has undoubtedly started to implement numerous policies that have a climate change mitigating effect (Ellermann et al, 2009). In the deliberations of the 12th Five-Year Plan for China's development strategy, a general consensus exists for a more sustainable development path. However, proponents of a low-carbon future for China face opposition by others who suggest that China should focus on unrestrained business-as-usual development until 2030 before worrying about (unilateral domestic) climate change mitigation. The 12th Five-Year Plan covers the years 2011 to 2015 and will among other things provide guidance for economic restructuring and major investments in infrastructure and capital with long turnover rates such as energy generation and heavy industry facilities. Decisions made in year 2010 therefore predetermine to a large degree China's general emissions trajectory over half a century or so to come. A careful look into the future (up to the often-cited year 2030) and its potential responsibilities – including historical (pre-2005) and new emissions – therefore seems to be warranted. Figures 4.9 and 4.10 corroborate this point, as in the MATCH dataset emissions between 2006 and 2030 make up the largest part of total emissions since 1890, with an average annual contribution of over 1.6% after 2005.

We are mindful of the difficulty of predicting future emissions and rely directly on the MATCH calculations. The MATCH group used latest

Figure 4.9: Total contribution during different time periods (MATCH data)

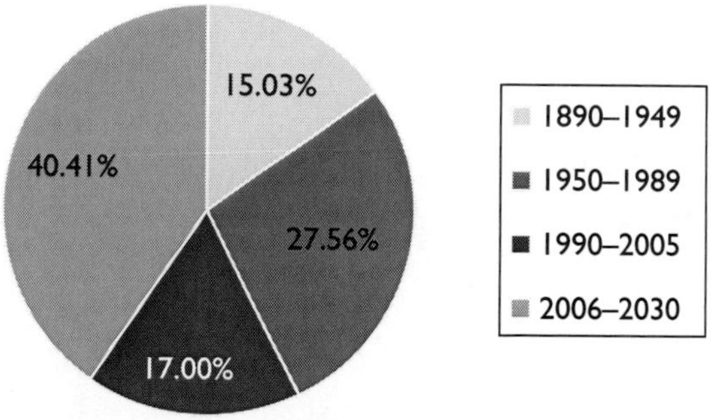

Source: Authors' calculations based on MATCH dataset.

available emissions data (2005) and extrapolated country emissions using an average of the six basic IPCC SRES (Special Report on Emissions Scenarios) scenarios for 17 world regions, avoiding a judgement on the probability of any single scenario to be more 'correct' than others. The point of this section is *not* to come up with a reliable number of future emissions, but to illustrate the potential future direction of responsibility for climate change. In contrast to the previous sections, this section cannot provide a clear ethical argument for the metric used (and as a consequence the use of the results), as it builds the sum of *actual* historical emissions and *potential* future emissions, complicating the interpretation of the results. The numbers provided are therefore simple results of a calculation based on the scientific consensus of the IPCC over future emissions, but lack the power of an ethical analysis of future historical responsibility.[19]

Figure 4.10: Annual contribution during different time periods

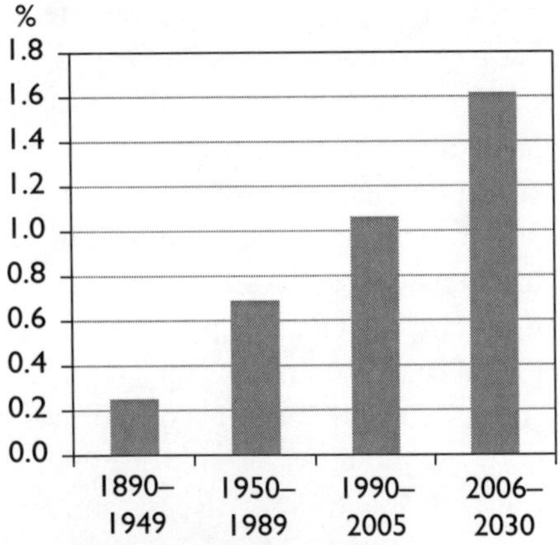

Source: Authors' calculations based on MATCH dataset.

The look into the future reveals potentially significant shifts in the shares of responsibilities of countries and regions (Figure 4.11, lighter colour shows actual historical responsibility, darker colour shows 'potential future responsibility'). Strict responsibility of Annex I countries would be 53.8% (–10.1 percentage points), epistemically constrained responsibility would be 45.2% (–8.1 percentage points). The shares of the US would decline by 5 percentage points to 20.6% and 3.9 percentage points to 16.2%, and EU25 to 15.8% and 12.6% respectively (–3.3/–2.1 percentage points). China's share of strict responsibility would rise sharply to 12.1% (plus 5.7 percentage points or 88.3%) and epistemically constrained responsibility would increase by 4.8 percentage points (or 40.4%) to 16.8%, overtaking the potential shares of the US and EU25 and potentially amounting to more than a third of the Annex I total by 2030. India's potential responsibility shares rise to 2.6% and 4% respectively (2.3 percentage points/3 percentage points and a drastic relative increase).

Figure 4.11: A scenario for future (historical) responsibility for climate change

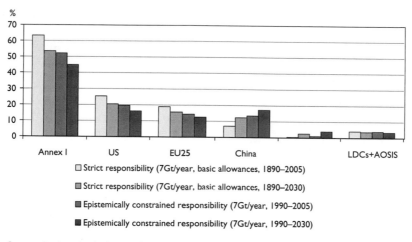

Source: Authors' calculations based on MATCH dataset.

The direction of these numbers – which as noted before should not be interpreted as an ethical analysis of future historical responsibility, but merely as a calculation based on commonly agreed emission scenarios – could potentially have significant implications for the ethical debate surrounding climate change. They point to the use of future emissions scenarios as an important research topic when looking at projected responsibility.[20] So far, there is no ethical concept for combining actual historical responsibilities and potential future responsibilities, and the calculations here cannot be used for their absolute numerical results. Their direction, however, suggests that by 2030, responsibility shares could be distributed quite differently from today, changing the force of the principle of 'common but differentiated responsibility' for some major players. China could by 2030 potentially become similarly responsible for climate change as the US or EU25, and India's responsibility could surpass that of Germany or Japan. This does not, however, affect the argument of limiting capabilities of current developing countries to combat climate change.

Conclusion

One aim of this chapter has been to put forward and discuss a methodology for the numerical differentiations of China's responsibilities for climate change as opposed to calculating causal contributions to climate change. For expository purposes, this was done on the basis of aggregate GWP-weighted historical emissions as a proxy. Moving to fully fledged climate modelling techniques as used in the MATCH project would change the relative contributions and resulting responsibilities by at most 10% for most countries.[21] Our aim was not to engage in a debate over which of the two conceptions of responsibility – 'strict' or 'limited' – with the chosen parameter values is more appropriate, or whether the causality of developing-country emissions should be partially attributed to Annex II countries, not least because the answer may well depend on what one wishes to do with the results. However, the order of magnitude difference in the responsibility of the two extremes of the scale under both conceptions is large. Further thought needs to be given to how these calculations of historical responsibility can inform the debate around burden sharing, particularly given the discrepancy between the affluence and wealth of the exponents at either end of the spectrum of responsibilities we considered in this chapter.[22]

While the ethical argumentation for these two conceptions of responsibility are pretty developed and less contentious, it is still not very clear how future potential emissions can be incorporated into a responsibility concept to include the most likely emission scenarios for the coming one to two decades. It is very likely that the responsibility of countries in 2030 will look quite different from today, and China's share will be hard to ignore by that time. Our ability to see this today raises interesting epistemic questions and points to the need for increased research on this matter, and particularly on the future of responsibility.

Notes

[1] Here we build on Müller et al (2009), giving particular attention to the role of China.

[2] In this chapter, the traditional definition of countries' 'anthropogenic' emissions, namely that from their sovereign territory, shall be followed, for determining both their relevant causal contributions and moral responsibilities.

[3] Strictly speaking, it is either blame- or praiseworthy, but in the present context the former suffices.

[4] As Müller et al (2009) emphasise, the methodologies could easily be adapted to be used with the full MATCH modelling techniques.

[5] Ultimately, however, they use country-wide emission contributions, adjusted for measures of income distribution in the population, to calculate global responsibility shares because it is impossible to express the percentage responsibility of a per-capita share.

[6] Note, however, that the two are *not* the same. To be allocated an emission permit per se is not tantamount to being given a responsibility allowance for the specified amount of emissions, in the same way that being given the legal licence to produce tobacco does not give one immunity from the consequences of tobacco use!

[7] For example, if it is agreed that all the emissions in question are harmful, then the basic global per-capita allocation would be $b = 0$, implying that the resulting basic country allocations are zero for all countries regardless of their population size, and thus that the allocation-based responsibility measures are independent of population figures. In contrast, per-capita measures by definition reflect population size.

[8] The calculations that follow are based on data from a variety of sources (Klein Goldewijk and Battjes, 1995; Marland et al, 2003; USEPA, 2006; UNFCCC, 2007). See Höhne et al (forthcoming, section 2.1) for a detailed discussion of the emissions dataset.

[9] This percentage is in the same range as the MATCH results for the same type of emissions and time period (72.3%). Taking all Kyoto gases into account, the Annex I share for this time period drops to 54%.

[10] According to the MATCH calculations, non-Annex I annual emissions (all gases) surpassed non-Annex I emissions in 1992, and developing-country cumulative historical emissions (all gases) will have surpassed developed countries by 2024.

[11] Based on the Chinese presentation at the AWG-LCA Shared Vision workshop at COP14 in Poznan in 2008. This simplified metric circumvents the problem that there is no logically meaningful expression of average per-capita and per-year emissions.

[12] Based on a side event at the 15th Conference of the Parties (COP15) to the UNFCCC in Copenhagen in 2009 (Pan et al, 2009). Note that Chinese

researchers are generally working only with energy CO_2 emissions rather than all gases and sectors in the Kyoto Protocol. We assume they did the same here.

[13] The data before 1890 are much less complete. Roughly 10% of the effect of total aggregate emissions is left out when starting in 1890 instead of 1750, the year normally identified as the start of industrialisation. See Höhne and Blok (2005).

[14] Strictly speaking, we should also have allocated basic allowances according to the terrestrial sinks capacity of the respective sovereign territory, but given the uncertainties on how much these are, we decided to err on the side of caution and just consider oceanic sinks.

[15] The position of Japan in this strict responsibility scale (2.8%) also suggests that burden sharing according to responsibility alone may not really be tenable, and that it would have to be complemented with some 'respective capacity' component, as referred to in Article 3.1 of the UNFCCC.

[16] See Müller et al (2009) for a full sensitivity analysis for varying choices of basic and subsistence allowances.

[17] It can be questioned whether the difference in hypothetical to actual emissions growth would have been the same as the difference in hypothetical to actual population growth. Economic growth, industrialisation and modernisation since the end of the 1970s could have been hampered by overpopulation, leading to an elasticity lower than 1.

[18] Per cent, *not* percentage points.

[19] The question of the use of future emissions – modelled in emission scenarios – to calculate the historical responsibility at an end year that lies in the future would be an interesting research topic in this field. An argumentation could perhaps start in this direction: in the case one considered pre-2030 emissions completely predetermined by today's decisions on energy strategy and so on, and considered the modelled emission scenario an accurate description of future development, these future emissions could already be assumed to be historical today. Then they could be summed up with actual historical emissions.

[20] Chen et al (1999) early on pointed out the changing trend of contribution shares, comparing pre-1990 historical contribution with estimated contribution over the period 1990-2010.

[21] Per cent, *not* percentage points.

[22] Affluence (GDP per capita, PPP, 2005): US = US$41,890, India = US$3,452. Wealth (GDP, PPP, 2005): India = US$3.8 trillion, US = US$12.4 trillion (World Bank, 2006).

References

Agarwal, A., Narain, S. and Sharma, A. (eds) (1999) *Green politics*, New Delhi: Centre for Science and Environment.

Aristotle (1908) *Nicomachean ethics*, Oxford: Clarendon Press.

Baer, P., Athanasiou, T., Kartha, S. and Kemp-Benedict, E. (2008) *The Greenhouse Development Rights Framework*, Berlin: Heinrich Böll Foundation, Christian Aid, EcoEquity and the Stockholm Environment Institute.

Botzen, W.J.W., Gowdy, J.M. and Van den Bergh, C.J.M. (2008) 'Cumulative CO_2 emissions: shifting international responsibilities for climate debt', *Climate Policy*, vol 8, no 6, pp 569-76.

Brown, D., Tuana, N., Averill, M. et al (22 other authors) (2006) *White paper on the ethical dimensions of climate change*, University Park, PA: Rock Ethics Institute, Penn State University.

Chen, Y., Pan, J. and Zhuang, G. (1999) '防范全球变暖的历史责任与南北义务 [fangfan quanqiu biannuan de lishi zeren yu nanbei yiwu] Historical responsibility and north–south obligation for preventing global warming', *World Economy*, vol 2, pp 62-65.

den Elzen, M.G.J., Fuglestvedt, J.S., Höhne, N., Trudinger, C., Lowe, J., Matthews, B., Romstad, B., Pires de Campos, C. and Andronova, N. (2005) 'Analysing countries' contribution to climate change: scientific uncertainties and methodological choices', *Environmental Science Policy*, vol 8, no 6, pp 614-36.

Ellermann, C. and Mayer, M. (2010) *Climate change with Chinese characteristics: A study of discourse*, Washington, DC: American Association of Geographers Annual Meeting.

Ellermann, C., Oliver, P., Li, X., Yowargana, P. and Wang, C. (2009) *Enhanced actions*, London: E3G.

Eshleman, A. (2004) 'Moral responsibility', *Stanford Encyclopaedia of Philosophy*, Stanford, CA: Stanford University.

Friman, M. (2007) *Historical responsibility in the UNFCCC*, Linköping: Centre for Climate Science and Policy Research, Linköping University.

Friman, M. and Linnér, B.-o. (2008) 'Technology obscuring equity: historical responsibility in UNFCCC negotiations', *Climate Policy*, vol 8, no 4, pp 339-54.

Gardiner, S.M. (2004) 'Ethics and global climate change', *Ethics*, vol 114, no 3, pp 555-600.

Harris, P.G. (2010) *World ethics and climate change: From international to global justice*, Edinburgh: Edinburgh University Press.

He, J., Zhang, A. and Liu, B. (2000) '全球气候变化问题与我国能源战略 [quanqiu qihou bianhua wenti yu woguo nengyuan zhanlüe] Issues of global climate change and energy strategy in China', *Journal of Tsinghua University (Philosophy and Social Sciences)*, Issue 4.

Höhne, N. and Blok, K. (2005) 'Calculating historical contributions to climate change: discussing the "Brazilian proposal"', *Climatic Change*, vol 71, no 1, pp 141-73.

Höhne, N., Blum, H., Fuglestvedt, J., Bieltvedt, R., Skeie, B., Kurosawa, A., Hu, G., Lowe, J., Gohar, L., Matthews, B. and Nioac de Salles, A.C. and Ellermann, C. (2010) 'Contributions of individual countries' emissions to climate change and their uncertainty', *Climatic Change*, DOI: 10.1007/s10584-010-9930-6

Hope, C.W. (2008) 'Optimal carbon emissions and the social cost of carbon over time under uncertainty', *Integrated Assessment*, vol 8, no 1, pp 107-22.

IPCC (Intergovernmental Panel on Climate Change) (1996) *Climate change 1995: Economic and social dimensions of climate change*, Cambridge: Cambridge University Press.

Ito, A., Penner, J.E., Prather, M.J., de Campos, C.P., Houghton, R.A., Kato, T., Jain, A.K., Yang, X., Hurtt, G.C., Frolking, S., Fearon, M.G., Chini, L.P., Wang, A. and Price, D.T. (2008) 'Can we reconcile differences in estimates of carbon fluxes from land-use change and forestry for the 1990s?', *Atmospheric Chemistry and Physics Discussions*, vol 8, no 1, pp 3843-93.

Klein Goldewijk, C.G.M. and Battjes, J.J. (1995) *The IMAGE 2 hundred year (1890-1900) data base of the global environment (HYDE)*, Bilthoven: National Institute of Public Health and the Environment (RIVM).

Klinsky, S. and Dowlatabadi, H. (2009) 'Conceptualizations of justice in climate policy', *Climate Policy*, vol 9, no 1, pp 88-108.

MacGregor, J. (2006) *Ecological space and a low-carbon future: Crafting space for equitable economic development in Africa*, Agrifoodstandards.net.

Marland, G., Boden, T.A. and Andres, R.J. (2003) 'Global, regional, and national fossil fuel CO_2 emissions', *Trends: A compendium of data on global change*, Oak Ridge, TN: Carbon Dioxide Information Analysis Center, US Department of Energy, http://cdiac.esd.ornl.gov/trends/emis/meth_reg.htm

Marland, G., Boden, T.A. and Andres, R.J. (2005) 'Global, regional, and national fossil fuel CO_2 emissions', *Trends: A compendium of data on global change*, Oak Ridge, TN: Carbon Dioxide Information Analysis Center, US Department of Energy, http://cdiac.ornl.gov/trends/trends.htm.

MOFA (Ministry of Foreign Affairs) (2008) 'Position paper of the People's Republic of China at the 63rd session of the United Nations General Assembly on climate change issue (extract)', Beijing: MOFA, www.ccchina.gov.cn/en/NewsInfo.asp?NewsId=14978

Monbiot, G. (2007) *Heat: How to stop the planet burning*, London: Penguin Books.

Müller, B. (2001) 'Varieties of distributive justice in climate change', *Climatic Change*, vol 48, no 2, pp 273-88.

Müller, B., Höhne, N. and Ellermann, C. (2009) 'Differentiating (historic) responsibilities for climate change', *Climate Policy*, vol 9, no 6, pp 593-611.

NDRC (National Development and Reform Commission) (2007) '中国应对气候变化国家方案 [zhongguo yingdui qihou bianhua guojia fang'an] China's National Climate Change Programme, Beijing: NDRC.

NDRC (2008) '中国应对气候变化的政策与行动 [zhongguo yingdui qihoubianhua de zhengce yu xindong] China's policies and actions on climate change', Beijing: NDRC.

NDRC (2009) *China's position on the Copenhagen climate change conference*, Beijing: NDRC.

Pan, J., Luo, Y., Teng, F. et al. (2009) *Carbon equity in global efforts to combat climate change*, Bonn: UNFCCC, http://cop15.meta-fusion.com/kongresse/cop15/templ/play.php?id_kongresssession=2403&theme=unfccc

Prather, M.J., Penner, J.E., Fuglestvedt, J.S. et al (12 other authors) (2009) 'Tracking uncertainties in the causal chain from human activities to climate', *Geophysical Research Letters*, vol 36, doi: 10.1029/2008GL036474.

Retallack, S. (2005) *Setting a long-term climate objective*, London: Institute for Public Policy Research.

Stern, N. (2006) *Stern Review: The economics of climate change*, London: HM Treasury, www.hm-treasury.gov.uk./independent_reviews/stern_review_economics_climate_change/stern_review_report.cfm

UNFCCC (United Nations Framework Convention on Climate Change) (1997) *Paper no 1: Brazil: Proposed elements of a protocol to the United Nations Framework Convention on Climate Change*, Bonn: UFCCC Sekretariat.

UNFCCC (2007) 'National inventory submissions 2007', http://unfccc.int/national_reports/annex_i_ghg_inventories/national_inventories_submissions/items/3929.php

USEPA (United States Environmental Protection Agency) (2006) *Global anthropogenic non-CO_2 greenhouse gas emissions: 1990 – 2020*, Washington, DC: ESEPA, www.epa.gov/nonco2/econ-inv/international.html

Wang, T. and Watson, J. (2007) 'Who owns China's carbon emissions', *Tyndall Briefing Note*, Norwich: Tyndall Centre for Climate Change Research.

World Bank (2006) *World Development Indicators 2006*, Washington, DC: World Bank.

WRI (World Resources Institute) (2009) *CAIT climate analysis indicators tool*, Washington, DC: WRI.

Xu, H. and Yu, S. (2008) '气候变化的责任与中国的努力 [qihou bianhua de zeren yu zhongguo de nuli] Climatic change responsibility and China's endeavor', 中国能源 *Energy of China*, vol 4.

Zhao, R. (2007) '气候变暖凸显富国责任 [qihou biannuan tuxian fuguo zeren] Climate warming highlights the responsibility of rich countries', 时事报告(高中版) *Current Affairs (High School Edition)*, vol 1, pp 34-37.

FIVE

The 'non-cooperator pays' principle and the climate standoff

Jonathan Symons

Analysis of distributional justice in the global climate regime typically focuses on how historical responsibility, present-day capacity, vulnerability and rights to development should shape the international allocation of duties and entitlements associated with climate change (see Chapters Two and Four). This chapter argues that state *cooperation* in seeking an effective global response to climate change is an overlooked factor that should have a larger place in this ethical calculus, and it examines how an emphasis on cooperation might influence our assessment of China's climate policies. The proposed emphasis on cooperation follows from recognition that addressing climate change is a global collective action problem. Although states have the financial and technical capacity to reduce greenhouse gas (GHG) emissions, effective action has been delayed for want of international agreement over what contribution each party should make. The scale of the cooperation challenge is all the greater because an international collective action problem, wherein states have differing commitment to addressing climate change, is layered on top of a series of national collective action problems, whereby the interests of polluting industries tend to dominate within national political processes (Olson, 1971; Harris, 2007).

In the context of this intractable two-level collective action problem, contribution to international cooperation might be considered as important as emissions levels in an assessment of a state's responsibility for climate change. A state with low GHG emissions that works to undermine international agreement might potentially be as ethically blameworthy as a high emitter that sincerely seeks to achieve a cooperative outcome. The significance of cooperative effort is widely recognised in non-academic debates, as is demonstrated when a change of government alters popular assessments of national responsibility. When Barack Obama entered the White House and Kevin Rudd became Prime Minister of Australia, their states' emissions profiles did not suddenly change. However, popular assessments of each state's culpability for climatic harm shifted because the new administrations signalled their support for international cooperation. This intuitive understanding of the link between cooperative behaviour and national responsibility is not reflected in normative theoretical accounts of climate justice. This chapter argues that contribution to cooperation is a key measure of state responsibility for climate-related harm that should inform a just international distribution of climate change-related costs. The implications of this perspective are explored, particularly with reference to ongoing international negotiations under the United Nations Framework Convention on Climate Change (UNFCCC).

This chapter focuses on China's negotiating position, in the process providing a preliminary assessment of China's contribution to cooperation in the climate regime. The central argument is that non-cooperation in global climate negotiations should be a central element of any assessment of state responses to climate change. A normative framework emphasising cooperation would provide support for allocations of obligations and entitlements among states that would otherwise be considered unethical. In order to capture the cooperation-related elements of ethical responsibility, the chapter proposes a forward-looking 'non-cooperator pays' principle: under the condition of anarchy, actors negotiating to secure an essential public good that cannot be provided without widespread cooperation are justified in seeking to induce cooperation by imposing costs on non-cooperators, even if this cost allocation would be considered unjust in the absence of the collective action problem. If accepted, this principle would have significant implications. First, an emphasis on willingness to cooperate might lead us to view the positions of particular actors, in this case China, in a more or less critical light. Second, in the absence of an effective international climate agreement, the non-cooperator pays principle might justify measures that may not otherwise be considered just. Equalising 'border tax adjustments' on GHG emissions embedded in traded goods, notably those from China, are discussed in this context.

China and global climate negotiations

The full implications of the 15th Conference of the Parties (COP15) to the UNFCCC that was held in December 2009 in Copenhagen will be unclear for some time. Many commentators agree that the 'Copenhagen Accord' (hereafter, the Accord), which was the major outcome of the conference, contains some positive elements (UNFCCC, 2009). For example, by attracting developing-state emissions pledges, the Accord may be seen as an important step towards facilitating United States (US) congressional support for emissions reductions (Doninger, 2009).

However, overall, the Accord falls well short of the kind of ambition that would be required to put humanity on the path to averting dangerous climate change. The Accord is vague, lacks implementation detail and has failed to secure state emissions-reduction pledges of significant-enough magnitude to keep predicted warming below 2°C (Alessi et al, 2010, pp 1-5). Indeed, in the wake of widespread disquiet over the negotiations at Copenhagen, uncertainty surrounds the future role of the United Nations (UN) climate process (Müller, 2009).

Accounts of China's role at Copenhagen are polarised. They range between the view that China's pledges are comparatively substantial and those who allege that China was a deliberate saboteur that worked assiduously to thwart agreement on firm targets and commitments (Curtin, 2010, p 7). The disparity between these perspectives points to the difficulty of finding an impartial measure of cooperative contribution. China's defenders maintain that its pledge, to lower emission intensity by 40-45% between 2005 and 2020, amounts to a 25% reduction below business as usual and that this absolute reduction below business as usual far exceeds the current commitments of Europe, the US and Japan (Jotzo, 2010). If fully implemented, this pledge would also be consistent with targets assigned to China under some independent allocations of global action, such as that developed by the Australian Garnaut Review (Garnaut, 2008; Jotzo, 2010). Confidence that China is committed to implementing this pledge should be bolstered by economic analysis showing that China's existing policies create an 'implicit price of carbon' through incentives for low-carbon electricity generation that is comparatively high (significantly higher than in the US, Japan or Australia) (Vivid Economics, 2010, pp ii-iv) and suggestions in the Chinese media that a carbon tax might be introduced in coming years (*China Daily*, 2010). Given that objections to the friends of the chair process created such disquiet at Copenhagen, China's defence of the principles of consensus decision making and state equality might also be considered markers of its significant commitment to global cooperation.

An opposing and more critical view emphasises the significance of China's insistence that its emission-reduction pledge should be neither binding nor verifiable. Given the scale of Chinese emissions, an effective international agreement addressing global warming cannot be achieved without credible commitments from China. Other states are reluctant to commit to economically costly action in the absence of credible assurance concerning China's policies. China is predicted to double its emissions in the next 15 years even if it meets its Copenhagen pledge (Alessi et al, 2010, p 4), and it has already become the largest national emitter with responsibility for around 18% of global emissions (Garnaut, 2008, p 65). Under a business-as-usual scenario, this figure would rise to approximately 33% of global emissions by 2030 (Garnaut, 2008, p 65). Awareness that China will be an indispensable nation within any successful climate agreement underpins the US' (and others') insistence that China must eventually accept targets that are both binding and verifiable. The demand for verification seems justified given evidence that published emissions data in China do not match satellite observations (Akimoto et al, 2006).

Implementing the norm of common but differentiated responsibility

The dispute over enforceable, verifiable developing-world emissions forms part of a much larger struggle over the application of the norm of 'common but differentiated responsibility' (CBDR) in the climate regime. The CBDR norm was established in Article 1 of the UNFCCC:

> [T]he global nature of climate change calls for the widest possible cooperation by all countries and their participation in an effective and appropriate international response, in accordance with their *common but differentiated responsibilities* and respective capabilities and their social and economic conditions.

The practice of differentiating responsibilities in multilateral agreements is longstanding, and 'differential and more favourable' treatment has previously been given to developing countries. However, the UNFCCC departs from precedent by adopting differentiated responsibility as a central principle (Stone, 2004, pp 278-9). Inclusion of CBDR in the UNFCCC followed from earlier acceptance of the 'right to development' (Shue, 1995, p 459; see Harris, 1999). States recognised that restrictions on GHG emissions would limit development and so needed a framework for a global agreement that would both limit total emissions and not stifle developing-world growth.

While the UNFCCC contains no binding emissions targets, the CBDR norm found practical expression in the differentiated targets negotiated at the Kyoto, Japan, third Conference of the Parties in 1997, which were codified in the Kyoto Protocol to the UNFCCC. The Kyoto Protocol establishes binding emission restrictions for 'Annex B' states (that is, developed states plus some former communist Eastern European states), but includes no mandatory targets for non-Annex

B (that is, developing) states. The decision to limit emissions targets to Annex B states in the first commitment period appears to have been largely a tactical move to delay dealing with the thorny question of emissions limits for developing powers such as China and India (Vanderheiden, 2008, p 69). During Kyoto negotiations it was already abundantly clear that a climate treaty that excluded China or India could not avert dangerous climate change, but neither would these states accept emissions limits that restricted their capacity to develop. By deferring resolution of this impasse to another day, negotiators lowered the ambition of the Kyoto Protocol and left unanswered the question of whether it would be politically possible to achieve a climate regime that was both fair (consistent with the CBDR norm) and sufficiently ambitious as to avert dangerous climate change.

A deadlock over how strictly the CBDR norm should be applied has developed and deepened since Kyoto and now dominates (some might say paralyses) climate negotiations. At Copenhagen, Chinese Premier Wen Jiabao reiterated China's long-held view that 'developed countries must take the lead in making deep quantified emission cuts and provide financial and technological support to developing countries' (Wen, 2009). In this view, developing states should accept binding limits only after developed states have led the way, and the developed world should meet the cost of developing-world action. China justifies this strict interpretation of CBDR by reference to both the moral obligation of developing states to prioritise sustainable development and poverty eradication, and the counterbalancing obligation of developed states to provide compensation for damages caused by their historical GHG emissions. Even the foreword to China's National Climate Change Programme stresses China's moral obligation to maximise economic growth. Tellingly, it does this by repeating wording from Article 4, paragraph 7 of the UNFCCC (1992), which states that 'economic and social development and poverty eradication are the first and overriding priorities of the developing country Parties'. At Copenhagen, Premier Wen Jiabao also described the responsibilities of developed states under CBDR in stark moral terms. He reiterated that leadership by developed states is 'an unshirkable moral responsibility as well as a legal obligation that they must fulfil' (Wen, 2009).

Developed states have accepted an obligation to take the lead in mitigation, and the Accord contains an unenforceable promise of significant new adaptation funding. However, despite having accepted that only developed states would assume targets under the Kyoto Protocol, developing states must take on binding obligations if a more ambitious international agreement is to replace the Kyoto Protocol. In fact, the allocation of responsibility under Kyoto may have been more 'differentiated' than domestic politics will allow. Major states that took on significant reductions below a business–as–usual scenario in Kyoto refused to ratify (as in the case of the US), ratified but subsequently announced an intention to not comply (Canada) or have adopted compliance plans based on investment in international flexibility mechanisms rather than domestic taxation or regulation (Japan) (Harrison and Sundstrom, 2007). While it is not possible to assert that opposition to strict CBDR was the reason for this backsliding, it is clear that a strict interpretation of CBDR in which the developed states lead by cutting emissions and providing resources to the developing world has not proved popular among Western publics. The depth of the antagonism to strong interpretations of CBDR was clearly illustrated by the US Senate's rejection of the Kyoto Protocol in the 1997 Byrd–Hagel Resolution (S. Res. 98, 2001) (see Harris, 1999). The resolution stated that the US should not be a signatory to any protocol that does not include binding targets for developing nations as well as industrialised nations. The US Senate passed the resolution unanimously.

Much of the disagreement on specific issues at Copenhagen (and in climate negotiations generally) can be attributed to this underlying disagreement over the appropriate application of CBDR. For example, in Copenhagen, China and the other 'BASIC' countries (Brazil, South Africa, India and China) stressed the primacy of the Kyoto negotiation track over the long-term commitments track, which was a new negotiating track that might be created by the Copenhagen Accord. This position was motivated by a desire to entrench the strict Kyoto interpretation of CBDR, wherein developed states would accept binding commitments for the post-Kyoto period (Spencer et al, 2010, p 6). Likewise, when China worked to head off an agreement that would have raised adaptation funding via a global measure targeting bunker fuels, it was also seeking to defend CBDR (Greenair Online, 2010).

The centrality of the CBDR dispute to the ongoing success of climate negotiations raises the question of whether China's position is justifiable. Should China be seen as a brave defender of developing states and vulnerable populations? Or is its insistence on a tough application of CBDR unethical, given that such an application works against the interests of vulnerable populations by unreasonably undermining the prospect of negotiating an effective global climate agreement? To answer this question we need to first assess what constitutes fair terms of cooperation in the context of polarised conceptions of fairness.

Cooperation and the commons

In his paper 'The tragedy of the commons', Hardin (1968, p 1245) famously outlined the principle that 'the morality of an act is [in part] a function of the state of the system at the time it is performed'. Hardin's insight concerning the situational nature of ethics is apposite to GHG pollution. Some actions, such as an individual taking a joy-ride in a private jet or a state constructing a coal-fired power station, which might otherwise be ethically neutral, become harmful, and possibly unethical, once a level of pollution is reached where the global climate system is threatened. Many scholars have drawn on such a situational understanding of ethics to suggest that some discount should be applied to the ethical responsibility attached to the historical emissions of affluent states (Marburger, 2008, p 51; Vanderheiden, 2008, pp 163-4; Harris, 2010a, p 144; see also Chapter Four). Here I propose that recognition of the situational aspect of ethics should be extended further so that assessment of the 'state of the system' includes not only natural systems (for example, the global atmospheric system) but also human regulatory systems (for example, the global climate regime). Acts should be judged for their contribution towards cooperative regulatory efforts as well as on the basis of their direct physical consequences.

This argument might be illustrated through a reconfiguration of Hardin's 'tragedy of the commons' scenario. Begin by picturing a pasture open for use by all residents of a village. Historically, most villagers have been too poor to afford cattle and so have been content to allow the village's two rich herders to utilise it for grazing. Use has remained at a level where the commons has not been degraded. Finally, however, comes the day when poorer villagers can afford a few cattle each. They begin to graze these cattle on the common land and soon the commons begins to deteriorate from overuse. There is no formal system of government in the village to which the rich herders can appeal. Realising that even if they withdraw their entire (larger) herds from the commons they will be unable to save it, the rich villagers become alarmed and call a meeting where they propose that each villager should agree to graze only one cow on the commons. If everyone agrees, the rich herders will accept equal restraints. They point out that the cooperation they propose will save the commons and thus benefit each person.

The new cattle-owners are outraged that rights to the commons will be rationed at the very moment at which they are first able to enjoy them. They insist that they should have the same unlimited usage rights that their rich neighbours have traditionally enjoyed. If they are to accept grazing limits, they wish to be compensated in full by those who previously benefited from greater access. The richer villagers calculate that not only would they be better off with no cooperation than cooperation on these terms, but also that they lack the capacity to pay the level of compensation that has been demanded. Since their efforts to save the commons have failed, they decide to extract maximum value from the commons in the little time remaining before its complete degradation.

Hardin intended his original commons scenario to refute the idea that an 'invisible hand' automatically aggregates rational individual actions in pursuit of self-interest to provide an optimal collective outcome. This revised scenario illustrates that individuals acting in compliance with privately held standards of fairness can also fail to arrive at optimal levels of cooperation. However, my interest is in the normative questions raised: how should the villagers have acted, and how should each be judged? Each has offered to cooperate according to standards that they perceive to be fair. Each has also continued to maximise individual utility by over-exploiting the commons when cooperation on terms they consider fair has been rejected. Does this mean that each is equally ethically blameworthy? The answer depends on the behaviours we regard as relevant to the assessment. If we are concerned only with polluting behaviours, or pollution after the environmental system passes a threshold of endangerment, then the rich herders are clearly most responsible. They have grazed the greatest number of cows on the commons and so have contributed the greatest amount of environmental harm. By this account the poorer villagers are less blameworthy. But is this assessment appropriate?

If we extend Hardin's proposal regarding 'situational morality' to include the state of human governance systems within our ethical appraisal, then we might reach a different conclusion. While early use of the commons had no environmental impact, once the system passed a threshold where further utilisation was harmful the rich herders proposed a cooperative scheme to address the problem. Significantly, in this scheme the benefits of collective action would have been distributed equally among all actors. Only after this cooperative scheme was rejected, and the commons' fate was sealed, did the rich herders resume their polluting activity. In contrast, the poor villagers might be held more ethically blameworthy. Not only have they contributed (albeit more modestly) to the pollution of the commons, but they have also refused to accept a cooperative management scheme that would have enhanced the wellbeing of each actor.

Now suppose that the rich herders had pursued a different plan. Worried that the village would not survive the loss of its commons, they decide to enforce cooperation on the terms they proposed. They hire helpers to warn off and then physically expel any villager who tries to graze more than one cow on the common land. They hope that after a short period the enforcement will become unnecessary and all will accept the value of cooperation. How should we judge the herders for using force against their neighbours? Should ethical appraisal of their conduct be influenced by their motivation to resolve a challenging cooperation problem?

I suggest that this context is relevant because, if protection of a public good is held to be an independent normative goal, then proportionate actions that are necessary to achieve this goal may be justified. However, to assess whether the threats of physical coercion were justified we would need information about the value of the public good and whether there were alternative ways in which it could be secured. For example, if food from the common land provided such vital nutrition that the survival of the village children would be jeopardised by its degradation, then we might accept that enforcement of cooperation on reasonable terms is justified. However, if preservation of the commons is of less importance, we might be less inclined to accept the constraint on individual freedom. Without going into these details we can observe that the presence of a collective action problem influences our intuitive judgements about appropriate behaviour. We could express this intuition by expanding Hardin's maxim to observe that the morality of an act is (in part) a function of the state of the system at the time it is performed *and the act's impact on cooperative efforts to protect the system.*

The 'non-cooperator pays' principle

The 'cooperative' element of situational ethics might be formulated as a 'non-cooperator pays' principle (NCP principle), which states that *under the condition of anarchy, actors negotiating to secure an essential public good that cannot be provided without widespread cooperation are justified in seeking to induce cooperation by imposing costs on non-cooperators, even if this cost allocation would be considered unjust in the absence of the collective action problem.* In order to justify and explain this principle, I will first outline two key conditions that limit the scope of its application before examining how the NCP principle relates to obligations and entitlements of individuals versus those of states.

The scope of the NCP principle is limited to actors negotiating to provide (a) an *essential public good* (b) under the *condition of anarchy*. Public goods are commonly defined as goods that are both 'non-excludable' and 'non-rival' (Barrett, 2007, p 1). This means that once a public good has been provided, no person can be prevented from enjoying it, and no person's enjoyment of the good impinges on others. A habitable global atmosphere is a public good in the sense that by simply being alive and enjoying a safe climate I do not diminish the capacity of anyone else to do the same. Because public goods are non-excludable, they are amenable to free-riding and so, in the absence of government, are likely to be undersupplied. For example, a state deciding whether to spend money on climate change mitigation measures (for example, investing in capital-intensive low-emission energy infrastructure) will be aware that the vast majority of the benefits of expenditure will accrue to others. In contrast, the benefits of adaptation expenditure (for example, construction of new storm-resistant infrastructure) are exclusively local and are therefore likely to attract greater local political support. In the absence of a global agreement that guarantees proportionate state contributions to mitigation efforts, it may be rational for states to prioritise adaptation over mitigation even though each state would be better off if every state prioritised mitigation. For these reasons alone, the public good of climate safety is likely to be underprovided.

Here I am concerned with cases of *essential* public goods. I use the term 'essential public good' to refer to a public good that is likely to be necessary for the survival and flourishing of human communities. If a public good is likely to be essential for preserving people's 'fundamental interests', where fundamental interests are understood as interests that are 'sufficiently weighty as to generate obligations on others' (Caney, 2005, p 767), then provision of the public good should be given consideration by all actors. As the threat to fundamental interests increases, so does the weight that other actors must give to the goal of providing the good. Because of the scale of the threat posed by climate change, specific ethical standards apply to actors negotiating a global climate agreement that would not be relevant to actors negotiating provisions of a non-essential public good. For example, if an affluent state were to propose a global campaign to eliminate the virus causing the common cold, it would have no grounds on which to expect that developing states should contribute to this desirable but relatively unimportant public good. It is worth noting that cooperation to produce essential public goods will likely benefit the least advantaged members of the global community. If measures that promote cooperation provide benefits to the least advantaged, they are likely to be consistent with some widely accepted principles of justice (Rawls, 1999).

A second limitation to the application of the NCP principle is that it concerns only *actors negotiating under the condition of anarchy*. Anarchy is a key condition because governments are (ideally) capable of utilising legitimate forms of coercion to achieve the cooperation necessary to provide public goods. In the absence of government, public goods are more likely to be undersupplied. For this reason, the ethical imperative to promote cooperation is greater in the absence of government, and cooperation concerns might partially displace other normative goals.

Distinguishing between the obligations of states and people

Many normative theorists might find problematic the claim that special normative standards are appropriate for states negotiating under anarchy because they consider individuals to be the ultimate bearers of duties and entitlements, and thus only assign duties to institutions (such as states) if these duties derive from the duties of their members. However, there is some disagreement over this question among normative theorists analysing climate justice from a cosmopolitan perspective. While some argue that individuals are the ultimate bearers of moral duties even if they enlist institutions to discharge those duties (Jones, 2002, pp 68–9), others hold that only institutional actors are capable of resolving complex international problems and therefore only institutional actors should be held responsible (Scheffler, 2002, pp 40–5; Green, 2005). Yet, an account of justice that absolves individuals of moral responsibility in respect of so crucial an issue as climate change is repugnant to many as it seems to abandon the basic cosmopolitan recognition 'that every human being has a global stature as the ultimate unit of moral concern' (Pogge, 1992, p 49; see Harris, 2010b).

One possible resolution to this debate becomes apparent if we accept that prescriptions derived from ideal normative theory provide an appropriate guide for individual actors, but not for institutions. If ideal standards were to be accepted by everyone, all people would become advocates for ideal state actions. In this scenario, institutional action would conform to ideal standards and global cooperation problems would be instantly resolved. Regrettably, most people have not accepted the climate change-related duties suggested by ideal normative theory. Political leaders face significant opposition to action on climate change, and within developed states there is often hostility to strict interpretations of CBDR. Further, climate change is a time-critical issue. State negotiators are aware that if an effective agreement is not reached soon, the window of opportunity in which it is possible to avert dangerous climate change will pass. Negotiators must also make decisions in a context where it is certain that other states will not adopt an ethically ideal course of action. Many state decision makers would also be constrained by their own domestic democratic institutions from pursuing policies that would be considered ideal from the perspective of justice. Given these political realities, international climate negotiations cannot hope to achieve an ideal agreement. In a choice between imperfect alternatives there are powerful reasons to prefer an agreement that is more effective in mitigating climate change over one that is less ambitious but better approximates distributional fairness.

A trade-off between effectiveness and fairness?

International climate change negotiations cover both *apportionment* of the global mitigation (and adaptation) effort and the *scale* of the global mitigation effort that will be pursued (that is, the level of atmospheric concentration of GHGs to aim for). Negotiators must therefore make decisions about the contemporary fairness of state contributions to mitigation efforts, and also make decisions about ambition and effectiveness that carry implications for intergenerational fairness. It might be argued that the Kyoto Protocol was a fair agreement in that it only imposed emissions limits on states that had significant historical responsibility for causing climate change. However, this fairness was achieved by lowering the agreement's ambition. As a consequence, Kyoto has proved ineffective at limiting global emissions growth. In a situation where swift cooperative action is required to avert a potential global catastrophe, normative analysis that uses ideal standards of justice as a guide for action has the potential to be dangerous if it leads states to make compromises that prioritise fairness over effectiveness.

The NCP principle is one attempt to encapsulate the normative value that should be attached to cooperation and effectiveness in the context of an intractable global collective action problem whose resolution may be essential for the wellbeing and possibly survival of billions of people in the future. This same tension between effectiveness concerns and fairness concerns can be seen in the climate regime's existing norms. For example, the justification for the CBDR norm draws on subsidiary normative principles, including the 'polluter pays' principle. The clearest international articulation of this principle is in the Rio Declaration on Environment and Development (Principle 16), which urges national authorities to use 'economic instruments' to ensure that costs of pollution are internalised and that the polluter 'bear(s) the cost of pollution'. This principle references a standard of *fairness* (that the beneficiary of pollution should pay for associated costs), but it draws its primary justification from an *efficiency* principle (that collective wellbeing is optimised if full costs of production are internalised rather than imposed on the community as a whole) (Shue, 1999, pp 534, 537; Gardiner, 2004, p 579). The polluter pays principle is consistent with the CBDR norm so long as developed states are asked only to bear costs that are proportionate to their historical emissions.

The CBDR norm also references normative principles that are much less connected to effectiveness. Most significantly, within many cosmopolitan accounts of atmospheric justice, the 'polluter pays' principle of compensation for harm is supplemented by an 'ability to pay' principle (Shue, 1999, p 537; Caney, 2005; Jagers and Goran, 2008, pp 581-2 or a 'beneficiary [of past GHG pollution] pays' principle (Page, 2008, pp 562-4), which is also akin to the concept of 'historical responsibility' pushed by many developing states. For many normative theorists, the allocation of costs on the basis of historical emissions raises questions about the fairness of penalising acts whose harmfulness was not clear at the time (in the case of emissions before 1990) or for imposing costs on the present generation for the actions of their parents and grandparents (Shue, 1999, p 537; Caney, 2005; Jagers and Goran, 2008, pp 581-2). Politically, the concept of historical responsibility is also contentious because it demands enormous transfers of wealth to the developing world. By way of example, the World Bank's most recent estimate is that adaptation costs in developing countries will be US$75–100 billion *annually* from 2010 to 2050 (Margulis et al, 2009, p 1). The dispute over how CBDR should be applied in the global climate regime is, in part, a dispute over how these various normative concerns should be balanced. Recognition of the normative significance of cooperation and effectiveness in international negotiations should assist us in judging the ethics of various state positions from a new vantage point.

Assessing China's interpretation of CBDR

If one accepts that cooperation should be a central factor in an assessment of the ethics of state climate policy, how would this influence our assessment of China's negotiating position? More specifically, how should we appraise China's insistence on a very strict interpretation of CBDR? In responding to this question it is helpful to draw on a typology of three types of CBDR proposed by Stone (2004). 'Rational bargaining CBDR' emerges from rational bargaining between parties who obtain an efficient agreement (that is, it is Pareto-improving in the sense that it leaves at least one party better off without disadvantaging others). Rational bargaining CBDR simply means that parties accept that their contributions and benefits will differ (Stone, 2004, pp 278-9). 'Equitable CBDR' describes a negotiation where parties are still committed to a Pareto-improving outcome (that is, all parties benefit to some degree) but agree to constraints on bargaining that limit possible outcomes to those that 'tilt the cooperative surplus more favourably toward a designated group of parties' (Stone, 2004, pp 278-9). In contrast to these two Pareto-improving forms, 'inefficient CBDR' awards the poor more than the entire net surplus of cooperation. Here the negotiated outcome seeks to correct previous injustices by transferring wealth from some parties to others (Stone, 2004, pp 278-9).

Where rational bargaining and equitable CBDR are both potentially consistent with global cooperation to address climate change among a community of self-interested states, inefficient CBDR is not. As such, even if there are persuasive ethical arguments in favour of inefficient CBDR, this standard would most likely undermine the possibility of global cooperation. China's position cannot be neatly placed on a spectrum between inefficient and equitable CBDR. Its pledges to reduce the carbon intensity of its economy may be quite ambitious, and in the context of current negotiations are probably consistent with either equitable or rational bargaining CBDR. However, China's refusal to make these pledges binding and verifiable, especially when combined with rhetoric concerning the historical responsibility of the West, amounts to a refusal to enter a binding deal on these terms. Instead, China is effectively demanding that developed states agree to inefficient CBDR, but is promising (without giving a guarantee) that it will make a greater contribution than it is legally bound to make.

As we have seen, climate regime negotiations are finely balanced and challenging. If China's rhetoric demands that developed states conform to the standards of inefficient CBDR, its position can be judged to militate against international cooperation. Thus, although China's arguments about the historical responsibility of developed states and its own responsibility to lift vulnerable populations out of poverty have merits, its negotiating position undermines the possibility of global cooperation. Arguably, this makes China's position unjustifiable, and means that China has significant responsibility for future climate harms even though its per-capita emissions remain below the global average. Since practical effectiveness should be the overriding goal of climate negotiations, even a principled refusal to take on binding and verifiable emission targets can be considered an unjust obstacle to global cooperation. Judged by the standard of contribution to global cooperation, China's climate policies can be found wanting.

Practical implications of the NCP principle

As we have seen, acceptance of the NCP principle alters our appraisal of state responsibility for climate change. This in turn might alter our assessment of what constitutes a just international distribution of climate costs. A distribution that promotes climate action by imposing penalties on states in which emissions are unregulated might be justified by the NCP principle even if such a distribution would otherwise be judged as unfair. Here, I will consider the example of trade measures against states that do take effective steps to limit GHG emissions. Other measures, such as tying adaptation assistance to mitigation action, might also be justified by the same principle.

Addressing climate change is an unusually challenging political problem because the immediate costs of action are high, the costs of inaction are delayed and an effective response requires cooperative multilateral action. Given the barriers to international cooperation, the capacity to impose costs on non-cooperators via border tax adjustments (BTAs) would promote international cooperation in three ways. BTAs (or carbon tariffs) would:

- act as an incentive promoting participation in an effective international agreement;
- reduce domestic political opposition to emissions restrictions by protecting trade-exposed industries (protecting domestic industries from international predation also encourages technological innovation); and
- enable GHG emissions to be taxed at the point of consumption rather than production (a point with important equity implications).

BTAs are taxes or subsidies that level the playing field between domestic industries subject to GHG-limiting measures and competitors in states that do not take on binding emissions limitations. BTAs seek to equalise the taxation of carbon on goods sold in a national market by imposing taxes on imports from states where GHG emissions are not regulated, and granting subsidies or tax relief to exports. Such measures promise to reduce GHG emissions by limiting 'carbon leakage' while creating incentives for all states to participate in a post-Kyoto successor agreement. The 'reserve allowance' scheme included in the US Waxman-Markey Climate Bill is an example of the kind of BTA measure that is likely to be adopted if developed states take serious steps towards limiting their emissions. The legality of BTAs under World Trade Organization rules is unclear (Tarasofsky, 2008, p 11). BTAs are commonly critiqued for amounting to a form of 'green protectionism' that is both economically damaging and unjust (Biermann and Brohm, 2005, p 291). According to this view, it is unjust to impose Western environmental standards on the developing world since doing so stifles economic development and defies the polluter pays principle. A counterargument – that BTAs are normatively justifiable – can be constructed in terms of the NCP principle and based on evidence concerning their capacity to induce global cooperation.

Restructuring incentives to make cooperation attractive

As Barrett (2007, p 93) argues, '[t]he essential challenge of a treaty is to restructure incentives so that countries are better off participating than not participating, and better off complying than not complying'. In the past, global environmental cooperation has often been achieved through what DeSombre (2000) terms the 'internationalisation' of US domestic policies. Once environmental standards have been adopted domestically by the US, industry and environmentalists often find common cause in demanding that these standards be imposed on other states through economic threats. While US environmental policy has been effectively internationalised on many occasions in the past, internationalising US emissions limitations may be a harder task. The cost of the overhaul of global energy systems necessary to combat global warming is of an order of magnitude several times greater than any of the cases DeSombre has analysed, such as protection of endangered species, air pollution limits or fisheries conservation. Further, the US is neither able nor willing to unilaterally impose global limitations on GHG emissions. However, it may be that if a group of large economies were to agree to place a price on GHG emissions and to seek to internationalise this policy through trade measures, the developing world may agree to more substantial emissions limitations than could be achieved through a purely voluntary scheme.

The 1987 Montreal Protocol on Substances that Deplete the Ozone Layer, although tackling a much simpler problem than global warming, offers an instructive model as to how this process might work. This protocol limited the global use of chlorofluorocarbons, which were suspected to destroy stratospheric ozone. By offering funds to assist developing countries with adjustment costs, and using market access as both a carrot and a stick (parties to the Montreal Protocol were given continued market access during a phase-out period, but non-parties were immediately excluded), this agreement gained almost universal acceptance and was subject to minimal normative critique despite involving limited 'differentiation' (Haas, 1992, p 197).

Existing efforts to encourage developing-world participation in a post-Kyoto successor agreement centre on 'carrots' such as technology transfer funding, adaptation funding and participation in an emissions trading market. These carrots all involve transfers of resources from industrialised states to developing states and, presumably for this reason, have to date been poorly funded and ineffective. It seems unlikely that these inducements alone will be sufficient to motivate developing-world acceptance (and enforcement) of emissions limits. The developing world also makes a strong argument that this assistance should not be conditional. Since industrialised states' emissions have created climate change, assistance is viewed as repayment of a historic debt. The limited leverage exerted by these inducements is a key argument supporting the 'stick' of BTAs. If non-participation in a global climate agreement gives a state a trade advantage, this militates against its participation in a climate agreement. If non-participation instead carries an economic cost (via carbon tariffs), the incentives favour participation.

The changing economic power of the industrialised world vis-à-vis developing powers such as China and India prompts a likely riposte to this argument: it is no longer possible for a small group of powers to impose solutions on the globe. Instead, emerging developing powers are only likely to accept an agreement that they consider to be fair. It is true that the greater equality in the contemporary world probably means that only a negotiated multilateral response to climate change would be practicable. The views of China and potentially other major developing states, such as Brazil, India and Russia, will need to be accommodated in any effective global response to climate change. However, if the divide between the conceptions of fairness held within developing and developed states is to be reconciled, established conceptions of fairness held by both sides will need to be reconsidered.

Changing incentives within domestic politics

The argument that unilateral action to place costs on GHG emissions will put domestic industry at a disadvantage is an important contributor to domestic opposition to GHG emission limitations in many states. For example, Steven Chu, the US Energy Secretary, has said that '[i]f other countries don't impose a cost on carbon, then we [the United States] will be at a disadvantage [and] we would look at considering perhaps duties that would offset that cost' (cited in Talley and Barkley, 2009, unpaginated). Carbon tariffs address this argument by re-establishing an even playing field between domestic and foreign production. Obviously, this measure would not completely neutralise domestic opposition to emission limitations. Polluting domestic industries will usually continue to resist emissions regulation. However, a key domestic political advantage of BTAs is that they enable advocates of regulation to refute nationalist fairness arguments about the risk of disadvantage in international competition. BTAs neutralise this nationalist rhetoric by shielding domestic industry from international competition. Without the claim of being disadvantaged internationally, polluting industries would be forced to argue against emissions restrictions on other grounds. It seems likely that public opinion will be less sympathetic to polluters' arguments once the cloak of shared national interest is removed. By protecting domestic industry from unregulated international competition, BTAs would also increase the incentive for emissions-reducing technological innovation and create economic incentives promoting the transfer of low-emissions technologies to developing-world manufacturers exporting to states that impose carbon tariffs.

A third advantage of a carbon tariff regime is that it allows emissions to be taxed at the point of consumption. At present, domestically produced goods face carbon taxes in Europe, but imports do not. The developing world's argument that its right to development and improved living standards should not be sacrificed to protect first-world overconsumption is persuasive. Yet, this argument is entirely consistent with BTAs. If exports from China to the European Union were subject to equalising BTAs, this would mean that European consumers would be taxed on their GHG emissions but Chinese consumers would not. The ethical argument for differentiated treatment of states ultimately rests on a concern for the wellbeing of people in developing states. This argument justifies opposition to limits on emissions that contribute to developing-world consumption. It does not justify opposition to restricting emissions on developing-world production that is destined for first-world consumption. BTAs in fact offer an ideal mechanism for targeting emissions that are linked to developed-world consumption without penalising so-called 'survival emissions', while at the same time promoting cooperative global action.

Conclusion

This chapter has worked from the premise that part of the purpose of norms and normative reasoning is to promote behaviour that promotes collective wellbeing. Norms frequently coordinate action so as to resolve collective action problems. In areas of social interaction around which humans have long experience, our moral intuitions tend to be very finely defined. However, when changing circumstances create new or unusual challenges, our moral intuitions may need refinement. As Gilbert (2006, p 9) notes 'although all human societies have moral rules about food and sex, none has a moral rule about atmospheric chemistry'. The challenge posed by anthropogenic climate change has few precedents in human history. It has a number of features – such as the long time delay between emissions and their environmental consequences, a global scale involving millions of actors, the difficulty of observing emissions, the non-excludable nature of mitigation efforts and the absence of an authority to enforce compliance – that might make norms that have evolved in other contexts ineffective in solving this global cooperation problem. The proposal of a non-cooperator pays principle is an attempt to articulate a new norm that is appropriate for this extraordinary cooperative challenge.

If it is accepted that the goal of cooperation should influence an assessment of the ethical responsibilities and entitlements of states, then we will also view state conduct in a different light. Although China maintains per-capita emissions that are slightly below the global average, its negotiation position is not currently supportive of international cooperative action to address climate change. A focus on cooperation may therefore lead us to judge China's position as unjust and to accept that the imposition of carbon tariffs on China by states that do limit their emissions is normatively justifiable. Developing states, such as China, make a strong argument that developed states have certain responsibilities to the developing world for damage already inflicted on the global climate system. However, when assessing such arguments we should recognise that an argument that a state owes or is owed assistance is quite distinct from a claim that particular people are owed assistance (Harris and Symons, 2010). We might endorse the idea that vulnerable people are owed assistance without accepting the argument that international negotiations must adopt an inefficient form of CBDR.

Acknowledgement
Initial preparation of this chapter was supported by the Hong Kong APEC Study Centre, Lingnan University, Hong Kong.

References

Akimoto, H., Ohara, T., Kurokawa, J. and Horii, N. (2006) 'Verification of energy consumption in China during 1996-2003 by using satellite observational data', *Atmospheric Environment*, vol 40, pp 7663-7.

Alessi, M., Georgiev, A. and Egenhofer, C. (April 2010) *Messages from Copenhagen: Assessments of the Accord and implications for the EU*, Brussels: Centre for European Policy Studies, www.ceps.eu/book/messages-copenhagen-assessments-accord-and-implications-eu

Barrett, S. (2007) *Why cooperate? The incentive to supply global public goods*, Oxford: Oxford University Press.

Biermann, F. and Brohm, R. (2005) 'Implementing the Kyoto Protocol without the USA: the strategic role of energy tax adjustments at the border', *Climate Policy*, vol 4, no 3, pp 289-302.

Caney, S. (2005) 'Cosmopolitan justice, responsibility, and global climate change', *Leiden Journal of International Law*, vol 18, pp 747-75.

China Daily (2010) 'Carbon tax likely, expert forecasts', *China Daily*, 10 May, www.chinadaily.com.cn/china/2010-05/10/content_9826546.htm?source=cmailer

Curtin, J. (2010) *The Copenhagen conference: How should the EU respond?*, Dublin: Institute of International and European Affairs.

DeSombre, E.R. (2000) *Domestic sources of international environmental policy: Industry, environmentalists, and U.S. power*, Cambridge, MA: MIT Press.

Doninger, D. (2009) *The Copenhagen Accord: A big step forward*, Washington, DC: Natural Resources Defense Council, http://switchboard.nrdc.org/blogs/issues/solving_global_warming/

Gardiner, S.M. (2004) 'Ethics and global climate change', *Ethics*, vol 114, pp 555-600.

Garnaut, R. (2008) *The Garnaut climate change review*, Melbourne: Cambridge University Press Australia.

Gilbert, D. (2006) 'If only gay sex caused global warming', *Los Angeles Times*, July 2, p 9.

Green, M. (2005) 'Institutional responsibility for moral problems', in A. Kupper (ed) *Global responsibilities: Who must deliver on human rights?* (pp 117-34), New York, NY: Routledge.

Greenair Online (2010) 'Bunker fuels and Copenhagen – the disappointing outcome that leaves the aviation industry adrift on GHG emissions', 19 January, www.greenaironline.com/news.php?viewStory=726

Haas, P.M. (1992) 'Banning chlorofluorocarbons: epistemic community efforts to protect stratospheric ozone', *International Organization*, vol 46, no 1, pp 187-224.

Hardin, G.J. (1968) 'The tragedy of the commons', *Science*, vol 162, pp 1243-8.

Harris, P.G. (1999) 'Common but differentiated responsibility: the Kyoto Protocol and United States policy', *N.Y.U. Environmental Law Journal*, vol 7, pp 27-48.

Harris, P.G. (2007) 'Collective action on climate change: the logic of regime failure', *Natural Resources Journal*, vol 47, no 1, pp 195-224.

Harris, P.G. (2010a) 'China and climate change: from Copenhagen to cancun', *Environmental Law Reporter (News & Analysis)*, www.epa.gov/ogc/china/harris.pdf

Harris, P.G. (2010b) *World ethics and climate change: From international to global justice*, Edinburgh: Edinburgh University Press.

Harris, P.G. and Symons, J. (2010) 'Justice in adaptation to climate change: cosmopolitan implications for international institutions', *Environmental Politics*, vol 19, no 4, pp 617-36.

Harrison, K. and Sundstrom L. (2007) 'Introduction: the comparative politics of climate change', *Global Environmental Politics*, vol 7, no 4, pp 1-18.

Jones, C. (2002) *Global justice: Defending cosmopolitanism*, Oxford: Oxford University Press.

Jotzo, F. (2010) *Comparing the Copenhagen emissions targets*, CCEP Working Paper 1.10, Canberra: Centre for Climate Economics & Policy, Crawford School of Economics and Government, The Australian National University.

Marburger, J. (2008) 'A global framework – International aspects of climate change', *Harvard International Review*, vol 30, no 2, pp 48-51.

Margulis, S. et al. (2009) *The costs to developing countries of adapting to climate change, new methods and estimates: The global report of the Economics of Adaptation to Climate Change Study: Consultation draft*, Washington, DC: World Bank Group, http://siteresources.worldbank.org/INTCC/Resources/EACCReport0928Final.pdf

Müller, B. (2009) *Copenhagen 2009: Failure or final wake-up call for our leaders?*, Oxford: Institute for Energy Studies.

Olson, M. (1971) *The logic of collective action: Public goods and the theory of groups*, Cambridge, MA: Harvard University Press.

Page, E.A. (2008) 'Distributing the burdens of climate change', *Environmental Politics*, vol 17, no 4, pp 556-75.

Pogge, T. (1992) 'Cosmopolitanism and sovereignty', *Ethics*, vol 103, no 1, pp 48-75.

Rawls, J. (1999) *The law of peoples*, Cambridge, MA: Harvard University Press.

Scheffler, S. (2002) *Boundaries and allegiances: Problems of justice and responsibility in liberal thought*, Berkeley, CA: University of California.

Shue, H. (1995) 'Ethics, the environment and the changing international order', *International Affairs*, vol 71, no 3, pp 453-61.

Shue, H. (1999) 'Global environment and international inequality', *International Affairs*, vol 75, no 3, pp 531-45.

Spencer, T., Tangen, K. and Korppoo, A. (2010) *The EU and the global climate regime: Getting back in the game*, Briefing Paper 55, Helsinki: The Finnish Institute of International Affairs, http://www.ciaonet. org/pbei/fiia/0018327/f_0018327_15694.pdf

Stone, C.D. (2004) 'Common but differentiated responsibilities in international law', *American Journal of International Law*, vol 98, no 2, pp 276-301.

Talley, I. and Barkley, T. (2009) 'Energy chief says U.S. open to carbon tariffs', *Wall Street Journal*, 18 March, http://online.wsj.com/article/ SB123733297926563315.html?mod=googlenews_wsj

Tarasofsky, R.G. (2008) 'Heating up international trade law: challenges and opportunities posed by efforts to combat climate change', *Carbon and Climate Law Review*, vol 1, pp 7-16.

UNFCCC (United Nations Framework Convention on Climate Change) (2009) *Copenhagen Accord*, New York, NY: United Nations, http://unfccc.int/home/items/5262.php

Vanderheiden, S. (2008) *Atmospheric justice: A political theory of climate change*, Oxford: Oxford University Press.

Vivid Economics (2010) *The implicit price of carbon in the electricity sector of six major economies*, Sydney, NSW: The Climate Institute, www. climateinstitute.org.au/

Wen J. (2009) 'Build consensus and strengthen cooperation to advance the historical process of combating climate change', Address at the Copenhagen Climate Change Summit by Wen Jiabao, Copenhagen, 18 December.

Part Three
Policy implications

SIX

Evaluating ethical obligations across scales of governance

Erich W. Schienke

China is one of the most significant and necessary players in addressing global climate change. Further, China is a country comprised of complex heterogeneous socioeconomic conditions, a wide range of ecosystems, diverse cultures and geographically differing access to energy and resources. Because of these diverse factors, it is difficult to take a generalised stance on how China ought to address climate change as an internal matter. It is important for actors and institutions inside and outside of China to comprehend these obligations across the nation's governmental levels, economic sectors and ecosystems. Assuming that all nations have an ethical obligation to reduce emissions to their fair share of a global target, it is therefore imperative that an analysis be conducted of China's ethical obligations to address climate change both as a nation and at various scales of governance within the state.

In this chapter, ethical obligations play out across various political-economic sectors at multiple scales in China. To develop an ethical baseline, in this chapter China's national obligations are analysed according to the eight ethical dimensions first developed in a *White Paper on the ethical dimensions of climate change* (hereafter referred to as EDCC White Paper) (Brown et al, 2006). Then, a framework is provided for further granularity in scalar analysis of ethical imperatives, which is referred to here as China's 'climate box'. The conclusion is that the ethics of China's climate problem should be understood in terms of a series of interrelated issues requiring the consideration and coordination of policies across multiple scales.[1]

The United Nations Framework Convention on Climate Change (UNFCCC) assumes nation states to be the main actors in negotiations on global limits (Harris, 2010). However, producing a normative analysis only of China's *national* obligations does not fully reveal clear ethical directives for regional, local or urban governance. While China may eventually arrive at a clear ethical directive as to how much it needs to mitigate to reduce overall national emissions, it is less clear how to ethically distribute mitigation efforts to regions with diverse geography and distribution of wealth. The lack of procedural clarity here comes about mainly because of China's economic geography and how wealth is distributed within the nation.

The problem of ethically distributing China's mitigation costs and efforts internally is made even more complex when one takes into account mismatches between scales (levels) of governance, such as the size and scope of institutional effectiveness, and the scales of certain ecosystems that need to be managed, such as standing carbon sinks in forests or permafrost that may cross multiple municipalities or regional authorities. That is, saying what China's ethical obligations to address global climate change are as a nation is more straightforward than determining how China may go about ethically addressing global climate change as an internal matter of good governance.

Chinese science and climate change negotiations

A main point argued in the EDCC White Paper is that the best scientific research available must be used as the basis for developing an ethical response to climate change.[2] Chinese climate and carbon-cycle scientists and their research play a significant role in informing and shaping national policies and perspectives on climate change. For external observers, it is difficult to have a complete understanding of the state of Chinese climate science because much of the research is reviewed and published in Chinese-only research journals. However, many of the current findings within Chinese climate science are discussed in an informative and revealing scientific report by Ding et al (2009). This report was published shortly before the December 2009 Copenhagen Conference of the Parties (COP) to the UNFCCC, the main position of which was argued by China with even further resolve in the 2010 Tianjin meetings leading up to the 2010 Cancun COP.

From Ding et al (2009), which was produced mainly by members of the Chinese Academy of Sciences (CAS), we can see a scientific foundation being developed to support China's climate regime position on future emissions obligations and rights. The Chinese scientific position emerging from this paper, mainly looking at a global comparison of historical and projected future emissions, is one that is:

- based on emissions rights, which should then be
- based on the concept of cumulative emissions per capita, which underlies an interpretation of common but differentiated responsibility;

- assumes a 470 parts per million volume (ppmv) global target for carbon dioxide (CO_2) levels, but argues that this will be globally very difficult to achieve; and
- divides emitters globally into four categories, namely countries and regions with (a) emissions deficits, (b) the need to reduce gross emissions, (c) the need to reduce emission growth rates and (d) the ability to maintain current growth rates.

The most important 'scientifically based' ethical question from China's perspective is how emissions ought to be divided globally, particularly when considering both current and historical per-capita emissions. In light of the findings of Ding et al (2009), it is not surprising that the Chinese delegation to the COP in Copenhagen and Tianjin argued for the need to confront and address the issue of historical emissions directly, before any future emissions limits would be agreed on by China. While it does have a significant and sober argument regarding historical emissions, China also has an undeniable obligation to reduce emissions as soon as possible for the benefit of future generations, especially its own.

Analysis of China's ethical obligations

There are at least eight significant dimensions in evaluating any nation's ethical obligation to address climate change. According to the EDCC White Paper, these are:

- responsibility for damages;
- atmospheric targets;
- allocation of global emissions among nations;
- use of scientific uncertainty in policy making;
- costs to the national economy;
- independent responsibility to act;
- potential for new technologies; and
- procedural fairness.[2]

Here, I will look at how these dimensions can be interpreted as they inform us on China's obligations as a nation, that is, at a national scale of governance.

Responsibility for damages

The EDDC White Paper asks: 'Who is ethically responsible for the consequences of climate change, that is, who is liable for the burdens of (a) preparing for and then responding to climate change (i.e. adaptation) or (b) paying for unavoided damages?' (Brown et al, 2006, p 10). China has contributed far less to historical emissions than most countries of the Organisation for Economic Co-operation and Development (OECD) with higher Human Development Index (HDI) profiles, particularly in relation to the United States (US) (with an HDI of .951, compared to .77 for China). Therefore, when comparing it to the US, China's obligation to take on such costs is lower because its past emissions have been relatively quite low and its current level of development is also relatively low, particularly outside of the top-tier cities. Further, as climate change progresses, various regions across China are already experiencing higher frequency and severity of floods and droughts, along with decreased glacial/snow runoff feeding essential river basins. These impacts will only grow worse in the future.

According to various models used in the Intergovernmental Panel on Climate Change's (IPCC) Fourth Assessment Report on impacts and vulnerability (IPCC, 2008), Sichuan's eastern regions and the Gobi desert will most likely experience more frequent and more severe droughts, in addition to more severe flooding events in the region. Mountainous regions in Sichuan, Tibet, Xinjiang and Yunnan are already subject to increased flooding (and even under the threat of glacial lake outburst floods) and the eventual decrease of snow and ice pack during winter months. With a decrease in glacial run-off, both fresh water and hydropower in the regions along the Mekong, Yangtze and Yellow Rivers (as well as the Ganges to the west) are projected to experience a long-term decline in water resources. Continued damming along these rivers will exacerbate this process. The coastal regions where China's population is most dense are also subject to increased risks due to rising sea levels, and some regions will be vulnerable to an increased frequency and intensity of storm activity (for example, typhoons).

China will clearly be negatively affected by climate change, even if there may be short-term agricultural and energy benefits in some regions. The risks posed by climate change also extend to Asia as a whole. The risks to China's interior and coastline justify taking immediate and appropriate action to mitigate. China will incur significant costs to its own future generations of vulnerable populations if it does not bring near-future emissions down to its global fair share, regardless of past emissions. Further, China is quickly closing the historical emissions gap in terms of gross emissions. However, from China's perspective, the emissions gap is still significant in terms of per-capita historical emissions, which is likely why per-capita emissions numbers (historical and projected) are favoured by Chinese officials in international negotiations on climate change.

As it is now the world's largest emitter nation, regardless of historical emissions, China is ethically obligated to respond to climate change as soon as possible within its capacity to do so. With an HDI of .77, China is by no means among the least-developed nations in the world. Since the mid-1990s, it has been developing a significant affluent population in urban regions such as Beijing, Shanghai and Shenzhen. As such, China will inevitably be required to tap its growing affluent populations first, particularly in the coastal regions, to adequately support the costs of mitigating and adapting to climate change (Harris, 2010, pp 125-7; see Chapters Nine and Ten).

In addressing the distribution of the harms and benefits resulting from climate change, China's central, provincial and urban governments will need a policy framework for addressing the disparities between the wealthier regions along the coast and the poorer interior, particularly as the increase of droughts and floods impacts the interior areas while infrastructure and development continue to lag behind in those regions. In addition, as China becomes a more affluent nation in the wider Asian region, it also becomes a more attractive migration destination for populations in other countries bordering it. For example, climate impacts in the Democratic People's Republic of Korea (DPRK, that is, North Korea) regardless of the dire political-economic situation the DPRK faces, could bring about a massive influx of refugees if severe famine were to occur due to drought or severe flooding. Such a condition would add further instability to an already unstable situation.

China's responsibility for climate impacts based on past emissions is still relatively low, as explained in Ding et al (2009). However, being the world's largest emitter of CO_2 requires a sober consideration of China's future responsibility for climate impacts, and this indicates a clear and present ethical obligation towards immediate action to reduce greenhouse gas (GHG) emissions. That is, China is not ethically responsible for most of the world's past emissions, but moving forward this will not be the case.

Atmospheric targets

The second major issue addressed in the EDCC White Paper concerns the actual targets for levels of atmospheric CO_2:'What ethical principles should guide the choice of specific climate change policy objectives, including, but not limited to, maximum human-induced warming and atmospheric greenhouse gas targets?' (Brown et al, 2006, p 15).This is a question with solutions that need to be worked out at different scales, from global to national, provincial, urban, community and individual levels.As the world is already committed to some warming in the 1-2°C range regardless of what we do, arriving at an ethically satisfactory level of global emissions ought to be determined by the degree of warming and ensuing damages that would not cause exceptional harm or endangerment to particularly vulnerable populations, especially those poorer populations who cannot afford adaptation costs.Again, a relatively 'safe' level of warming would be at 2°C or under, projected at an atmospheric level of approximately 450ppmv of CO_2, based on various IPCC reports (although China seems to be working with the number of 470ppmv, as discussed above).The global level of emissions is already projected to realistically surpass the 450ppmv mark, and thus global temperature will go beyond 2°C above historical levels.To meet the global goal of limiting the increase to 2°C, total emissions need to be reduced as soon as possible to about 70-80% of current levels.

While reductions ultimately need to be carried out at a local scale, the overall system being affected is still global in scale.As such, climate change and the obligations to adhere to a global agreement towards reduction are first supported by a theory of global ethics. Global ethics are primarily argued in some form of the ethical theory referred to as *cosmopolitanism*, that is, a universal ethic applying to everything within the 'cosmos' (Dower, 2002; Appiah, 2006). Cosmopolitanism in the case of climate change would argue that the global majority problem posed by climate change ought to override local or individual interests, in that local or individual interests should not be elevated above global or universal interests.

In terms of reducing GHG output, China considers its primary obligation to be to its own population and economy first, followed by those nations that support its interests, then followed by global interests. China's impact and influence globally is continuing to increase in the areas of economy, trade, security, public health, sporting and cultural events, and technology. Speaking for its national interests alone, Chinese officials cannot make the argument, within the framework of a cosmopolitan ethics, for strong global participation in the case of economic matters and not also acknowledge a supporting role in aggressively addressing climate change. Following the logic of a cosmopolitan ethic, one could even argue that China's climate commitment ought to reflect its percentage of current ownership of the global economy.[3] Further, China as a nation needs to participate in global emissions limits to prevent 'leakage' of emissions, such as the displacement of emissions from moving manufacturing from countries with heavier emissions regulations to those with more lax standards.

Setting and achieving atmospheric targets is a global ethical issue. Many nations that are already being negatively affected by climate change have had no choice in the matter, and they have done very little to contribute to the overall problem. As an issue of sovereignty, climate change is an external force already changing internal behaviour and impacting local livelihoods. Setting global atmospheric targets will force nations to set their own targets, which will inevitably impact their own economies in a mostly negative way. Because climate change is a global issue with a wide variety of local problems, adhering to an ethic of cosmopolitanism becomes the only reasonable theoretical foundation for developing a global response that will stem the severity and frequency of local impacts. In terms of global climate change, a nation such as China can only protect its local interests through global participation and adherence to strict global targets. Therefore, taking a cosmopolitan stance when agreeing on and adhering to a global target will be in China's and other nations' best interests.

Allocating global emissions among nations

While the previous question concerns setting global atmospheric targets, the next question concerns the ethical reasoning behind how the global emissions target will be allocated among nations: 'What ethical principles should govern the allocation of responsibility among people, organization, and governments at all levels to prevent ethically intolerable impacts from climate change?' (Brown et al, 2006, p 19). Because of the costs, allocation should depend significantly on each nation's development and CO_2 output. Here, the main issue at stake is the determination of an ethically appropriate and relevant GHG output for China. As is argued in Ott et al (2004), various ethical systems converge on the conclusion that overall atmospheric levels of GHGs ought to be stabilised at the lowest possible levels of concentrations. Determining precisely what this level ought to be for China is, politically, a highly contentious issue.

As a nation, China's per-capita emissions are relatively low. From 1990 to 2004, its per-capita emissions of CO_2 grew from 2.1 tons to about 3.84 tons (CDIAC, 2010), which is still at levels about one quarter to one sixth of that in the US. Nevertheless, in 2004, China was the world's second highest emitter nation, just behind the US, and shortly thereafter surpassed those levels to become the largest emitter. Further, as China continues to develop infrastructure, increases use of private cars and expands housing footprints in a sprawling mega-block approach to urban development, the country, particularly urban areas, will continue to rapidly expand per-capita GHG footprints in the coming decades. There is also a widening disparity between per-capita emissions for those living in the affluent urban areas versus those living in the much poorer rural and agricultural regions.

Based on principles of an egalitarian distributive justice across the globe, some account of per-capita emissions needs to be considered when determining China's fair share of global emissions. However, this obligation must internally extend to how emissions ought to be determined at a per-capita level within the country. Based on both egalitarian and welfare (Rawlsian) approaches to distributive justice, China is ethically obligated to ensure that per-capita emissions are fairly distributed across its population. China cannot reasonably argue that a per-capita emissions approach should be used to determine its national fair share at a global level, and at the same time allow per-capita emissions levels to range from 0.6 tons per year in rural regions, where over 70% of the nation's population resides, to per-capita levels of around 25 tons per year in the wealthiest urban areas. Ethically, as a distributive justice issue, China arguably cannot allow its poorer populations to displace the emissions of the wealthier populations of the country (see Harris, 2010). Determining a per-capita fair-share distribution within China, therefore, would require a per-capita cap for the wealthier regions as the poorer regions continue to develop.

Overall, there are a variety of scenarios with which one could use to determine China's fair and ethical share of global emissions. For example, emissions could be distributed based on China's: per-capita historical emissions; percentage of global GDP; current emissions outputs; national rank in the Human Development Index (HDI); imports versus exports of carbon; percentage of overall energy portfolio produced by renewables; or some combination taking into account any or all of these. When national limits are set and a mixture of approaches is implemented, China is unlikely to be satisfied. This was evident during the 2009 Copenhagen negotiations, during which China insisted on no hard emissions targets for any nation, including the developed nations. Moving forward, ethical responsibility requires China to take a lead in determining global and national targets and ensuring that they are equitably distributed internally.

Scientific uncertainty in policy making

In making climate change projections and predictions, it is very difficult to assure certainty. How can we be certain about how to take action on a matter we have primarily modelled and not directly measured impacts? The primary problem with questions concerning scientific uncertainty in projections is that it has been and continues to be used in politically divisive ways by many governments. This prompted the EDCC White Paper to ask:'What is the ethical significance of the need to make climate change decisions in the face of scientific uncertainty?' (Brown et al, 2006, p 23). Many countries and political communities have deliberated over some aspect of the certainty, cause and severity of climate change, and have argued against taking action based on claims of scientific uncertainty. The perception that climate change still contains a lot of uncertainty is not entirely unreasonable in so far as the immediate costs of mitigation and political consequences of actions are certain and will also induce definitive near-term impacts to political careers (particularly to four- to six-year election cycles). From the standpoint of the politician, the benefits of taking action are neither immediate nor certain as climate change action is riddled with political uncertainties. For years, claims about scientific uncertainty underpinned many of the justifications for not taking action in the US, that is, because the cost of action to industry and transport would supposedly far outweigh any possible cost of impacts. Since the 2007 IPCC report, the reality of climate change and the tremendous costs of projected impacts are considered unequivocal and too significant to ignore; they are about as certain as the science can possibly be about future events (that is, more than 95% certainty that climate change is anthropogenic). By 2009, most national governments acknowledged the reality of climate change, although most continue to hesitate in adopting strict caps on GHG emissions and in developing comprehensive mitigation plans moving forward to bring down global emissions levels.

For the most part, China has tended to adopt some of the more optimistic projections about climate change impacts while choosing to take less seriously the higher-risk scenarios, such as projections of more extreme drought in already-dry regions. However, Chinese civilisation is all too familiar with the problems of sometimes-severe flooding along its major rivers that have toppled dynasties. Thus, ignoring such warning signs seems socially, economically and politically unwise.[4] Further, using claims of scientific uncertainty to argue against confronting political-economic problems, such as what to do about the nation's massive dependence on coal, will only intensify the severity of actions that need to be taken in the future. On the other hand, scientific uncertainty cannot be ignored when proposing higher-risk mitigation solutions, such as waiting for development and use of carbon capture and storage (CCS) techniques (see below), which are intended to recapture carbon from the burning of fossil fuels and pump it underground. In the case of CCS, ignoring uncertainties, such as underground fault structures, could lead to local loss of life if a CO_2 leak were to occur during a seismic event.

To help confront internal debates over uncertainty, China needs to increase its scientific capacity in measuring and studying the global and regional carbon cycle, particularly with regards to its own industrial output. Gathering good data on carbon emissions across sectors is a significant challenge. Further rationalising and more closely governing planning processes, such as urban development, would go a long way towards improving efficiency in infrastructure. Increasing the capacity of scientific research networks will allow China to better monitor and understand its overall terrestrial carbon flux. Improving and enforcing industrial monitoring standards for all GHGs, particularly in the capacity of the local and regional offices of the Ministry of Environmental Protection, will significantly reduce uncertainty and margins of error in carbon accounting. However, even with significant scientific certainty about the location, severity and costs of climate impacts, scientific results alone will not provide policy makers with an appropriate framework for action, as harms and benefits will need to be weighed. That is, science does not provide the 'roadmap'; rather, it indicates what the terrain is. Ultimately, when and what China ought to do about climate change require making ethical decisions about its own population and about its own impact on the global commons, and these decisions will need to be grounded in good data and analysis.

Costs to national economies

Uncertainty in terms of future climate change impact often becomes one of the main arguments against taking actions in the present, bringing up the question: 'Is the commonly used justification of cost to a national economy for delaying or minimizing actions to reduce the threat of climate change ethically justified?' (Brown et al, 2006, p 29). Many nations have resisted calls to reduce their GHG emissions, first based on the costs to national economies across various sectors and, second, because many cost-benefit analyses used to determine or justify action do not conclude that reduction of GHG emissions is a worthwhile investment now rather than in the future (Brown, 2002; Nordhaus, 2007). Both the US and China have, time and time again, used the argument that 'the present costs are greater than the future benefits' in international negotiations. This same logic was argued by the US as the primary reason for not ratifying the Kyoto Protocol.

As a 'non-Annex I' (that is, developing) nation in the terms of the Kyoto Protocol, China has argued that its first priority is to its own continued economic development, which has been roughly 8-10% per year for roughly the past 30 years. The nation is currently mandating a sustained 8% growth rate ('protect 8') into the foreseeable future. However, China's rapid and peaceful rise as one of the world's leading economic superpowers has not come without significant costs in emissions. An underlying problem is that the very broad category of non-Annex I countries provides very little granularity in definition or degree of development, especially as distributed within the nations. According to development indices such as the Human Development Index, China is certainly not among the least-developed nations, and it cannot continue to leverage the poverty argument and its developing-nation status in international accords as though it is the same as the least-developed countries (Hu, 2009).

Costs of emissions reductions will adversely impact the economies of some regions more than others. Dislocating coal jobs in the poorer regions will have a greater political-economic impact than on the wealthier coastal and urban regions where the energy from coal is primarily used. As Hu (2009) argues, it is the wealthier regions that need to make the reductions first, allowing interior and western regions to continue developing while wealthier regions take on the burden of beginning the process of contraction and convergence across sectors.

China cannot reasonably argue in terms of the costs of taking action on its economic growth while practically ignoring the costs of not taking action. If one were to account for the full costs of environmental pollution from industry, the high growth rates would be down around 5-6% compared to GDP figures that do not take into account environmental impacts, that is, a green versus non-green accounting of GDP. Further including overall pollution costs on human and ecological health, in some particularly polluted areas, can bring the GDP growth rate into negative figures. If measuring GDP in this manner, some towns and smaller cities would have a growth rate as low as −2-3%. Continuing development with a business-as-usual approach in China will likely exacerbate the medium- and long-term bottom-line costs on development, doing little to improve overall efficiency across various sectors of industry and infrastructure. Further, cost-benefit analyses to determine whether, how much, what kind and when to begin mitigation actions are typically employed without the complete tally of costs of a full inclusion of critical climate system thresholds, such the loss of the Greenland ice sheet (which would dramatically raise sea levels) or the loss of snow pack and glaciers in the Himalayas.

Thus, any nation, and particularly the leading emitter nations, cannot ethically argue costs to national interests alone when the impacts affect populations around the world. This is because 'no person or nation has a right either to harm others as a means to achieve their economic health or to endanger others' life, health or security' (Brown et al, 2006, p 30).

Independent responsibility to act

How a global emissions target will be divided among nations is a crucial question, because this will directly impact national and local economies. However, disagreements about which nations take the first steps and when has led to many nations, such as the US and China, stalling sufficient action. Regardless of obligations to the international community, each country has the obligation to act due to the possible severity of climate change. The EDCC White Paper poses this question: 'Is the commonly used justification for delaying or minimizing climate change action – that any government need not act until all others agree on action – ethically justified?' (Brown et al, 2006, p 32). Throughout its engagement with the UNFCCC process, China has strongly argued that it is not obligated to reduce its emissions before the US and other nations because of the potential setbacks this would have on China's economic development.[5] In contrast, the US argues that it will not reduce its emissions until China joins with the Kyoto/ post-Kyoto Protocol, and at the very least, begins to provide good data on emissions releases.

If the US were to begin significant reductions before China, this would likely result in accelerated displacement of manufacturing in the US and European Union to China. This would likely be the case for many consumable goods, steel, aluminium and other energy-intensive manufacturing. That is, in terms of comparative advantages, labour would not be the cheaper commodity as much as lax emissions regulations would be. In other words, comparative advantages from off-shoring emissions will likely be the case if some nations go first, while others continue in a business–as–usual fashion. At the time of writing in 2010, China is committed to reducing emissions intensity, as demonstrated by its push towards cleaner energy. However, reducing GHG emissions intensity per unit of GDP does not address the problem of gross emissions, which need to be lowered globally.

Under the UNFCCC, developed (Annex I) nations such as the US agreed to be the first to reduce GHG emissions, based on issues of equity and to prevent dangerous changes to the climate system based on human activity. As has been readily argued by China, signatory nations acknowledged a 'common but differentiated responsibility' (CBDR) to take action on emissions reduction (see below). However, in practice, no significant responsibility or action has been taken thus far on the part of either the US or China. Such a standstill has actually proven to be mutually beneficial to the political-economic elements that are proponents of business as usual.

There is a tolerable limit to global emissions, where nations can emit without adversely affecting the global climate system. To achieve this, worldwide emissions would have to be reduced to approximately less than 20% of 2004 levels as soon as possible. While determinations of what precisely is a just/fair share of global emissions continues to be a contentious issue among nations, countries that refuse to reduce their emissions (including China and the US) have the burden of demonstrating that emissions are below their nation's equitable share. For the US, this would require somewhere in the region of a 90% reduction from current levels. According to a recent Global Carbon Project report (GCP, 2008; Gregg et al, 2008), China alone accounted for at least 18% of 2004 global emissions, with an increase since then. Much attention has been put on China's increased energy consumption in the form of coal, but building materials such as cement are likely a significant factor as well, as one ton of cement equals one ton of CO_2 emissions. In terms of current estimated gross emissions, if China were the only nation to hold steady at these emissions levels and the rest of the world were to cease any emissions, China would still continue to increase global emissions at an unsafe rate (that is, at a rate greater than the Earth's capacity to absorb those emissions). Based on these criteria, China in particular can make no ethically justifiable argument at this point for not taking immediate action towards GHG emissions reductions, let alone put forth a justifiable argument for the continued dramatic growth of emissions levels as it develops.

Actions such as excessive emissions or pollution may be considered as wrongful under international law, 'even in the absence of a violation of a specific agreement such as the UNFCCC' (Brown et al, 2006, p 33). Thus, China has an ethical obligation to begin reducing emissions immediately, regardless of the actions taken by other nations. Conversely, all developed nations have an obligation to begin reducing emissions immediately, regardless of China's actions.

Potential new technologies

Many nations argue that reduction of emissions should be delayed until newer, more appropriate and less costly measures are developed and become available on the market. However, the EDCC White Paper asks: 'Is the commonly used justification for delaying or minimizing climate change action until less costly technologies are invented ethically justified?' (Brown et al, 2006, p 34). The question of waiting for new technologies is perhaps one of the most difficult to model in terms of the practicality of waiting for cleaner technologies to be developed. The reasons given for waiting tend to be premised on at least some combination of the following four main assumptions:

- existing technologies are too costly and will harm the economy;
- new technologies that can help to reduce emissions now will be less costly in the future;
- waiting for new or less costly innovations will not cause harm; and
- there are no unintended consequences or high risks that come with the new technologies (Brown et al, 2006).

Further, it is assumed that market pressures and demands will catalyse the development of newer technologies. However, considering the recent condition of global financial markets, it may be unwise to wait for market incentives to drive the demand for such innovation. Incentivising innovation of cleaner energy technologies will likely only come at the level of national government interventions to force hard targets for energy efficiency and emissions reductions, such as increasing fuel-efficiency standards.

There are a wide variety of technologies that China needs to consider carefully when adopting a technology and innovation strategy and for the purposes of GHG mitigation and efficiency improvements. I will briefly discuss two of these potential technologies: (a) carbon capture and storage and (b) biofuels. These two technology paths may seem appropriate for China, but adopting them can create a variety of ethical problems.

Carbon capture and storage

The first technological mitigation path considered here is that of carbon capture and storage (CCS), a process that is intended to capture CO_2 from coal-fired and natural gas-based power plants and store it in underground geological formations, such as saline aquifers and spent oil fields. The primary problem is that, in 2009, coal provided China with approximately 75% of its energy, and coal releases more GHGs per unit of energy than any other form of fossil-fuel combustion. Thus, the idea of capturing carbon from either burnt coal or natural gas seems quite appealing at the outset, particularly because it might be used in the retrofitting of some existing power plants. Because of its appeal and the opportunities it presents for China to continue burning one of its cheapest and most abundant sources of energy, many local governments have lauded the possibility of CCS strategies and have counted them as among the best strategies for GHG sequestration from the energy production.

However, the technology of geologic carbon storage is unproven over longer timeframes and can pose significant risks to human and ecosystem health. The geologic sequestration of CO_2 is limited in space and time. If the burning of coal were to continue at currently projected rates, it is highly unlikely that there will be enough ideal space for storing CO_2 over the long term because many saline aquifers could be saturated in a matter of a few decades. Furthermore, CCS is a technology primarily available to only new plant installations unless a coal plant is geographically located near an ideal site and it can be retrofitted to use CCS technology. It is unclear whether the 'cap rock' used to seal the CO_2 will withstand great pressure and prevent leakage over long periods of time. Long-term studies about the suitability of sites have not been conducted. CCS is primarily based on models and maps of best-possible locations, not on experimental evidence. At best, CCS will prove useful over the short term in newer sites using coal and natural gas for energy production. Over the long term, however, funds for innovation might be better directed elsewhere.

For a nation such as China, which depends on its own fossil-fuel supplies for about three quarters of it energy, CCS will likely seem very appealing as a way forward in terms of mitigation. However, the problem and biggest risk associated with CCS is not necessarily the suitability and plausibility of the technology, but rather basing business-as-usual practices of burning coal at ever-increasing rates on the less-than-certain promise of how much and how safely CCS can deliver in terms of safe CO_2 mitigation (Brown, 2008). The Chinese government and industries should not be overconfident in the potential of CCS to be a cornerstone for their mitigation strategies.

Biofuels

Another possible technology in the mitigation pipeline is the use of biofuels in automobiles, heating and power generation. Biofuels are combustible fuels extracted from feedstocks through a variety of fermentation and extraction processes. Methanol, ethanol, methane and biodiesel are the most common forms of biofuels available today, and many are in wide use around the world. Common feedstocks include corn, soybean, palm oil, sugarcane, pulpy wood fibres, grasses and discarded foodstuffs. Different types of biofuel are not equal in efficiency and output.[6] Beyond obvious choices about energy efficiency, many biofuel feedstocks are coming under increasing demand, which are directly competing with food in many regions. In addition to competing with food, biofuels present extensive challenges to land-use policies. They present tremendous challenges for densely populated China, where land-use trade-offs for producing biofuel crops make it a prohibitive option (except for a few promising possibilities with cellulosic methanol processes also used in desert reclamation). Nevertheless, use of biogas digesters in rural areas seems efficient and just. Thus, projects such as biogas should receive further investment from the government and non-governmental organisations.

The promise of new technologies in helping China to address its emissions problem is less than certain, although for some applications solar holds significant promise. Other technologies requiring further ethical analysis would include transportation (all sectors), other forms of 'clean energy', building- and urban-layout plans, nuclear energy, land-use strategies, sanitation and food. Overall, China will likely gain significantly more emissions reductions per Yuan through an overall improvement in infrastructure efficiency in power transmission, planning urban development along with smart transportation systems, and investments in simple things such as better insulation and efficient heating and cooling. The upside is that all of these technologies are already available.

Procedural fairness

Due process in China's climate decision making is of particular importance and relevance because decision making is being done within a nascent rule-of-law system (Peerenboom, 2002). The question posed by the EDCC White Paper is thus: 'What principles of procedural justice should be followed to assure fair representation in climate change decision-making?' (Brown et al, 2006, p 35). Procedural justice in the global climate regime requires that all significant interests be taken into account, regardless of national size, wealth and so forth. Both within China and in relation to the nation's engagement on the world stage, adhering to the principles of procedural justice in climate policy development will require vigilance.

Procedural justice demands the participation of stakeholders. In this case, stakeholders who will be subject to climate impacts must have a representative voice in the decision-making process. At the international level, this would likely take multiple forms. First, China needs to assure the global community that it is fully participating in the IPCC and post-Kyoto climate regimes and not blocking commitments willingly made by other countries (see Chapter Five). Second, China should continue to be a leading voice for the robust participation of developing nations. At the same time, China's size and scale cannot entirely overshadow the discourse and procedures for other developing countries, particularly within East Asia and Africa, where China continues to move forward with industrial investments and commercial expansion. At the national level and below, China will need to ensure that the voices of those being affected the most will be part of the decision-making process. However, the current political-bureaucratic arrangement does not support this kind of input from communities and this is unlikely to change without further domestic and international pressure. Direct action in local politics may not be the most appropriate approach for China's current political structure, but some form of public-based accountability, observation and reporting would be helpful and could easily be based on public participation and local community involvement.

China's 'climate box'

While directives implemented at the national level are crucial to fulfilling climate change obligations, the scalar aspects of problems in China suggest that an analysis of national directives alone would not get at the deep complexity and the conflicts facing the country across multiple levels of governance. After China's ethical obligations as a nation are made apparent, further analysis can be conducted as to how national-level obligations should be ethically worked out as a matter of internal governance. For China, comprehensive internal mitigation will require a strategy that addresses challenges at global, regional, national, intra-regional, provincial, urban, firm, small town and village enterprise (TVE) levels. However, foreign interests engaging China only at the national level will not ensure the robust participation or transparency of the many levels below the central government. As such, foreign interests collaborating with China to address climate change will need to do so across multiple levels, and proper funding and support will need to follow in kind.

There are two global climate regime approaches that, when scaled down, are particularly applicable to conditions in China. First, the principle of CBDR states that all countries have a common responsibility to mitigate emissions but that the responsibility is differentiated between richer and poorer nations. As development in China is geographically uneven and mainly clustered along the coast, the nation must implement differentiated mitigation policies to ensure that the poorer regions do not bear the brunt of the costs. Second, contraction and convergence (C&C) is a strategy where various nations would converge on a per-capita emissions target by a set date, where the nations with highest per-capita emissions drop the most while least-emitting nations are allowed to still increase per-capita emissions. The idea is that once global convergence of per-capita emissions is achieved, further contraction of all per-capita emissions continues towards 470ppmv. In the case of China, Hu (2009) argues that, to address CBDR across the country's population, a framework similar to C&C needs to be adopted internally, where the country's wealthier regions (with a higher HDI) must take the first major steps towards mitigation (lowering per-capita emissions) while poorer regions continue to catch up. Due to China's complexity in both size and diversity, an internal C&C approach requires a more nuanced and granular articulation of the ethical issues and practical problems across political scales, such as the differences between provincial per-capita emissions and the per-capita emissions of citizens within a specific municipality.

In addition to being geographically distributed, China's problems and directives for effective climate-mitigation policies differ depending on levels of administrative authority or governance, as Table 6.1 illustrates. In some cases, both ethical directives and policy directives can be in conflict with directives at other levels of governance. In particular, emissions 'slippage' could still occur while regulating significantly at one level, such as the national or provincial level, and not at the other urban/local, small TVE levels. For example, it would be inadequate for meeting reductions if energy policy at the national level were directed towards the overall reduction of coal-fired plants coordinated with a move towards renewable energy sources, while at the urban/local levels efficiency gains are lost through lack of regulation and enforcement of building codes concerning something as simple as proper and sufficient insulation for the heating and cooling of residential buildings. Logistically, this will require a significant increase in the capacity to accurately measure, monitor and federate GHG emissions data at these various levels.

Each of the levels of governance in Table 6.1 represents a place for further intervention or participation from both the Chinese government and other actors and institutions outside of China. Of particular importance for ethical oversight will be the compliance with regulations at the small TVE level, where the palpable pressure to increase GDP encounters opposition with the need to rigorously comply with and adopt cleaner and more efficient energy solutions. Following closely behind this trend, firms and industrial facilities are pushing hard to increase profits and exploit a comparative advantage in an ever-more competitive global economic setting. The first thing to be sacrificed in such situations may be cleaner production methods and investments in newer, more efficient facilities. Outside firms operating or cooperating with local Chinese firms are going to need to be vigilant in demanding that less carbon-intensive production is demonstrated thoroughly and robustly, and that local Chinese firms are not shifting production to other, dirtier facilities in the country or region. Moving forward, dimensions of Chinese carbon governance will need to work coherently together across scales if an internal C&C towards a national cap is to be implemented properly and cohesively without exacerbating problems around the distribution of harms and benefits, particularly to China's poorer regions.

Table 6.1: Ethical obligations and policy goals across scales of governance

Scale/level	Ethical obligation for China	Policy goals
Global	Working to ensure that global safe levels of CO_2 are agreed on and met. CBDR.	Ensuring participation and support of global climate regime and that safe levels of CO_2 are met. Not blocking relevant policies, particularly on measuring.
Supra-regional	Assuring a fair share of burdens with regional partners, in this case East Asia. Sharing data and technical capacity for regional decision making.	Responsibility to manage regional carbon flux and industrial outputs between cooperating nations. Ensuring that nations do not make a comparative advantage out of different emissions regulations.
National	Ensuring that China's just/fair share of global emissions is met. Addressing independent responsibility to act and bring emissions to fair share.	Ensuring compliance across all economic sectors and at all levels of governance below national scale. Determining directives for energy sector, infrastructure, innovation and technology transfer.
Intra-regional	Cooperative and procedurally fair planning across provinces and ecosystems. Ensuring that emissions 'slippage' does not occur.	Emissions balance across regions within China on economic- and ecosystem-based collaborations. Encouragement of collaboration between urban regions.
Provincial	Determination of fair share among provinces and ensuring that the fair share is met within the province even if growth is sacrificed.	Implementing provincial-level emissions caps. Increasing procedural capacity and representation of participation of various levels of authority within the province.
Urban/regional	Ensuring cost-effective emissions reductions and active urban planning goals around CO_2 reduction.	Planning goals for urban development, anti-sprawl measures, coherent transportation networks, inter-urban collaborations.

Scale/level	Ethical obligation for China	Policy goals
Urban/local	Ensuring onsite implementation of efficiency regulations and controlling unregulated development. Improvement of local participation in procedural processes, such as environmental impact assessments.	Strict implementation of planning codes. CO_2 reduction in project choice. Support for choosing green buildings. Regulating developers. Improving insulation in buildings.
Firms/ businesses	Ensuring that companies are complying with CO_2 regulation and that emissions leakage is not happening internally. If in building industry, not taking on cheaper costs if long-term costs are in emissions leaks.	Increasing CO_2 reduction compliance. Installing cleaner, more energy efficient technologies. Demanding proof of compliance with other partner firms. Engaging in robust technology transfers for efficiency gains.
TVEs	Enforcing cleaner production and adoption of cleaner technologies in cottage industries (typically dirtiest). Ensuring compliance on the ground.	Implementing clean development and production strategies on the ground. Most difficult regulatory issues here, and impetus for business-as-usual is strongest. Micro loans or grants used to fund efficiency.
Individual	Reducing personal GHG footprint as much as possible. Supporting policies for regulation and data collection.	Conscious effort of consumption habits. Changing personal preferences and transport. Understanding personal carbon footprint.

Conclusion

An analysis of China's ethical obligations based on the eight main considerations within the EDCC White Paper indicates that China's interests are aligned with those of global human development. Based on this analysis, the three most challenging issues for China are likely to be:

- its responsibility to other nations for damages due to climate change;
- the potential for new technologies and investments into cleaner energy technologies and paths that support innovations in efficiency; and

• ensuring procedural fairness internationally and at the level of local public participation.

While it is still a developing nation, because of its geographic and economic size, access to resources and risk posed to its own population, China has an undeniable obligation to move forward in global negotiations and in taking extensive measures to mitigate as soon as possible. Further, China cannot continue to block the agreement on definitive emissions targets and measurements for countries, as its representatives did at the 2009 COP in Copenhagen. While the preliminary meeting in Tianjin did not develop clear prerogatives for the 2010 COP in Cancun, the Tianjin meeting did serve to demonstrate that China has already made significant progress in solar and renewable energy and other mitigation efforts (Stone, 2010).

In developing a national C&C roadmap, China's climate governance will require a scalar methodology of oversight, resembling the approach introduced as the *climate box*. Ensuring that this climate box is tightly sealed is a difficult problem for the government, as emissions slippage will almost certainly occur at multiple levels. Furthermore, each of these scales of governance represents an opportunity for intervention by foreign governments, non-governmental organisations, firms and other parties that have an interest in seeing China converge its CO_2 output and contract towards the nation's fair share of global emissions. The primary challenges facing China will be onsite compliance and accountability of climate strategies, and the development of more robust forms of public participation to ensure that they are measurably effective.

Notes

[1] Extending from similar approaches to the use of scale in adaptive management (Gunderson and Holling, 2002; Gunderson et al, 2009), scale is used here in three significant ways: the *scale of governance*, the *scale at which ecosystems need to be managed* and the *scale of mitigation*.

[2] See Chapter Four of this volume as an example of a robust ethical analysis based on comprehensive data.

[3] Following this line of thinking, based on a 2008 global gross domestic product (GDP) of US$61.1 trillion, China would only be responsible for 7% of all GHG reductions, whereas the US would be responsible for 24%.

[4] The Changjiang river (Yangtze) is colloquially known as 'China's sorrow' because of the eternal return of devastating floods. Flood control is also one primary justification for building the Three Gorges Dam.

[5] Let there be no confusion here. The US must reduce gross emissions output as soon as possible, no matter how it is argued.

[6] A study conducted by Adler et al (2007) found that 'compared with the lifecycle of gasoline and diesel, ethanol and biodiesel from corn rotations reduced GHG emissions by ~40%, reed canarygrass by ~85%, and switchgrass and hybrid poplar by ~115%' (Adler et al, 2007, p 683).

References

Adler, P., Grasso, S.J.D. and Parto, W.J. (2007) 'Life-cycle assessment of net greenhouse-gas flux for bioenergy cropping systems', *Ecological Applications*, vol 17, pp 675-91.

Appiah, A. (2006) *Cosmopolitanism: Ethics in a world of strangers*, New York, NY: W.W. Norton.

Brown, D. (2002) *American heat: Ethical problems with the United States' response to global warming*, Lanham, MD: Rowman & Littlefield.

Brown, D. (2008) 'Ethical issues raised by waiting for geological carbon storage', *ClimateEthics.org*, http://climateethics.org/?p=38

Brown, D., Tuana, N., Averill, M., Bear, P., Born, R., Brandåo, C.E.L., Cabral, M.T. S., Frodeman, R., Hogenhuis, C., Heyd, T., Lemons, J., Mckinstry, R., Lutes, M., Müller, B., Miguez, J.D.G., Munasinghe, M., Araujo, M.S.M.D., Nobre, C., Ott, K., Paavola, J., Campos, C.P.D., Rosa, L.P., Rosales, J., Rose, A., Wells, E. and Westra, L. (2006) *White Paper on the ethical dimensions of climate change*, University Park, PA: Rock Ethics Institute, Penn State University, http://rockethics.psu.edu/climate

Carbon Dioxide Information Analysis Center, Tom Boden, Gregg Marland, and Robert J. Andres. (2010) *National CO2 emissions from fossil-fuel burning, cement manufacture, and gas flaring: 1751-2007 – China data*, Oak Ridge, TN: Oak Ridge National Laboratory.

Ding, Z., Duan, X., Ge, Q. and Zhang, Z. (2009) 'Control of atmospheric CO_2 concentrations by 2050: a calculation on the emission rights of different countries', *Science in China Series D: Earth Sciences*, vol 52, pp 1447-69.

Dower, N. (2002) *An introduction to global citizenship*, Edinburgh: Edinburgh University Press.

GCP (Global Carbon Project) (2008) *Carbon budget and trends 2007*, Canberra: Global Carbon Project.

Gregg, J., Andres, R. and Marland, G. (2008) 'China: emissions pattern of the world leader in CO_2 emissions from fossil fuel consumption and cement production', *Geophysical Research Letters*, vol 35, doi: 10.1029/2007GL032887.

Gunderson, L.H. and Holling, C.S. (2002) *Panarchy: Understanding transformations in human and natural systems*, Washington, DC: Island Press.

Gunderson, L.H., Allen, C.R. and Holling, C.S. (2009) *Foundations of ecological resilience*, Washington, DC: Island Press.

Harris, P.G. (2010) *World ethics and climate change*, Edinburgh: Edinburgh University Press.

Hu, A. (2009) 'A new approach at Copenhagen (Parts 1, 2, 3)', *China Dialogue*, 6 April, www.chinadialogue.net/article/show/single/en/2892-A-new-approach-at-Copenhagen-1

Intergovernmental Panel on Climate Change (IPCC) Working Group II (2008) *Climate change 2007: Impacts, adaptation and vulnerability: Working Group II contribution to the Fourth Assessment Report of the IPCC Intergovernmental Panel on Climate Change*, Geneva: IPCC Secretariat.

Nordhaus, W. (2007) 'To tax or not to tax: alternative approaches to slowing global warming', *Review of Environmental Economics and Policy*, vol 1, pp 26-44.

Ott, K., Klepper G., Linger S., Schaeffer, A., Sheffran J. and Sprintz D. (2004) *Reasoning goals of climate protection, specification of Article Two UNFCC*, Bonn: German Federal Ministry of the Environment.

Peerenboom, R. P., and ebrary Inc. (2002) *China's long march toward rule of law*, Cambridge, UK; New York: Cambridge University Press.

Rawls, J. (1971) *A theory of justice*, Cambridge, MA: Harvard University Press.

SEVEN

Short-lived greenhouse gases and climate fairness

Frances C. Moore and Michael C. MacCracken

The United Nations Framework Convention on Climate Change (UNFCCC), signed at the Rio Earth Summit in 1992, set as its objective the stabilisation of greenhouse gas (GHG) concentrations at a level that would avoid 'dangerous anthropogenic interference with the climate' (Article 2). Although 'dangerous' is perhaps deliberately subjective terminology, a limit of no more than 2°C above pre-industrial temperatures has been widely discussed and has been adopted as a target by the European Union, the Group of 20 (G20), and signatories to the December 2009 Copenhagen Accord. In order to have a reasonable chance of meeting this target, total global emissions need to peak and begin declining no later than about 2020 (Meinshausen, 2006).[1] Despite the urgency of the climate change problem, the current international regime has been relatively ineffective. The Kyoto Protocol that came into force in 2004 imposed emissions limits on relatively few nations and set a goal of only 5% emissions reductions below 1990 levels in the 2008-2012 compliance period. In addition to the United States (US) not being a signatory, a number of the participating nations, including Canada, Japan and New Zealand, and are unlikely to meet even the limited commitments they have undertaken through the Kyoto Protocol (Barrett, 2008).

Efforts to reach agreement on global climate action following the Kyoto first commitment period are currently stalled, with the long-awaited Copenhagen negotiations at the end of 2009 producing only the aspirational and non-binding Copenhagen Accord (see Chapter One). A key element of the post-Kyoto climate negotiations has revolved around how to engage major industrialising countries in mitigation activities. Emissions from developing countries currently account for only about 25% of global radiative forcing,[2] but this will grow to over 70% by 2100 if emissions controls are not implemented (Moore and MacCracken, 2009).[3] Developing countries have nevertheless refused to accept caps on emissions, pointing to the substantially larger per capita emissions in the developed North as well as the historical association between use of fossil fuels and economic development (for example, Singh, 2008). On the other hand, developed nations have pointed to the rapid growth in emissions from industrialising countries as a reason why a future climate agreement should have full participation from all major emitters (for example, Connaughton, 2007).

China plays a critical role in this dynamic of the international climate change negotiations. In 2006, it surpassed the US to become the world's largest emitter of GHGs. Moreover, its rapid economic growth caused emissions to increase by a remarkable 80% between 2000 and 2006 alone (Boden et al, 2009). Nevertheless, its per capita emissions are only just above the global average (1.27 tons of carbon per person per year in China in 2006 as compared to a global average of 1.25), its per-capita gross domestic product (GDP) is less than half the global average, and more than a quarter of its population lives on an income of less than US$2 a day (WRI, 2008). Although China must therefore be central in efforts to solve the climate change problem, China, along with other developing countries, has strongly opposed any proposal that would require it to cap its carbon dioxide (CO_2) emissions. Overcoming the current deadlock between developed and developing countries will therefore require finding ways around the major standoff over who should act first to reduce CO_2 emissions so that nations can get on with identifying and adopting energy sources and mitigation options that are at once consistent with national development strategies and have the potential to substantially mitigate global warming.

This chapter will propose one such strategy, namely the mitigation of short-lived GHGs that are also air pollutants, and will evaluate this strategy with respect to principles of fairness embodied in the international climate regime, particularly the principles of responsibility and capability. In short, the proposal envisions using, or leveraging, the different atmospheric lifetimes of elements contributing to global climate change in order to both overcome the negotiation stalemate between developed and industrialising countries and to maximise the near-term climatic effectiveness of global climate action. The following section summarises the role played by short-lived GHGs that are also air pollutants and outlines the key elements of the 'lifetime-leveraging' proposal (Moore and MacCracken, 2009). The burden sharing of mitigation efforts that would result from such an agreement is also assessed relative to fairness principles based on both responsibility and capability metrics.

Short-lived GHGs and the lifetime-leveraging proposal

Climate change has for a long time been considered the quintessential long-term environmental problem, with the most serious impacts affecting the grandchildren and great-grandchildren of current decision makers. While it is true that a significant fraction of the CO_2 released now will remain in the atmosphere for many thousands of years, it is also the case that some pollutants are comparatively short-lived (that is, have an atmospheric lifetime of weeks to decades) and yet have a substantial impact on climate over policy-relevant timescales (Archer, 2005; Jackson, 2009). For example, the atmosphere already contains enough long-lived GHGs to raise global average temperature by over 2°C (assuming a climate sensitivity of approximately 3°C). Of that, 0.8°C of warming has already been realised, 0.6°C will be realised as the oceans warm and the climate system comes to equilibrium, and the remainder is being offset by the cooling effect of very short-lived sulphate aerosols (a major contributor to air pollution) (IPCC, 2007b, p 204).

Table 7.1 summarises the major warming agents, their present contribution to radiative forcing as an indication of relative importance for global climate change, atmospheric lifetime, and principal sources.[4]

The Intergovernmental Panel on Climate Change (IPCC) estimates radiative forcing from black carbon at 0.44 W/m², making it the third most important anthropogenic warming agent after CO_2 and methane (IPCC, 2007b, p 207). More recent results from Ramanathan and Carmichael (2008) that include new observations suggest that forcing from black carbon may be as high as 0.9 W/m², which would make it the second most significant warming agent.[5] Black carbon, in addition, has a disproportionate warming effect in vulnerable regions; for example, it is scavenged out of the atmosphere by ice and snow particles, so falling onto snow pack and glaciers and decreasing the albedo (that is, light reflection) in sensitive areas such as the Arctic and alpine regions (Hansen and Nazarenko, 2004; Jacobsen, 2004). Shindell and Faluvegi (2009) conclude that short-lived pollutants caused up to half the warming experienced in the Arctic in the 20th century. In addition, black carbon emissions in South Asia have had a particular impact on China because a large fraction of the black carbon remains in the region and contributes to the formation of clouds of air pollution known as 'atmospheric brown clouds', the largest of which sits over the Himalayas where it (a) contributes to the retreat of glaciers on the Tibetan Plateau that form the headwaters of the Yangtze and the

Huang He rivers and (b) disrupts the Asian monsoon cycle (Menon et al, 2002; Ramanathan et al, 2007, 2008). Although tropospheric ozone is not included in Table 7.1 because it is not emitted directly, the IPCC (2007b, p 207) estimates that its radiative forcing is $0.39 \, W/m^2$, making it the fourth most significant warming influence.

In addition to their role in global climate change, black carbon and tropospheric ozone both contribute to air pollution. Approximately 20% of black carbon emissions come from the burning of traditional

Table 7.1: Change in radiative forcing from 1750 to 2005 due to emission of various agents[a] and more recent results for black carbon[b]

Agent emitted	Net change in radiative forcing in 2005 due to emissions 1750-2005 (W/m^2)	Atmospheric lifetime	Primary sources
CO_2	1.56	Centuries-millennia	Fossil-fuel burning, deforestation and land-use change, cement production
CH_4	0.86	~12 years	Landfills, natural gas leakage, agriculture
N_2O	0.14	~114 years	Fertilizer use, livestock sector, fossil-fuel combustion
CFC/HCFC	0.28	100-1,000 years	Aerosols, cleaning products, refrigerants
CO/VOC (tropospheric O_3 precursors)	0.27	CO – months VOC – hours (O_3 – days)	CO – incomplete fossil-fuel combustion; VOC – petroleum production and consumption, solvents
Black carbon	0.44-0.9	1 week, except longer for increase in snow albedo in some regions	Fossil-fuel combustion, biomass burning

Notes: CO_2 = carbon dioxide, CH_4 = methane, N_2O = nitrous oxide, CFC/HCFC = chlorofluorocarbon/hydrochlorofluorocarbon, CO/VOC = carbon monoxide/volatile organic compound, O_3 = ozone

Sources: [a] IPCC (2007b, pp 33, 207) [b] Ramanathan and Carmichael (2008)

biomass fuels (IGSD, 2008). These emissions are a major component of indoor air pollution, globally the eighth most important health risk factor and responsible for 2.7% of the global burden of disease (WHO, 2005). In China alone, indoor air pollution is estimated to be responsible for over 380,000 deaths each year, or 16% of the annual total (WHO, 2007). In addition, both pollutants contribute to urban air pollution, which is estimated to cause an additional 275,000 premature deaths in China each year (WHO, 2007). Finally, ozone pollution causes cellular damage in plants and has a substantial effect on primary productivity in both natural and agricultural ecosystems. Ozone-associated agricultural losses in Asia are expected to reach US$8 billion by 2020 (Wang and Mauzerall, 2004).[6]

The order-of-magnitude differences in atmospheric lifetime shown in Table 7.1 have significant policy implications. The long-lived GHGs regulated by the Kyoto Protocol are 'stock' pollutants in that a reduction in emissions will reduce the rate of increase of atmospheric concentration, but will not lead to a reduction in the total amount of gas in the atmosphere.[7] In contrast, black carbon and tropospheric ozone are 'flow' pollutants, meaning that a reduction in emissions will decrease the atmospheric concentration and the corresponding radiative forcing. Figure 7.1 shows the implications of this difference for climate policy.

Because of its long lifetime, halting emissions of CO_2 today would result in a decrease in associated radiative forcing of only 38% by 2050. In contrast, halting emissions of black carbon, methane and ozone precursors would eliminate the radiative forcing from these pollutants soon thereafter.[8] With the world already flirting dangerously with a commitment to the 2°C warming threshold, sharp reductions in the emissions of short-lived GHGs offer one of the only opportunities to actually reduce radiative forcing in the near term, so 'buying time' to control and begin reducing emissions of the long-lived GHGs.

Moore and MacCracken (2009) outlined a 'lifetime-leveraging' proposal for a global climate agreement that would use mitigation of short-lived GHGs to achieve early reductions in radiative forcing to offset continued growth in CO_2 emissions from industrialising countries (see also MacCracken, 2009). In the 'lifetime-leveraging' architecture, developed nations (those with a per-capita GDP greater than US$10,000) would commit to ambitious reductions in emissions of all GHGs, while middle-income nations (those with a per-capita GDP of US$3,000 to US$10,000) would commit to similarly ambitious reductions in emissions of black carbon, tropospheric ozone and methane, as well as improvements in energy efficiency and carbon intensity.[9] Countries would graduate from the middle-income group of nations and take on additional mitigation commitments as they developed, with graduation based on both per-capita emissions and per-capita GDP indicators. Preliminary modelling shows that for realistic, but ambitious, emissions cuts by developed countries, on the order of 80% by 2050 and 90% by 2100, this proposal would result in an equilibrium temperature increase of between 2 and 2.5°C above pre-industrial temperatures (MacCracken and Moore, 2009).[10]

Figure 7.1: Radiative forcing from CO_2 due to fossil-fuel burning, CO_2 due to land-use change, methane, nitrous oxide, soot (black carbon) and tropospheric ozone in 2000 and 2050

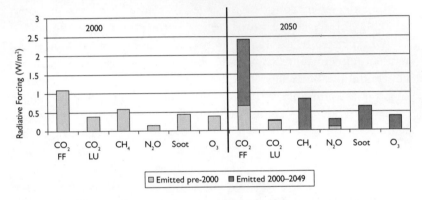

Note: Light tint represents the warming influence from emissions that have already occurred. Darker tint represents the projected warming influence from emissions taking place between 2000 and 2049, most of which can therefore be controlled through emissions policies put in place today.

FF = Derived from Fossil Fuel combustion; LU = Derived from Land Use change

Source: Adapted from Moore and MacCracken (2009)

In order to be effective, any climate agreement must be both climatically rigorous, with a reasonable chance of limiting warming to less than 2°C above pre-industrial temperatures, and within the 'political-contract zone' of major emitters if it has any chance of being agreed to and enforced (Winkler and Vorster, 2007). Climatically, in addition to the sharp emissions cutbacks in the developed nations, the key to the 'lifetime-leveraging' proposal is the early abatement of short-lived GHGs in both developed nations and middle-income countries such as China. These collective efforts would produce a reduction in radiative forcing that would offset continued growth in CO_2 emissions in industrialising nations, which remain uncapped for up to several decades, depending on the rate of development of the industrialising nations.[11] Politically, the question is whether the central trade-off in which middle-income countries begin working on short-lived GHG mitigation in return for uncapped CO_2 emissions in the near term will be considered fair and politically acceptable to those governments and constituencies involved. The following sections will consider the fairness question by evaluating the 'lifetime-leveraging' framework with respect to the fairness principles of 'common but differentiated responsibility' (CBDR) and respective capabilities embodied in the UNFCCC under Article 3.

Responsibility

Perhaps because it is a principle that can mean many things to many people, the CBDR principle has become near universal in mitigation burden-sharing proposals. Because of its resonance for those involved in the climate negotiations, it is a useful lens through which to analyse policy prescriptions (as seen previously in Chapters Four and Five). CBDR is usually understood to mean that while all nations have an interest in the protection of the Earth's climate, their duty to protect it is linked to the degree of responsibility they bear for the problem and their resources to take action. Nevertheless, its interpretation has not been uncontested since the signing of the UNFCCC in 1992. While developing countries argue that CBDR means that they should have no binding emissions-reduction commitments until developed countries have made substantial progress on cutting emissions, developed nations, particularly the US, have focused on the 'common' nature of the responsibility to argue for universal participation early on in the mitigative effort (Harris, 1999).

Even if the CBDR principle is accepted in theory, implementing it in practice by assigning mitigation commitments according to some responsibility metric is not a purely objective exercise. Instead, the flexibility of CBDR interacts with national political and economic circumstances to produce a multitude of proposed responsibility criteria, usually not unrelated to the self-interest of those proposing them (Albin, 2001; Ringius et al, 2002). A principal question is whether responsibility should be differentiated according to current emissions or, given the long atmospheric lifetime of CO_2, whether historic emissions should be taken into account (see Chapters Four and Nine). With a long industrial history, the US has repeatedly rejected taking past emissions into account (Grubb, 1995).[12]

Basing responsibility purely on absolute emissions is also unsatisfactory because it fails to take into account variations in national circumstances between countries. For example, China and the US produce roughly the same amount of GHG emissions, but China has four times as many people and so many would therefore argue that China should be considered less responsible for climate change than the US. The principle of per-capita emissions as a metric for assigning responsibility, stemming from the idea that all should have equal access to the atmospheric commons, is perhaps the most widely accepted responsibility metric (for example, Baer et al, 2008). Nevertheless, other normalising criteria have been suggested. For example, in the US, the Bush administration evaluated progress on combating climate change based on carbon intensity (emissions per unit GDP), reflecting an assumption that economic growth and production are socially beneficial and should not be sacrificed to protect the climate (White House, 2002). Similarly, Russia, the largest country in the world, proposed that responsibility should be based on GHG density (emissions per unit land area; Ringius et al, 2002).

In this chapter we look at per-capita, absolute emissions and intensity metrics (ignoring the GHG density proposal because it has received little support in the international negotiations), while recognising that the per-capita principle is better established as a responsibility metric and that significant controversy remains around the use of carbon intensity. Our discussion will also focus on black carbon and fossil-fuel CO_2 emissions (for which relatively good emissions data are available) as representative examples of short- and long-lived GHGs, respectively.

Figure 7.2 shows emissions of fossil-fuel CO_2 and black carbon in major regions, as well as emissions normalised by population and GDP. The per-capita emissions graph is particularly interesting, showing that the order of magnitude differences in per-capita CO_2 emissions between developed and developing countries, which are such an important issue in the climate negotiations, are largely absent for black carbon. Instead, per-capita black carbon emissions are far more even among regions, with somewhat higher values in North and South America and relatively lower values in Europe, Asia and Sub-Saharan Africa. This difference in the distribution of per-capita emissions results from the fact that black carbon is not intrinsically linked to economic activity in the same way that CO_2 currently is. Because black carbon is a product of incomplete combustion, lower black carbon emissions go hand in hand with more efficient combustion. Other abatement technologies such as particulate traps for diesel engines have been developed and widely deployed in developed countries in order to improve public health.

Figure 7.2: (a) per-capita CO_2 and black carbon emissions, (b) absolute emissions, (c) CO_2 and black carbon intensity (normalised by GDP)

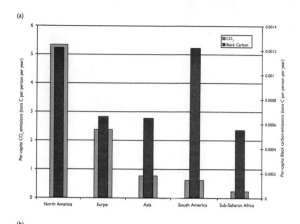

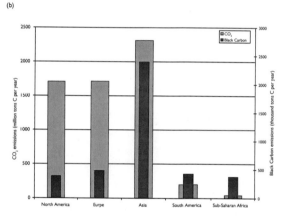

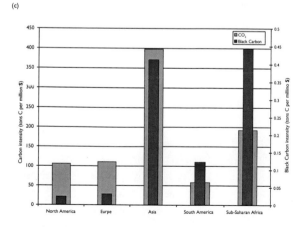

Note: C = carbon.

Sources: Bond et al (2007); World Bank (2008); WRI (2008); UNPOP (2009)

Assigning responsibility solely on the basis of absolute emissions would result in North America and Europe being assigned high responsibility for CO_2 emissions, but far lower responsibility for black carbon. Asia is responsible for high levels of both species, while South America and Sub–Saharan Africa release minimal levels of both. In the context of this chapter, it is interesting to note the relative responsibilities for CO_2 and black carbon emissions. While North America, Europe and Asia are responsible for roughly equal proportions of total CO_2 emissions (30–40%), Asia is responsible for a far greater proportion of the black carbon emissions (66%) than either Europe (12%) or North America (9%). Similarly, Africa is responsible for less than 1% of CO_2 emissions but over 10% of black carbon emissions.

Using the carbon intensity metric, the service-based economies of North America and Europe exhibit low responsibility, while the resource-based and industrialising economies of both Asia and Africa are significant contributors. As noted above, however, the intensity metric is of dubious value as an indicator of responsibility because it obscures the historical contributions to overall GHG emissions associated with GDP growth, which is a key structural fact of the climate change problem. Nevertheless, comparing the most efficient economy with the least efficient, gives a sense of the potential scope for improvement of energy use in industrialising economies. At present, a unit of wealth produced in Asia is associated with 3.5 times more CO_2 emissions, but almost 20 times more black carbon emissions, than an equivalent unit produced in North America. At first glance, this suggests that there may be significant scope for improvement, although this conclusion is questioned by some researchers who point to an off-shoring of environmentally damaging production by rich countries to poorer countries, resulting in artificially low carbon intensities in wealthy nations (Heil and Selden, 2001; Roberts and Parks, 2006, pp 163-9).

Fairness principles based on responsibility are more difficult to apply than it would first appear because widely varying political and economic national circumstances lead to conflicting claims over fair ways of evaluating responsibility. In a complex and morally ambiguous world in which understandings of fairness are contextual and socially constructed, it is counterproductive to arbitrarily select any one definition of responsibility. Instead, a useful way forward is to evaluate multiple metrics and develop policy based on findings that are robust under multiple assumptions. The analysis above shows that, under several measures of fairness, Asia is responsible for a relatively high proportion of the black carbon problem whereas North America and Europe have lower levels of responsibility, particularly in terms of absolute emissions and emissions intensity. In contrast, the two commonly used measures of responsibility (per-capita and absolute emissions) show the developed world as having a large responsibility to mitigate CO_2 emissions. Moreover, all responsibility metrics show the developing world as *relatively* more responsible for black carbon than for the CO_2 problem. In the face of resource constraints that limit spending on mitigation, this finding suggests that it is fair for mitigation actions to be differentiated according to the 'lifetime-leveraging' proposal so that industrialised nations work on reducing long-lived GHG emissions and industrialising nations, notably China, work initially on short-lived emissions, particularly black carbon and methane (MacCracken, 2009).

Capability

Although less frequently cited as a principle of mitigation burden sharing than CBDR, differentiating responsibilities based on 'respective capabilities' is also an important principle of the UNFCCC (Article 3). The principle finds its roots in a longstanding and fundamental tradition of international environmental policy – that developing nations should not have to sacrifice scarce resources to environmental improvement in the face of more pressing basic development needs (Bernstein, 2002). Implementation of this principle has meant that many international environmental treaties include temporary exemptions for developing countries or financial transfers from the North to the South to aid compliance with commitments (Harris, 2010, pp 58-70).

In terms of climate change specifically, implementation of the capability principle has been developed through research into the determinants of mitigative capacity. Originally proposed by Yohe (2001), mitigative capacity has been defined by the IPCC as 'a country's ability to reduce anthropogenic greenhouse gases or enhance natural sinks' (IPCC, 2007a, p 696). The determinants originally proposed by Yohe (2001) include the range of viable technological options available to a country or community, viable policy instruments, institutional structure, and human and social capital. In developing the concept further, Winkler et al (2006) explicitly link mitigative capacity with development pathway and use two indicators of capability – the Human Development Index and per-capita GDP. Similarly, indicators proposed by the World Resources Institute include life expectancy, literacy rate, per-capita GDP and energy use (Jones, 2009, citing WRI, 2008).[13]

A solid theoretical foundation for differentiating mitigation commitments based on capacity (essentially synonymous with level of development) exists in the literature and is being employed in the international climate regime. However, the lack of any empirical evidence that high mitigative capacity actually corresponds to mitigation (Jones, 2009) suggests that the mitigative capacity concept may be playing a normative role; that is, it is not so much that countries with high mitigative capacity (developed countries) can or do mitigate more, so much as they *should* mitigate more. Seen this way, the capability-based fairness principle is already playing an important role in the negotiations.

As can be seen from Table 7.2, there are significant disparities in the proposed mitigative capacity/development indicators, particularly in the GDP-per-capita and energy-use variables. Not only are the developing countries of Asia, South America and Africa less responsible for the CO_2 problem, they are also less able to implement solutions. This may be part of the reason why so much of the climate negotiation process seems to revolve around entrenched divisions between developed and developing countries (Grubb, 1995). Nevertheless, climate change cannot be solved by developed countries alone: even if emissions in countries of the Organisation for Economic Co-operation and Development were to go to zero in 2013 after the expiry of the Kyoto Protocol, the 2°C threshold of radiative forcing would be reached before 2050 based solely on emissions growth in the developing world (Moore and MacCracken, 2009). Given that key industrialising countries will have to be part of an effective climate agreement, the rest of this section will ask whether these nations are *more* capable of mitigating short-lived as opposed to long-lived GHGs, again using black carbon and fossil-fuel CO_2 emissions as representative examples.

Table 7.2: Selected capability indicators from WRI (2008)

	Life expectancy	Literacy rate	Per-capita GDP	Energy use
	Years	%	US$ per year (PPP)	Tons of oil equivalent per person per year
North America	78.1	99	41,141	7.9
Europe	74.8	98.7	21,513	3.8
Asia	68.9	78.4	4,547	1.1
South America	72.4	90.8	8,263	1.2
Sub-Saharan Africa	49.9	59.9	1,755	0.7

Source: WRI (2008)

Figure 7.3 summarises the key differences between mitigation of short-lived and long-lived GHGs, using the US and East Asia as examples of developed and developing regions, respectively. Technologies to reduce black carbon (and to a lesser extent tropospheric ozone) have already been developed and deployed in the US in order to abate air pollution, resulting in a reduction of black carbon emissions by over half between 1950 and 2000, and by almost three quarters since emissions peaked in 1920. Similar declines have occurred in Western Europe since the 1950s. In contrast, no developed nation has managed to truly bring fossil-fuel CO_2 emissions under control and there are no examples of large, wealthy countries with per-capita emissions low enough to be considered sustainable. In other words, it is as yet unclear what a low-carbon society with a high standard of living would look like, which is not the case for short-lived GHGs that are also air pollutants.

Figure 7.3: Left: black carbon emissions in the US and East Asia. Right: fossil-fuel CO_2 emissions

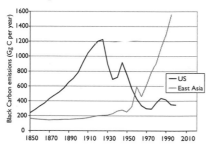

Note: Gg = gigagram; C = carbon

Sources: Bond et al (2007); WRI (2008)

The fact that air pollution abatement technologies were deployed in the North long before global warming became a serious policy concern speaks to another element of the capability principle. Pollution control confers benefits as well as costs and a country is more capable of controlling pollution to the extent that it can benefit from those efforts. Not only do the benefits make pollution control more economically beneficial, they also make pollution control more politically feasible in that measures can be justified to constituents on the basis of local environmental and health improvements. However, in the case of long-lived GHG emissions, this aspect of capability becomes irrelevant because it would require states likely to suffer the most from climate change to be responsible for the most mitigation.

This not only runs in direct opposition to the responsibility principle, but is entirely impractical given that the most vulnerable states are the least developed countries that have extremely limited resources (Ringius et al, 2002). Nevertheless, in the context of mitigating short-lived GHGs, which has substantial local and regional co-benefits, the distribution of abatement benefits may have a significant impact on a country's capability to take action.

Table 7.3 compares the geographical and temporal distributions of direct benefits from the abatement of short-lived GHGs and fossil-fuel CO_2 emissions. Industrialising countries will be more capable of mitigation to the extent that a greater fraction of benefits occurs locally and immediately as opposed to globally and in the distant future. In this respect, it is clear that abatement of short-lived GHGs is a far better fit with the capabilities of industrialising countries in that it would result in an immediately apparent improvement of local air quality. In fact, governments in developing countries are already implementing policies to improve local air quality: New Delhi is switching its municipal bus system to compressed natural gas to reduce air pollution, while Beijing is considering making pollution-control measures implemented for the 2008 Olympics permanent (Oster, 2008). Integrating these existing and emerging policies with climate change mitigation efforts could both generate significant improvements for the climate and overcome the developed–developing nation deadlock in the negotiations.

This analysis suggests that industrialising countries will be more capable of mitigating short-lived GHGs than CO_2 emissions. Not only does the technology to reduce these emissions exist, but it has already been widely deployed in developed countries with demonstrated success. Moreover, these policies were implemented because of air quality concerns alone, which are becoming increasingly serious in major industrialising countries. Many of these countries are already looking to improve air quality. Because of this, incorporating these policies into the climate regime, with its associated financing and technological transfer benefits, is far more likely to be within the capacity of developing countries than setting a cap – even an expanding cap – on fossil-fuel emissions.

Table 7.3: Comparison of the geographical and temporal distributions of benefits for short-lived GHGs and fossil fuel-CO_2 emissions

		Local	Regional	Global
Black carbon and O_3	Benefit:	Reduced morbidity and mortality from indoor and urban air pollution	Reduced atmospheric brown cloud formation and associated glacier melt, monsoonal disruption and surface dimming	Reduced impacts from global climate change
	Relative magnitude:	Substantial	Small to moderate	Moderate
	Timescale:	Immediate	Immediate to decadal	Multi-decadal
Fossil-fuel CO_2	Benefit:	None	None	Reduced impacts from global climate change
	Relative magnitude:	NA	NA	Very substantial
	Timescale:	NA	NA	Multi-decadal

Note: The magnitude of the benefits is subjectively assessed and is relative to the total benefits for that action. Variations in timescale result from differential responses of different natural systems.

Sources: Based on WHO (2005)

Conclusion

Returning to the theme of this volume, we ask how the analysis presented above relates to the question of China's responsibility for the climate change problem and its responsibility to mitigate emissions. We suggest that a useful approach is to disaggregate analysis on the basis of both the atmospheric lifetimes of GHGs and their contribution to local environmental and public health problems. This has the advantage of decomposing the monolithic (and perhaps somewhat abstract) question of China's responsibility for climate change into more tractable questions from which feasible and policy-relevant approaches can be developed.

Despite the fact that it is still an emerging economy, as the world's largest GHG emitter China is coming under increasing pressure to address its role in global climate change. Partly in response to these concerns, the Chinese government has already adopted ambitious energy-intensity, carbon-intensity and renewable-energy targets (Wong and Light, 2009). Moreover, the country is one of the world's largest investors in renewable energy, with a rapidly growing wind-energy sector and the world's largest solar hot water market (Martinot and Junfeng, 2007). Nevertheless, China has continued to resist accepting a binding cap on its GHG emissions in the international negotiations (Doyle, 2009).

Adopting aggressive mitigation of short-lived GHGs such as black carbon, tropospheric ozone and methane, as proposed in the 'lifetime-leveraging' architecture, would reduce China's contribution to climate change by reducing the atmospheric burden of these pollutants and the associated radiative forcing. It would also address the country's substantial air quality problems. China contains four of the 10 most polluted cities in the world and urban air pollution is responsible for approximately one in 10 deaths in China (WHO, 2007). Policies to improve industrial combustion efficiency, to regulate particulate emissions from transportation, to replace traditional biomass burning with improved stoves and to reduce tropospheric ozone formation all have substantial health co-benefits consistent with China's national development strategy. Moreover, the technologies to implement these policies exist and have already been deployed in developed nations.

'Lifetime-leveraging' thus appears to be a fair and highly effective way for China to engage in the international effort to mitigate climate change, being consistent with fairness principles based on both responsibility and capacity. Furthermore, engaging in such a strategy would give China political leverage to demand more ambitious mitigation targets for long-lived GHGs from the developed world as well as reductions in short-lived GHGs from other industrialising nations. Taken together, these actions by developed and industrialising countries would put the world on a path that has a good chance of staying below the 2°C threshold and of achieving the UNFCCC objective of avoiding 'dangerous anthropogenic interference with the climate'.

Notes

[1] An additional determinant will be the magnitude of the offsetting cooling influence created by sulfur dioxide emissions, which are chemically transformed to sulfate and create a whitish haze that reflects back a small fraction of the incoming solar radiation.

[2] Radiative forcing is a useful measure for directly comparing diverse factors of global warming that affect the Earth's climate. Measured in watts per

square meter (W/m^2), the value describes the change in net energy flux at the tropopause (top of the troposphere), positive downward, caused by a given climate driver (for example, an increase in GHG concentration or a change in albedo, that is, surface reflectivity).

[3] Based on the Intergovernmental Panel on Climate Change's (IPCC) B2 scenario (IPCC, 2000).

[4] Although tropospheric ozone and black carbon are, for convenience, collectively referred to in this chapter as 'short-lived GHGs', it should be noted that black carbon is, strictly speaking, not a gas but an aerosol particle.

[5] Semi-direct effects of black carbon on clouds, which make estimating the climatic significance of black carbon difficult, may reduce the estimate somewhat (Koch and Del Genio, 2010).

[6] Ozone is also an important part of what may become a significant carbon-cycle feedback. Warmer temperatures due to global warming accelerate the rate of ozone production, which in turn harms forest ecosystems, weakening the land carbon sink and accelerating the build-up of CO_2. Modelling studies indicate that the indirect radiative forcing from this feedback effect in 2100 will be comparable to the direct forcing from elevated ozone concentrations (Sitch et al, 2007). Ozone abatement policies can thus directly mitigate global warming while also protecting the land carbon sink.

[7] Methane, the only one of the bundle of six GHGs regulated by the Kyoto Protocol with an atmospheric lifetime of less than a century, is the exception. With a 12-year residence time, methane might be considered a stock pollutant for the purposes of the (five-year) Kyoto commitment period, but is a flow pollutant for the purposes of long-term (multi-decadal) policy making.

[8] Within weeks to a month for black carbon and ozone, and roughly two decades for methane.

[9] Low-income countries (those with a per-capita GDP of less than US$3,000) would be encouraged, but not required, to take the types of actions of the middle-income nations.

[10] This would not be the warming in 2100 because the Earth's temperature takes some time to equilibrate to changes in radiative forcing. Instead, this equilibrium temperature increase would be realised over the course of one to two centuries.

[11] To the extent that the industrialising nations can begin reducing the growth in their CO_2 emissions in order to prepare for a later cut in CO_2 emissions, there would be a further reduction in the warming influence of the uncapped portion of CO_2 emissions (Energy Modeling Forum, 2009).

[12] Note that the question of historic emissions is less relevant for short-lived GHGs because they are rapidly removed from the atmosphere. Nevertheless, because of a lag in the equilibration time between radiative forcing and global temperature, a long history of short-lived GHG emissions adds energy to the Earth system, and this energy exerts a warming influence even after emissions have ceased and the gases have been removed from the atmosphere.

[13] In its current formulation, mitigative capacity can become conceptually confused with responsibility because it is generally accepted that the capacity to reduce emissions increases with emissions (note both the technological options determinant proposed by Yohe, 2001, and the energy use indicator included by WRI, 2008). This is a result both of the observed relationship between economic development and emissions and of the idea of subsistence emissions (the emissions needed to provide basic human needs) as opposed to luxury emissions that are easier to mitigate (Shue, 1993). This not only makes it more difficult to distinguish between responsibility and capability principles, but also results in the paradoxical conclusion that enhancing mitigative capacity requires increasing emissions (Jones, 2009)

[14] Mitigation of fossil-fuel CO_2 emissions can have significant co-benefits in terms of reductions of co-emitted air pollutants such as sulfates, nitrogen oxide and particulate matter (including black carbon) (IPCC, 2007a, pp 619-90). The magnitude of these benefits will vary depending on mitigation strategies used. For example, they may be substantial for fuel switching to renewables, but minimal for carbon sequestration.

References

Albin, C. (2001) *Justice and fairness in international negotiation* (vol 74), Cambridge: Cambridge University Press.

Archer, D. (2005) 'Fate of fossil-fuel CO_2 in geologic time', *Journal of Geophysical Research*, vol 110, doi: 10.1029/2004JC002625.

Baer, P., Athanasiou, T., Kartha, S. and Kemp-Benedict, E. (2008) *Greenhouse Development Rights Framework: The right to develop in a climate-constrained world* (2nd edition), Berlin: Heinrich-Boll Foundation.

Barrett, S. (2008) 'Climate treaties and the imperative of enforcement', *Oxford Review of Economic Policy*, vol 24, no 2, pp 239-58.

Bernstein, S. (2002) *The compromise of liberal environmentalism*, New York, NY: Columbia University Press.

Boden, T.A., Marland, G. and Andres, R.J. (2009) *Global, regional and national fossil-fuel CO_2 emissions*, Oak Ridge, TN: Carbon Dioxide Information Analysis Center, Oak Ridge National Laboratory.

Bond, T., Bhardwaj, E., Dong, R., Jogani, R., Jung, S., Roden, C. et al (2007) 'Historical emissions of black carbon and organic carbon aerosol from energy-related combustion, 1850-2000', *Global Biogeochemical Cycles*, vol 21, GB2018.

Connaughton, J.L. (2007) *Testimony before the U.S. House of Representatives Committee on Oversight and Government Reform, March 19th 2007*, Washington, DC: US Congress.

Doyle, A. (2009) 'China to act on climate, warns of "unfair" demands', *Reuters*, 2 June.

Energy Modeling Forum (2009) 'International, US and EU Climate Change Control Scenarios: Results from EMF 22', edited by L. Clarke, C. Böhringer and T.F. Rutherford, *Energy Economics*, vol 31, supplement 2, pp S63-S306 (December).

Grubb, M. (1995) 'Seeking fair weather: ethics and the international debate on climate change', *International Affairs*, vol 71, no 3, pp 463-96.

Hansen, J. and Nazarenko, L. (2004) 'Soot climate forcing via snow and ice albedos', *Proceedings of the National Academy of Sciences*, vol 101, no 2, pp 423-8.

Harris, P.G. (1999) 'Common but differentiated responsibility: the Kyoto Protocol and United States policy', *N.Y.U. Environmental Law Journal*, vol 7, pp 27-48.

Heil, M.T. and Selden, T.M. (2001) 'International trade intensity and carbon emissions: a cross-country econometric analysis', *Journal of Environment and Development*, vol 10, pp 35-49.

IGSD (Institute for Governance and Sustainable Development) (2008) *Reducing black carbon may be the fastest strategy for slowing climate change*, Washington, DC: IGSD.

IPCC (Intergovernmental Panel on Climate Change) (2000) *Special report on emissions scenarios*, Geneva: IPCC.

IPCC (2007a) *Climate change 2007: Mitigation of climate change*, New York, NY: Cambridge University Press.

IPCC (2007b) *Climate change 2007: The physical science basis*, New York, NY: Cambridge University Press.

Jackson, S.C. (2009) 'Parallel pursuit of near-term and long-term climate mitigation', *Science*, vol 326, pp 526-7.

Jacobsen, M.Z. (2004) 'Climate response of fossil fuel and biofuel soot, accounting for soot's feedback to snow and sea ice albedo and emissivity', *Journal of Geophysical Research*, vol 109, D21201.

Jones, T.W. (2009) *On capacity, mitigation, and global governance: The importance of semantics in the international climate policy regime*, New Haven, CT: Yale School of Forestry and Environmental Studies.

Koch, D. and Del Genio, A.D. (2010) 'Black carbon absorption effects on cloud cover: review and synthesis', *Atmos. Chem. Phys.* vol, 10, pp 7685-96, doi:10.5194/acp-10-7685-2010.

MacCracken, M. (2009) 'Moderating climate change by limiting emissions of both short- and long-lived greenhouse gases', Paper presented at the Proceedings of the 42nd Session of the International Seminars on Planetary Emergencies, Erice, Sicily: Italy, 20-23 August 2009.

MacCracken, M. and Moore, F. (2009) 'Achieving agreement and climate protection by mitigation of short- and long-lived greenhouse gases', Paper presented at the Copenhagen Climate Congress, Copenhagen, 10-12 March 2009.

Martinot, E. and Junfeng, L. (2007) *Powering China's development: The role of renewable energy*, Washington, DC: Worldwatch Institute.

Meinshausen, M. (2006) 'What does a 2°C target mean for greenhouse gas concentrations? A brief analysis based on multi-gas emission pathways and several climate sensitivity uncertainty estimates', in J.H. Schellenhuber (ed) *Avoiding dangerous climate change* (pp 265-79), New York, NY: Cambridge University Press.

Menon, S., Hansen, J., Nazarenko, L. and Luo, Y. (2002) 'Climate effects of black carbon aerosols in China and India', *Science*, vol 297, pp 2250-3.

Moore, F. and MacCracken, M. (2009) 'Lifetime-leveraging: an approach to achieving international agreement and effective climate protection using mitigation of short-lived greenhouse gases', *International Journal of Climate Change Strategies and Management*, vol 1, no 1, pp 42-62.

Oster, S. (2008) 'Beijing considers pollution-control measures', *Wall Street Journal*, 24 September.

Ramanathan, V. and Carmichael, G. (2008) 'Global and regional changes due to black carbon', *Nature Geoscience*, vol 1, pp 221-7.

Ramanathan, V., Agrawal, M., Akimoto, H., Aufhanner, M., Devotta, S. and Emberson, L. (2008) *Atmospheric brown clouds: Regional Assessment report with focus on Asia*, Nairobi: United Nations Environment Programme.

Ramanathan, V., Ramana, M.V., Roberts, G., Kim, D., Corrigan, C., Chung, C. et al (2007) 'Warming trends in Asia amplified by brown cloud solar absorption', *Nature*, vol 448, pp 575-9.

Ringius, L., Torvanger, A. and Underdal, A. (2002) 'Burden sharing and fairness principles in international climate policy', *International Environmental Agreements*, vol 2, pp 1-22.

Roberts, J.T. and Parks, B.C. (2006) *A climate of injustice: Global inequality, North–South politics, and climate policy*, Cambridge, MA: MIT Press.

Shindell, D.T. and Faluvegi, G. (2009) 'Climate response to regional radiative forcing during the twentieth century', *Nature Geoscience*, vol 2, pp 294-300.

Shue, H. (1993) 'Subsistence emissions and luxury emissions', *Law & Policy*, vol 15, no 1, pp 39-60.

Singh, M. (2008) PM's speech on release of Climate Change Action Plan', www.pmindia.nic.in/lspeech.asp?id=690

Sitch, S., Cox, P.M., Collins, W.J. and Huntingford, C. (2007) 'Indirect radiative forcing of climate change through ozone effects on the land-carbon sink', *Nature*, vol 448, pp 791-4.

UNPOP (United Nations Population Division) (2009) *World population prospects: The 2008 revision*, New York, UNPOP, http://esa.un.org

Wang, X. and Mauzerall, D.L. (2004) 'Characterizing distributions of surface ozone and its impact on grain production in China, Japan and South Korea: 1990 and 2020', *Atmospheric Environment*, vol 38, pp 4383-402.

White House (2002) *President Bush announces clear skies & global climate change initiative*, Washington, DC: White House.

WHO (World Health Organization) (2005) 'Indoor air pollution and health' (Vol. Fact Sheet 292), Geneva: WHO.

WHO (2007) *Country profiles of environmental burden of disease: China*, Geneva: WHO.

Winkler, H. and Vorster, S. (2007) 'Building bridges to 2020 and beyond: the road from Bali', *Climate Policy*, vol 7, pp 240-54.

Winkler, H., Brounds, B. and Kartha, S. (2006) 'Future mitigation commitments: differentiating among non-Annex 1 countries', *Climate Policy*, vol 5, no 5, pp 469-86.

Wong, J. and Light, A. (2009) *Climate progress in China: A primer on recent developments*, Washington, DC: Center for American Progress.

World Bank (2008) 'Quick reference tables: GDP 2007', Washington, DC: World Bank, http://web.worldbank.org/WBSITE/EXTERNAL/DATASTATISTICS/0,,contentMDK:20399244~menuPK:1504474~pagePK:64133150~piPK:64133175~theSitePK:239419,00.html

WRI (World Resources Institute) (2008) 'Climate Analysis Indicator Tool', Washington, DC: WRI, cait.wri.org

Yohe, G. (2001) 'Mitigative capacity: the mirror image of adaptive capacity on the emissions side: an editorial', *Climatic Change*, vol 49, pp 247–62.

EIGHT

Sustainable consumption and production in global value chains

Patrick Schroeder

This chapter analyses China's responsibility for climate change by reference to the concept of 'sustainable consumption and production' (SCP). SCP has three main attributes. First, it is an integrative analytical perspective based on 'life-cycle' thinking for understanding the complex interrelationship between global economic activity and value chains, and between human wellbeing and global environmental degradation, including climate change. Second, it is an international political process to promote and support policies and actions necessary for systemic transition towards sustainable consumption and production patterns. Third, it is a set of practical solutions or 'tools' to be applied by policy makers, the private sector, civil society and individuals to address social, economic and environmental problems arising from unsustainable production and consumption patterns. Sustainable consumption and production as an integrative analytical perspective is based on the realisation that consumption and production are not separated from each other; they are inextricably connected and need to be considered as a coupled system (Lebel and Lorek, 2008).

For conceptual simplification, the SCP perspective is often separated into a production side and a consumption side, with consumption and production referred to as 'two sides of the same sustainability coin'. SCP is based on life-cycle thinking, for which the most important analytical tool is life-cycle assessment (LCA). LCA is the internationally standardised scientific approach behind modern environmental policies and business decisions. Through LCA, it is possible to consider resource use and pollution occurring during all stages of the life cycle of goods and services, from the resource-extraction phase to the end-of-life phase, or 'from cradle to cradle', thereby making the 'world behind the product' visible (de Leeuw, 2005). Conceptually, life-cycle thinking offers huge untapped potential for providing comprehensive information and data about products and their associated environmental impacts. That said, there is a wide gap between life-cycle information already generated and comprehensive practical applications that address environmental issues based on life-cycle thinking (Mont and Bleischwitz, 2007).

The SCP concept has been discussed since the early 1990s. However, tools and methodologies for practical implementation are still evolving. SCP as a practical approach developed from the principle of 'cleaner production', which, according to the United Nations Environment Programme, Division for Technology, Industry and Economics (UNEP-DTIE), 'is the continuous application of an integrated, preventive environmental strategy towards processes, products and services in order to increase overall efficiency and reduce damage and risks for humans and the environment' (www.unep.fr). Born out of the realisation that cleaner production alone will not be sufficient to achieve necessary reductions in environmental impacts (Mont and Plepys, 2008), and that overall increases in consumption can offset efficiency improvements on the production side through so-called 'rebound effects' (Sorrell, 2007), the cleaner production approach was extended by adding the 'consumption side', thereby creating the integrated SCP approach. SCP, with its life-cycle perspective, is necessarily a global approach because it is based on the total use of resources going into the production of goods and provision of services, as well as the resulting emissions and waste. It aims to account for all the entry points for remediation as well as possible synergistic interventions throughout global production and consumption chains.

SCP is gaining in importance on the international and multilateral political agenda. A 'political' SCP agenda first gained momentum at the World Summit for Sustainable Development (WSSD) in 2002, where it was stated that 'all countries should promote sustainable consumption and production patterns, with the developed countries taking the lead and with all countries benefiting from the process....' (WSSD, 2002). Responding to the call of the WSSD Johannesburg Plan of Implementation, in June 2003 UNEP and the United Nations Department of Economic and Social Affairs initiated a global action plan to promote sustainable consumption and production – the so-called Marrakech Process. This global multi-stakeholder process, which includes national governments, the private sector and civil society, aims to promote SCP and to work towards a 'Global Framework for Action on SCP', a 10-year set of programmes to support regional and national initiatives promoting the shift towards SCP patterns. One of the main goals of the Marrakech Process is the development of non-prescriptive guidelines to support the implementation of national SCP programmes and action plans that require the active participation of national governments (Clark, 2007). In the case of China, the national

SCP action plan is manifested in the 'Circular Economy Law', which is discussed below.

The Commission on Sustainable Development (CSD) took up the theme of SCP and the Marrakech Process during its 2010/11 two-year cycle. The CSD is reviewing progress on implementing policies related to SCP, and looking at constraints and barriers to achieving SCP. It is further expected that governments will consider the adoption of a related 10-year framework of programmes currently being developed under the Marrakech Process.

In addition to being an analytical approach and international process, the SCP approach also offers a 'toolbox' to be applied by policy makers, the private sector, civil society and individuals to address social, economic and environmental problems arising from unsustainable production and consumption patters. The SCP toolbox contains practices and solutions that are being used to address unsustainable consumption and production patterns (see Lebel and Lorek, 2008; Tuncer and Schroeder, 2009). Some of these SCP practices are technical and managerial, seeking to improve product properties and manufacturing processes to make them more energy and resource efficient, and to reduce the content of toxic substances and the output of industrial waste products. Examples include cleaner and leaner production practices, voluntary industry approaches, technological innovations (including Research & Development [R&D] for product innovation) and green supply-chain management.

Other practices are used to effectively communicate relevant information about products or companies' performance to stakeholders, such as policy makers and consumers. Such information-sharing and communication practices include, among other things, eco-labelling and certification, corporate sustainability reporting (including greenhouse gas [GHG] emissions), product information disclosure and consumer awareness raising. Further practices can be classified as demand-side management approaches that go beyond simply providing better information by actively influencing consumption behaviour towards becoming more sustainable. Examples include product-choice editing by retailers and regulators, and green public procurement undertaken by local and national governments. These practices are often closely related and mutually supportive; they can be combined as a package for more comprehensive cross-sectoral strategies to deal with the environmental, social and economic impacts of consumption and production systems – including climate change.

SCP and climate change

How does the pressing issue of climate change relate to the SCP perspective, SCP approaches and related policies? From the SCP perspective, climate change is one of the symptoms of unsustainable consumption and production patterns. While climate change is often perceived and discussed mainly as an energy issue, especially in the context of China, from the SCP perspective it becomes clear that many more economic sectors and activities need to be considered, including, among others, forestry, agriculture and waste management. Use of resources, including land and water, as well as their respective indicators, need to be considered to be able to assess the overall impacts on the climate and ecosystems, and impacts of climate change on society and livelihoods (Warhurst and Slater, 2010). The application of life-cycle thinking and a product–based value-chain perspective show that current efforts to reduce GHGs do not focus on the 'hot-spots' responsible for the main share of emissions. Large unrealised potentials for impact reduction exist 'upstream' in the value chain, in the resource extraction phase and in the early stages of raw material processing, as well as 'downstream' in the value chain, during use phases and during disposal of goods and services (see Figure 8.1).

Figure 8.1: Climate change mitigation potentials along the value chain

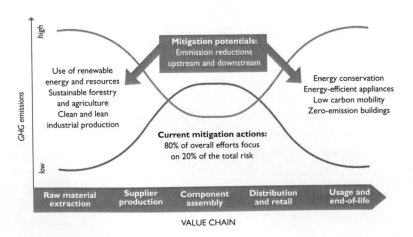

Source: Wei and Schroeder (2010); adapted from WWF-UK (2004)

Applying life-cycle thinking is crucial to achieving significant reductions in global resource use, lowered environmental impacts and reduced GHG emissions. LCA is a particularly important tool that can provide information to prevent the shifting of burdens from one life-cycle phase to another, the shifting of emissions from one sector to another and the shifting of emissions from one geographical location to another. Furthermore, LCA can provide information for full evaluation of environmental impacts, such as acid rain, summer smog, cancer effects or water and land use. When only carbon-footprint data are used for decision making, be it at the policy, company or consumer levels, this cannot be guaranteed (EC, 2010). The application of LCA data for decision making by different stakeholders, particularly businesses and policy makers, is referred to as 'life-cycle management' (LCM). LCM is making life-cycle thinking and product sustainability operational through the continuous improvements of production and consumption systems. LCM also supports the business assimilation of industrial policies and compliance to regulations (Remmen et al, 2007).

Currently, the main initiatives to reduce GHG emissions at global, bilateral and national levels, such as the Kyoto Protocol under the United Nations Framework Convention on Climate Change (UNFCCC), or the Asia-Pacific Partnership on Clean Development and Climate, focus mostly on production, such as technical efficiency improvements in electricity generation, industrial manufacturing equipment of key industry sectors and renewable energy development. While acknowledging the importance of these actions, the SCP perspective also shows that a variety of additional social and economic issues need to be considered in order to understand the underlying causes of climate change and to find comprehensive solutions to climate change. The most crucial contribution of the SCP approach to climate change is the realisation that in addition to technical solutions on the production side, other non-technical issues and options for changes on the consumption side need to be considered and supported, particularly for the reduction of emissions of high-impact behaviour through changes in lifestyles and habits (see Maréchal, 2010).

In addition to technological and industrial transformation towards renewable energy technologies, energy-efficient manufacturing processes and new technological innovations are required to successfully mitigate climate change. Consumer behaviour and lifestyles are also keys in finding solutions, as stated in the Fourth Assessment Report of the Intergovernmental Panel on Climate Change: 'there is ... high agreement and medium evidence that changes in lifestyle and behaviour patterns can contribute to climate change mitigation across all sectors.

Management practices can also have a positive role' (IPCC, 2007, p 59). Looking more specifically at which type of consumption patterns and lifestyles have climate change impacts, a comprehensive study about end-consumption-related activities in the European Union found that there are three consumption sectors (also called demand areas) responsible for about 70-80% of the overall environmental impact of human consumption and production systems: housing, mobility and food (Tukker et al, 2006).[1] For instance, LCA shows that more than 80% of GHG emissions over the life of a private passenger car occur while driving it (WWF-UK, 2008). Similarly, the use phase of a computer is responsible for three times more GHG emissions than are emissions resulting from manufacturing it (UNEP, 2008).

Examples of SCP practices that address climate change issues in these three consumption-demand areas include, for example, energy labelling for buildings and electric appliances, carbon labelling for food products and emissions standards for private vehicles. Interestingly, many of the consumption-based SCP practices simultaneously address other environmental, social and economic issues. Energy labelling of buildings encourages better insulation for energy efficiency, which not only reduces energy consumption for heating or cooling but also helps households save money in the long run. Using low-carbon or even zero-carbon transportation contributes to improving air quality in cities and has significant health benefits for inhabitants. In the demand area of food, consumer awareness raising can support efforts to reduce the intake of food with high-carbon footprints, particularly beef and dairy products, which can not only significantly lessen GHG emissions from agriculture and deforestation but also has positive health effects, such as by reducing the risk of cancer and heart disease.

In addition to mitigating climate change, SCP practices can provide opportunities for adaptation, particularly for the poor who are more vulnerable and will in many cases be seriously affected by climate change. Sustainable infrastructures with low resource intensity can enable 'leapfrogging' in human development, and they can support climate change adaptation in developing countries. Examples include decentralised and resilient renewable energy applications, such as solar photovoltaic (PV) home energy systems and small-scale wind power, and flexible and affordable mobile phone networks that do not depend on building expensive grids or landline infrastructures. Innovative business practices that collect and repair information-technology equipment and mobile phones from wealthy consumers, thereby avoiding e-waste, and donating or reselling them in developing countries, already contribute to this development. Sustainable innovative products for the poor include low-tech portable solar water purifiers, which will become increasingly important as water availability decreases in many developing countries. Organic farming can also contribute to climate change adaptation because it diversifies farm organisation, for example through more complex crop rotation. Especially for regions with drought or subsistence agriculture, organic farming is superior because yields are more stable. Other benefits include increased biodiversity, reduced environmental impacts and improved livelihoods due to high-value food chains (Niggli et al, 2009).

One important element of the SCP approach is the realisation that solutions can only be found by considering and involving *all* relevant stakeholders. Therefore, the following section discusses not so much the climate change responsibility of China as a country, but rather the responsibilities of some of the major value-chain stakeholders involved in China's complex consumption and production systems.

China's responsibility for climate change: an SCP value-chain stakeholder perspective

China's energy sector, which is heavily dependent on coal, accounts for the largest share of the country's GHG emissions. Emissions from industrial production processes are similarly significant. Electricity and heat generation, together with manufacturing industries and construction, were responsible for over 80% of China's carbon dioxide (CO_2) emissions in 2007 (IEA, 2009). Industry is responsible for the largest share of energy use, accounting for about 50-55% of the total (Fan et al, 2009). Primary and secondary heavy-industry sectors, such as mining, steel, cement, aluminium and chemicals, are particularly responsible for a large share of the industrial emissions (National Bureau of Statistics of P.R. China, 2009). Thus, a major responsibility lies with large utilities and companies operating in these energy- and emissions-intensive sectors.

Policy makers at national and local levels have responsibility to design and implement industrial and economic policies that facilitate the transition to a low-carbon economic structure. A great number of small- and medium-sized enterprises (SMEs) still use outmoded equipment and technologies that waste energy and resources, thus resulting in high levels of GHG emissions and other pollutants. Most of the current manufacturing capacity in China is still based on outmoded and energy-intensive technologies and only a small number of SMEs meets current international standards (Ho, 2005). Therefore, both private companies and state-owned enterprises need to upgrade their facilities and take measures that reduce emissions from their operations. Multinationals operating in China can play a positive role by supporting technology transfer and capacity building.

These measures would address a large share of emissions, but responsibility goes further than addressing 'in-house' activities; it is also necessary to look 'upstream' in the supply chain. Extraction of resources, such as minerals, oil and timber, involve land-use changes that have huge impacts on the climate. Often, these activities take place in other countries. For example, deforestation in Burma, Indonesia and Russia is closely related to manufacturing activities in China. In the early 2000s, Burma suffered one of the fastest rates of deforestation in the world, mainly fuelled by demand for timber from China. According to the environmental organisation Global Witness (2009), in 2005 China imported more than 1.5 million cubic metres of Burmese timber worth an estimated US$350 million. Almost all of these imports were illegal. Since 2007, the Burmese and Chinese governments have taken action and reduced the trade of illegal timber by 70%. However, the problem has not been solved completely, and China still accounts for about a quarter of the global illegal trade in timber. An effective SCP solution to addressing this issue involves both voluntary and mandatory product labelling of forest products. In 2007, the Forest Stewardship Council office in China launched an 'FSC National Initiative' for the promotion of responsible forest management inside and outside China, with support of China's State Forest Administration, the Chinese Academy of Forestry, WWF-China and other organisations.

Looking in another direction at the 'downstream' value chain, one needs to acknowledge the responsibility of final consumers. Chinese emissions from industrial production activities and impacts generated upstream during resource-extraction activities need to be considered in relation to consumption activities in other countries. Relatively little attention has been paid to the amount of emissions related to the consumption of goods and services. Thus, a consumption-based account of CO_2 emissions is helpful to understanding the impact of global trade. It differs from conventional emissions inventories because it considers imports and exports of goods that contain embodied CO_2 emissions (see Figure 8.2).

Consumption-based accounting shows that many consumption-related impacts on the climate from industrialised countries have shifted geographically (see Chapter Five). Many polluting and emissions-intensive manufacturing processes have, over the last two decades, effectively been outsourced to developing countries, in particular to China (Kuhndt et al, 2008). Overall, 22.5% of carbon emissions produced in China in 2004 were exported (Davis and Caldeira, 2010). The import of emissions–intensive products from China increases the per-capita carbon footprint of consumers in the countries doing the importing. For example, in the case of Norway, about 1.5 tonnes of CO_2 per person per year are generated in China to produce exports consumed by Norwegians (Reinvang and Peters, 2008). Consumers in industrialised countries therefore have responsibility for GHG emissions generated in China. Also, coming back to the issue of deforestation, many Chinese-manufactured wood products are destined for consumption in the United States (US) and Europe. Therefore, these consumers share some of the responsibility for illegal logging and deforestation in countries such as Burma, and thus for the resulting negative impacts on climate.

Figure 8.2: Consumption-based emissions accounting

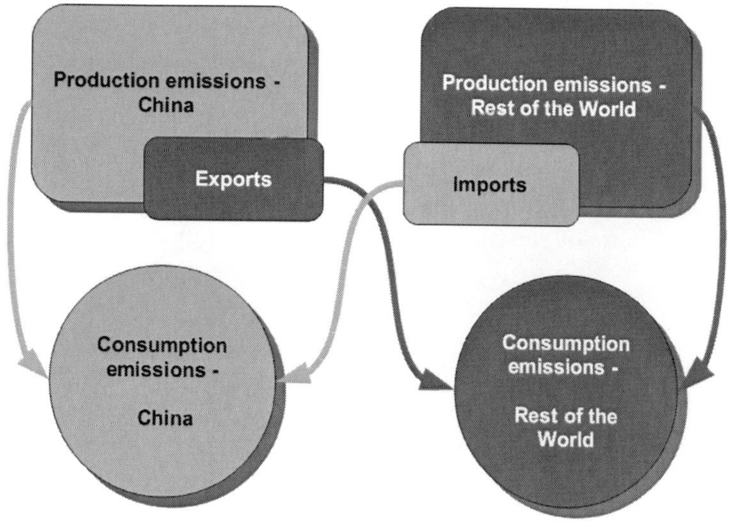

Source: After Carbon Trust (2006)

But domestic consumers within China are also responsible for the country's contribution to climate change (see Chapters Nine and Ten). LCAs show that household consumption is an increasingly important factor for growth of China's CO_2 emissions. According to a study by Liu et al (2010), which looked at increases in China's CO_2 emissions from 1992 to 2002, household consumption has offset improvements in technological efficiency on the production side. This shows that purely technological approaches are unlikely to lead to overall reduction in environmental impacts and to achieve climate stabilisation. In the last two decades, domestic Chinese households have increasingly contributed to the expansion of manufacturing activities in China, and will likely do so more in the future. Consequently, due to their demand for consumer goods and services, domestic Chinese households are becoming a more important contributor to CO_2 emissions.

Having said this, large gaps remain between different levels of human development and per-capita emissions within China, which displays a wide range of different consumption and production patterns. Stark differences exist between regions and social classes where poverty and Western-like, high-impact lifestyles often exist side by side. GHG emissions are, so far, clearly correlated with the level of economic and human development. Poor people in China have per-capita emissions comparable to those of many least-developed countries, well below the global average of around 5 tonnes per year. Hundreds of millions of Chinese people are still not consuming enough to meet their basic needs for water, food, shelter or energy services and increasingly they suffer from the environmental problems associated with industrial pollution. These people are not as responsible for climate change.

All the same, China's average per-capita emissions in 2009 were 6.1 tonnes (Olivier and Peters, 2010), slightly above the world average due to an increasingly affluent urban consumer class with emissions profiles similar to their counterparts in industrialised countries. China's urban consumers belong to the emerging 'global consumer class', which totalled about 1.7 billion people in 2004, with almost 40% in Asia (Worldwatch Institute, 2004), and which shares a lifestyle of conspicuous consumption regardless of cultural background or nationality. They are likely to live in modern apartments equipped with electronic appliances and gadgets, have access to information technologies and global luxury brands, own their own cars and travel by air. In China, rapid growth in economic activity and incomes has revolutionised access to modern consumer goods and services. The country has in the last three decades not only become a global manufacturing hub, but it is now home to an emerging consumer class. It is estimated that by 2020, about 700 million Chinese will be part of this global consumer class, compared with about 100 million in 2006, and in terms of spending, this increase in consumer numbers equals a five-fold increase in consumer spending, to US$2.3 trillion per year by 2020 (McKinsey Global Institute, 2006, p 17).

As for China's nouveau riche, especially the younger generation, consumption is no longer only about meeting basic daily needs. Following their counterparts in industrialised countries, China's new rich have entered a stage of conspicuous consumption, an 'enjoy now' phase where high-end purchases are no longer out of reach. According to Merrill Lynch's Asia Pacific Wealth Report, an estimated 415,000 Chinese had more than US$1 million in disposable assets in 2007, more than any other country (Merrill Lynch and Capgemini, 2008). Up to 170 million people, or 13% of the population, mostly aged between 25 and 40 and living in the highly developed coastal regions of China, can already afford luxury brands, and the number is predicted to reach 250 million by 2010. With a growth of 20–35% in the next five years, the Chinese Ministry of Commerce predicts that the country will become the world's largest luxury market by 2014, accounting for 23% of global business (*China Daily*, 2009). Wealthy urban Chinese consumers therefore contribute greatly to climate change and thus have a responsibility to reduce personal carbon footprints as much as their counterparts in industrialised countries do (see Chapters Nine and Ten).

Consumption behaviour is closely related to and dependent on the retail sector. Major changes have taken place in the Chinese retail sector over the last two decades. The transformation not only reflects the changing supply and demand relations of a globalised economy, but also interaction between production, retailing, consumption and economic policy (Wang and Song, 2008). To support low-carbon lifestyles of Chinese consumers, the retail sector in China, including international supermarket chains and luxury brands, would need to make stronger efforts to offer more sustainable products with lower carbon footprints, at the same time educating consumers about sustainable lifestyles. Examples include innovative retail models, such as the development of product-service systems that can be realised through closer partnerships and collaboration between suppliers, retailers and consumers (Morelli, 2006). An additional issue is that eco-labels, important tools for the identification of green and sustainable products, have low credibility and are not trusted by Chinese consumers. The retail sector can take responsibility to increase the effectiveness of product labels and to increase consumer confidence.

To get a full picture of the situation, a range of other stakeholders need to be included, such as global transportation and logistics companies, end-of-life product managers and institutional (public) consumers. Responsibilities and options for them to address their contributions to climate change are summarised in Table 8.1.

Table 8.1: Possible SCP solutions for stakeholders addressing climate change along China's value chain

Life-cycle phase activity	Stakeholder groups/sectors (and level of responsibility)	Contribution to climate change through	Technical SCP solutions	Managerial/behavioural SCP solutions
Resource extraction, agriculture, forestry	Coal and mineral mining sector (high); oil and gas sector (high); large-scale agri-business (high); logging companies (very high)	Deforestation; land-use changes; coal-bed methane emissions; gas flaring; livestock methane; releases of soil carbon	Coal-bed methane capture; flare gas utilisation; organic farming; technology innovation in mining and drilling	Sustainable forest management; certified sourcing; implementing supplier codes of conduct; CSR; voluntary industry standards
Raw materials processing and primary manufacturing	Resource- and energy-intensive industries, eg steel, aluminium, cement, non-ferrous metals, chemicals, paper (very high); electricity and heat generation (very high)	Outdated inefficient equipment; CO_2 emissions from fossil-fuel combustion; industrial gases (HFCs); methane emissions from industrial waste water	Cleaner and leaner production technologies; efficiency upgrades; fuel-switching; pollution control; resource efficiency; use of renewable resources; replacement of outdated equipment; renewable energies; smart electricity grids; technology transfer	Closed-loop production systems; industrial symbiosis; R&D; voluntary industry standards; corporate sustainability reporting; CSR
Supplier industries	Supplier industries (mainly SMEs) (medium); multinationals (medium)	In-house electricity use (for motor systems, air pressure, boilers, etc.); inefficient equipment; low-awareness of workforce	Equipment upgrades; technology innovation in production processes; closed-loop production; technology transfer	Green supply-chain management; sustainable sourcing guidelines; capacity building and awareness raising of workforce; CSR

Life-cycle phase activity	Stakeholder groups/sectors (and level of responsibility)	Contribution to climate change through	Technical SCP solutions	Managerial/behavioural SCP solutions
Component assembly	Automotive, electronics, information technology (low to medium)	In-house electricity use; manufacturing of low-quality, single-use products	Technology innovation for product design; reparability and recyclability of products	Design for sustainability; eco-design; R&D
Distribution	Transport and logistics companies (medium)	Emissions from road transport, aviation, black carbon soot from shipping	Increased fleet efficiency; vehicle electrification; second-generation biofuels	Switch transportation modes (to rail); optimised distribution networks; reverse logistics; reduced packaging
Retail	Retail chains, supermarkets (medium)	In-store electricity consumption; refrigeration and product storage	In-store energy efficiency (refrigeration, lighting); solar heating/cooling systems; product labelling (including carbon labels)	Local sourcing; consumer awareness raising; promoting low-carbon lifestyles; take-back schemes; choice editing; ethical marketing; product-service systems
Consumption	Consumers overseas (medium to high); Chinese urban consumers (medium to high); Chinese rural consumers (low); institutional consumers (high)	Space heating and cooling; lighting; private mobility; air travel; high-impact consumer products; high-impact diets	Zero-emissions buildings; energy-efficient appliances; low-carbon vehicles; green products; smart metering	Avoiding high-impact goods and services (including food, vehicles and air travel); responsible (re)use and disposal of products; green public procurement
End-of-life	Waste managers (low to medium)	Methane emissions from landfill; emissions from incineration	Technology upgrades for incineration plants; methane capture for landfill	Recovery and recycling management systems

Note: CSR = corporate social responsibility, HFC = hydrofluorocarbon, R&D = Research & Development.
Source: Author's assessment

Opportunities for Chinese stakeholders to leapfrog towards SCP

As China's society and economy are in flux and the momentum of rapid economic development is likely to continue over the next two to three decades, large parts of the country's future urban and industrial infrastructures are yet to be built. From the SCP perspective, this is as much a worrying trend as it is an opportunity. Decisive action towards setting up sustainable consumption and production systems in the early stages of development can still be realised and thus enable China to 'leapfrog' over locking its economy and society into unsustainable industrial and urban infrastructures, institutions and consumption patterns. As indicated in Figure 8.3, the concept of leapfrogging offers, at least in theory, the prospect that China and other developing countries can avoid replicating the historically polluting development trajectory of the industrial West and thereby shape their development to meet their own needs and requirements (Goldemberg, 1998). Since 1980, China's carbon intensity has been gradually decreasing, dropping by about 6%. In 1971, US$1 of GDP (using year 2000 prices) required 6.09 kilograms of CO_2 emissions, but in 2007 the amount was down to 2.31 kilograms (IEA, 2009). In comparison to many other countries, this is one of the best achievements in reducing carbon intensity. Despite these achievements, China's energy intensity is still high, and future emissions–intensity reductions, such as the government's target of a 40-45% reduction by 2020 (compared to 2005), are necessary. In this section I discuss selected leapfrogging opportunities (and barriers to them) for Chinese stakeholders that can contribute to further emissions reductions through establishing SCP systems in China.

China's renewable energy sector is a major stakeholder in the issue of climate change. It has experienced, and continues to experience, leapfrogging development, particularly the share of renewable energy, which is growing substantially faster than total energy supply. The share of renewables in total primary energy supply is increasing steadily. For example, wind energy increased in capacity from less than 1 gigawatt (GW) in 2004 to more than 25 GW at the end of 2009 (REN21, 2010). Wind power in China certainly has now moved beyond the status of a niche technology, and development already achieved is complemented by a 'leapfrogging' in ambition for planned wind-power capacity for 2020. China first announced a wind-power target of 30 GW for 2020 in 2007, but then revised the number to 100 GW by 2020 in May 2009 (Mo, 2009). An alternative energy-development stimulus plan draft is currently under development, which would see installed wind-power capacity increase to 150 GW by 2020, of which 30 GW would come from offshore wind farms (Zheng and Mao, 2009). Should China's wind-power capacity indeed reach 150 GW by 2020, wind power would certainly have reshaped the country's energy system. In this sense, leapfrogging in the wind sector may be imminent, an important contribution to the realisation of SCP.

Figure 8.3: The process of leapfrogging using strategies for SCP

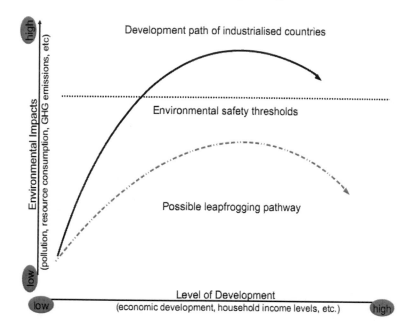

Source: After Goldemberg (1998) and Munasinghe (1999)

In addition, renewable energies have enabled many poor people in rural areas of Western China to leapfrog. Examples include solar photovoltaic (PV) home systems for renewable energy generation and solar water heaters. China's solar water heater market is already the largest in the world. China had an estimated installed capacity of 1.08 billion square metres in 2007 (Han et al, 2010), resulting in high savings in electricity. Through the adoption of solar PV home systems, many people in rural areas who have never been connected to the electricity grid have leapfrogged into a sustainable energy future without connecting to energy grids supplied by coal-fired power stations. Over the last decade, through a range of government-sponsored programmes, several million people in rural areas of Western China have been supplied with the solar PV systems, and related local industries have been built up that contribute to social and economic development in China's west.

Another major stakeholder is Chinese industry, which is already moving towards more energy- and resource-efficient production systems. One important approach for industrial development in China is the 'circular economy' concept, which promotes closed-loop and symbiotic industrial processes where waste products are reused and recycled. On a practical level, the circular economy model is a cleaner production approach that aims to ensure that industrial facilities' waste-product outputs (including heat, steam, wastewater and material scraps) can be used as other facilities' resource inputs. By preventing waste at source, as well as by turning waste into a resource, the circular economy concept aims to reduce both waste to be treated and levels of resource consumption of industry (NDRC, 2006). The approach has climate-related benefits because it results in energy savings during production processes and reduced GHG emissions from wastewater and landfills. However, despite efforts by Chinese government agencies and industries, knowledge and application of circular economy best practices is still inadequate, especially with regard to effectiveness, efficiency and appropriateness in specific Chinese circumstances (Geng et al, 2008).

China's new Circular Economy Law, which came into force on 1 January 2009, is extremely important in terms of underlining the government's intent to pursue a more sustainable model of industrial development. But to move from being a comprehensive legal framework to on-the-ground implementation requires further specification. Efforts to implement a circular economy currently focus mainly on large state-owned enterprises. To make the circular economy a nationwide common industrial practice, more attention is required to improve the environmental performance of SMEs, which constitute about 99% of all companies in China and generate about 60% of the value of industrial output (Ho, 2005). From an SCP perspective, the circular economy approach is an important step, but it is still too focused on production issues and thus does not sufficiently consider consumption issues. Furthermore, to effectively implement circular economic practices and to prevent shifting environmental impacts from one sector to another, companies and policy makers need to pay increased attention to life-cycle thinking. LCA data can provide important information about how to achieve overall impact reduction and to identify cases where 'false' reductions occur through burden shifting between sectors.

China's urbanisation trends are major drivers for economic development and social change, resulting in massive changes in consumption and production patterns, namely increases in energy and resource consumption. Cities in China are responsible for a large share of the country's GHG emissions. A study by the Global Carbon Project (Dhakal, 2009) shows that in 2006, China's 35 largest urban centres housed only 18% of country's population, but they produced 41% of its GDP, consumed 40% of its commercial energy and caused 40% of its CO_2 emissions. Thus, it is clear that, while the population share of large cities may be small, their energy and CO_2 impacts are disproportionately large. The carbon emissions of urban dwellers in China are comparable, and in cases even higher, to those of industrialised countries. In the cases of key cities such as Beijing (which has 11.9 tonnes of direct emissions per registered person), Shanghai (16.7 tons/registered person) and Tianjin (12.4 tons/registered person), the emissions are well above other key cities in the developed world, such as Tokyo (5.9 tonnes/person in 2003), Greater London (6.95 tonnes/person in 2003) and New York City (7.1 tonnes/person in 2005) (Dhakal, 2009). Looking at the total consumption-based carbon footprint of cities, these figures would possibly be even higher, as the example of Hong Kong shows, which in 2001 had an estimated annual carbon footprint of 29 tonnes per person (Hertwich and Peters, 2009).

Nevertheless, large leapfrogging potentials exist in China's future urban development, the building and construction sector being a major stakeholder. More than half of the construction currently going on in the world is taking place in China, and by 2030 the country is expected to have more than 200 cities with populations of over one million people each (McKinsey Global Institute, 2009). According to statistics of the United Nations Development Programme, China's per-capita housing space in both rural and urban areas has increased from 8.1 square metres in the year 2000 to 31.6 in 2007, and from 4.2 square metres in 2000 to 22.6 in 2007 respectively (UNDP China, 2010). Residential buildings now total over 40 billion square metres, which will increase by another 30 billion square metres by 2020. Nearly 95% of existing buildings consume high amounts of energy. Energy consumption for heating, for example, is two to three times what it is in developed countries in the same climatic zones. In 2007, China's residential electricity consumption accounted for 292 terrawatt hours (TWh), still low compared to the US (1,359 TWh), but an indication for the growth in demand to be expected (Seligsohn et al, 2009).

This suggests that there is great potential for 'leapfrogging' to avoid high electricity consumption in buildings. Through early introduction of low- or zero-energy building concepts, energy-intensive lock-in could be avoided. Retrofitting existing building stock through installation of heat-pump systems, solar hot water systems, better insulation and efficient lighting systems is also a feasible option. Smart metering is already being introduced in Shanghai and, in combination with efficient electric household appliances, will allow reductions in household electricity consumption. Furthermore, use of sustainable and renewable building materials can reduce other environmental impacts.

Urbanisation is not only driving construction; it is also a driver for new mobility patterns. Private urban car ownership per 100 families in China increased from 0.5 in 2000 to 6 in 2007 (UNDP China, 2010). At present, with only about 2% of the total population in China owning a motor vehicle, private car ownership is still low compared with 40-50% in Europe and North America. However, this level is expected to rise steeply, and estimates put the number of private passenger cars in China at 190 million by 2035 (ADB, 2006). Despite having strong regulation of vehicle ownership in cities such as Shanghai, CO_2 emissions from the transportation sector increased by eight times in the period from 1985 to 2006. Beijing registered close to a sevenfold increase in the same period (Dhakal, 2009).

In the area of personal urban mobility, positive developments towards sustainable consumption patterns and some form of leapfrogging can already be observed in the uptake of electric scooters and bicycles. Over the last decade, electric two-wheelers have made strong advances in quality, and the diffusion and commercialisation has accelerated dramatically since the early 2000s. In China, electric two-wheelers emerged from virtual non-existence in the 1990s to about 50 million by 2007 (ADB, 2009). Despite concerns about lead emissions from batteries, on almost all metrics electric bikes are more environmentally friendly than cars, taxis or motorcycles. Moreover, they provide cost-effective and environmentally efficient transportation where high-capacity public transport service is difficult to supply.

Another type of leapfrogging is 'lifestyle leapfrogging', an option for private consumers as stakeholders. Technology is one part of the solution to achieving systemic solutions in terms of consumer behaviour towards sustainable lifestyles. However, as noted above, technical solutions alone will not be sufficient to realise a low-carbon economy and sustainable development in China. While awareness about 'production-side' issues and the need to reduce industrial pollution and emissions is widely acknowledged in China, SCP practices addressing the 'consumption side' – consumption behaviour and lifestyles – have so far received little attention. They require more complex and integrative practices involving a larger range of stakeholders than conventional production-side practices. The reason is that consumption is not only an activity to fulfil basic needs for food, clothing and shelter; increasingly, it is driven by a complex set of forces rooted in different psychological, social, cultural and institutional settings (Mont and Plepys, 2008).

The concept of lifestyle leapfrogging would imply that consumers in China do not need to go through the stages of unsustainable consumption patterns, but can directly realise sustainable lifestyles. Although sustainable green lifestyles and products in China were at the time of writing in 2010 only within the reach of wealthy consumers, these environmentally conscious consumers can become agents of change supporting the transition towards SCP. Through their buying power they have the opportunity to take up their responsibility and support 'green' and low-carbon products, such as organic food and natural cosmetics, modern low-carbon buildings that use environmental technologies and sustainable building materials, organic fashion made from natural fibres and dyes, and low-carbon vehicles such as hybrid cars. The market share of green niche products would need to be increased and made available for mainstream consumers. However, green consumerism is probably not the final answer. The greening of markets and improving the quality of green products should instead be seen as a first step in the direction of sustainable consumption.

Other measures also need to be considered. Demand-side management approaches to control unsustainable consumption patterns will become increasingly critical in the future. Consumer choice editing – the practice of regulating or even banning the sale of particularly environmentally damaging products – is often not a viable political option in many Western countries where market-based mechanisms are preferred over top-down command and control mechanisms. In those cases, expanding consumption options and letting consumers decide for themselves is more feasible. However, China's policies for changing consumer behaviour based on a tradition of central planning could provide fast and effective results compared to those implemented in Western countries. Approaches developed and practised in Western countries could also be replicated and offer potential solutions for addressing challenges arising from Chinese consumption patterns and lifestyles. In addition, particular practices and strategies based on Chinese cultural, social and political contexts need to be considered for realisation of SCP in China (see Leong, 2008).

A major barrier to the acceptance of sustainable consumption in China, as much as in Europe, is the perception that it entails a restriction in consumption and a reduction in quality of life. In this respect, the challenges of promoting sustainable consumption among the consumers in China are similar to those in Europe and North America. While sustainable consumption might entail a reduction in the *quantity* of resources consumed, it also means improving the *quality* of consumption, thereby contributing to increases in quality of life. In addition to promoting green products, traditional Chinese cultural traditions and values have the potential to positively influence consumption behaviour and could help to deal with conspicuous consumption. With their emphasis on simplicity, contentment, moderation, frugality and harmony between humans and nature, Chinese traditions are still relevant today. The traditional concepts about quality of life and happiness can in principle enable individuals and society to leapfrog consumer culture beliefs about wellbeing and satisfaction through maximum consumption via material good accumulation (Daniels, 2010). While 'back to nature' in the proper sense of the phrase is not possible, these traditional cultural values can support awareness about the need of balancing rapid economic growth through industrialisation and environmental protection, including the global atmosphere.

Finally, the Chinese government as major institutional consumer and important stakeholder in the Chinese economy can further accelerate the shift towards sustainable consumption through implementing green public procurement (GPP) practices. The government is positively influencing the supply of green products through centralised GPP, particularly focusing on energy-saving products. In 2009, the commitment to 'The Government Green Procurement Regulations' were being reinforced by a China State Council order and subsequently many of China's local government procurement centres have increased their efforts to implement GPP (Kok, 2009). Nevertheless, barriers still exist to realise the full potential of GPP for climate protection, including lack of awareness and limited capacity of local authorities and higher costs of green products.

Conclusion

At present, SCP is mainly being promoted in China through the circular-economy approach, which has a strong focus on cleaner and leaner production processes, waste minimisation and recycling. It does, however, not yet explicitly include the issue of sustainable consumption. While the 'Circular Economy Law' is an important piece of legislation for improving environmental performance of industrial sectors, a comprehensive SCP approach will also need to consider the growing impact of new consumption patterns, particularly as they relate to growing GHG emissions. A more comprehensive national action plan for SCP in China would be an important next step.

The debate about China's responsibility for climate change, and related questions of environmental damage and sustainability, is complex. The SCP perspective shows that the responsibility of China cannot be discussed independently of, and without assigning responsibility to, stakeholders outside of China in industrialised countries, notably consumers of products 'made in China'. It also shows that Chinese stakeholders need to take responsibility for emissions produced through resource acquisition in other countries, as shown by the case of tropical deforestation. Due to the interconnected economic relations of global value chains, responsibility for China's emissions needs to be shared between producers and consumers. China's manufacturers have the responsibility to offer low-carbon and green products to their consumers both in China and overseas. At the same time, multinational companies operating in China have the responsibility to support the diffusion of environmentally friendly technologies and green products in China. 'Leapfrogging' to both sustainable production *and* consumption systems in China is an option for continued increases in human development without locking the country into unsustainable development pathways.

The conceptual and practical approaches of SCP offer a good opportunity for China to enable leapfrogging in various areas, including energy, industrial manufacturing, urbanisation and consumer behaviour. Realisation of SCP will reduce ecological footprints and GHG emissions simultaneously, and it can contribute to the creation of a resource-efficient and low-carbon economy and society in China.

Note

[1] These sectors are also thought to be the causes for about 70% of the global warming potential from the EU (ETC/RWM NAMEA database).

References

ADB (Asian Development Bank) (2006) *Urbanization and sustainability in Asia: Case studies of good practice*, Mandaluyong City, Philippines: ADB.

ADB (2009) *Electric bikes in the People's Republic of China: Impact on the environment and prospects for growth*, Mandaluyong City, Philippines: ADB.

Carbon Trust (2006) *The carbon emissions generated in all that we consume*, London: Carbon Trust.

China Daily (2009) 'Battered luxury brands eye Chinese market for growth', *China Daily*, www.chinadaily.com.cn/bizchina/2009-04/11/content_7669126.htm

Clark, G. (2007) 'Evolution of the global sustainable consumption and production policy and the United Nations Environment Programme's (UNEP) supporting activities', *Journal of Cleaner Production*, vol 15, no 6, pp 492-8.

Daniels, P.L. (2010) 'Climate change, economics and Buddhism – part I: an integrated environmental analysis framework', *Ecological Economics*, vol 69, pp 952-61.

Davis, S.J. and Caldeira, K. (2010) 'Consumption-based accounting of CO_2 emissions', *Proceedings of the National Academy of Sciences of the United States of America*, vol 107, no 12, pp 5687-92.

de Leeuw, B. (2005) 'The world behind the product', *Journal of Industrial Ecology*, vol 9, no 1-2, pp 7-10.

Dhakal, S. (2009) 'Urban energy use and carbon emissions from cities in China and policy implications', *Energy Policy*, vol 37, pp 4208-19.

EC (European Commission) (2010) *ILCD handbook: International reference life cycle data system handbook: General guide for life cycle assessment: Detailed guidance* (1st edition), Ispra, Italy: European Commission, Joint Research Centre, Institute for Environment and Sustainability.

ETC/RWM NAMEA database: Database of the European Topic Centre on Resource and Waste Management (ETC/RWM) on National Accounting Matrices including Environmental Accounts (NAMEA).

Fan, G., Stern, N., Edenhofer, O., Xu, S., Eklund, K., Li, L. and Hallding, K. (2009) *Going clean: The economics of China's low-carbon development*, Stockholm Environment Institute (SEI) and the Chinese Economists 50 Forum, Stockholm: SEI.

Geng, Y., Zhu, Q., Doberstein, B. and Fujita, T. (2008) 'Implementing China's circular economy concept at the regional level: a review of progress in Dalian, China', *Waste Management*, vol 29, no 2, pp 996-1002.

Global Witness (2009) *A disharmonious trade: China and the continued destruction of Burma's northern frontier forests: A review by Global Witness: 2006-09*, London: Global Witness.

Goldemberg, J. (1998) 'Leapfrogging energy technologies', *Energy Policy*, vol 2, no 10, pp 729-41.

Han, J., Mol. A. and Lu, Y. (2010) 'Solar water heaters in China: a new day dawning', *Energy Policy*, vol 38, pp 383-91.

Hertwich, E. and Peters, G.P. (2009) 'Carbon footprint of nations: a global, trade-linked analysis', *Environmental Science and Technology*, vol 43, no 16, pp 6414-20.

Ho, P. (ed) (2005) 'Greening industries in newly industrialising countries: Asian-style leapfrogging?', *International Journal of Environment and Sustainable Development*, vol 4, no 3, pp 209-26.

IEA (International Energy Agency) (2009) *CO₂ emissions from fuel combustion highlights* (2009 edition), Paris: IEA.

IPCC (Intergovernmental Panel on Climate Change) (2007) *Climate change 2007: Synthesis report*, Geneva: IPCC.

Kok, A. (2009) 'China's local govts embrace green procurement, Asia Pacific Future Gov, 28 April, www.futuregov.asia/articles/2009/apr/28/chinas-local-govts-required-make-green-procurement/

Kuhndt, M., Fisseha T. and Herrndorf, M. (2008) 'Global value chain governance for resource efficiency: building sustainable consumption and production bridges across the global sustainability divides', *Environmental Research, Engineering and Management*, vol 3, no 45, pp 33-41.

Lebel, L. and Lorek, S. (2008) 'Enabling sustainable production-consumption systems', *Annual Review of Environment and Resources*, vol *33*, pp 241-75.

Leong, B. (2008) 'Is a radical systemic shift toward sustainability possible in China?', in A. Tukker, M. Charter, C. Vezzoli, E. Stø and M.M. Andersen (eds) *System innovation for sustainability 1: Perspectives on radical changes to sustainable consumption and production* (chapter 12), Sheffield: Greenleaf.

Liu, J., Wang, R., Yang, J. and Shi, Y. (2010) 'The relationship between consumption and production system and its implications for sustainable development of China', *Ecological Complexity*, vol 7, no 2, pp 212-6.

McKinsey Global Institute (2006) *From 'made in China' to 'sold in China': The rise of the Chinese urban consumer*, Shanghai: McKinsey Global Institute.

McKinsey Global Institute (2009) *Preparing for China's urban billion*, Shanghai: McKinsey Global Institute.

Maréchal, K. (2010) 'Not irrational but habitual: the importance of "behavioural lock-in" in energy consumption', *Ecological Economics*, vol 69, pp 1104-14.

Merrill Lynch and Capgemini (2008) Third annual Asia-Pacific wealth report 2008, www.capgemini.com/resources/news/merrill-lynch-and-capgemini-release

Mo, K. (2009) 'Go with wind: China to dramatically boost its wind power capacity, again', Green Law Website, Natural Resources Defense Council and China Environmental Culture Promotion Association, www.greenlaw.org.cn/enblog/p=1538

Mont, O. and Bleischwitz, R. (2007) 'Sustainable consumption and resource management in the light of life cycle thinking', *European Environment*, vol 17, no 1, pp 59-76.

Mont, O. and Plepys, A. (2008) 'Sustainable consumption progress: should we be proud or alarmed?', *Journal of Cleaner Production*, vol 16, pp 531-7.

Morelli, N. (2006) 'Developing new product service systems (PSS): methodologies and operational tools', *Journal of Cleaner Production*, vol 14, no 17, pp 1495-501.

Munasinghe, M. (1999) 'Is environmental degradation an inevitable consequence of economic growth: tunneling through the environmental Kuznets curve', *Ecological Economics*, vol 29, pp 89-109.

National Bureau of Statistics of P.R. China (2009) *International statistical yearbook 2009*, Beijing: China Statistics Press.

NDRC (National Development and Reform Commission) (2006) *Five-year workplan for saving energy and reducing emissions: Official document*, Beijing: NDRC.

Niggli, U., Fließbach, A., Hepperly, P. and Scialabba, N. (2009) *Low greenhouse gas agriculture: Mitigation and adaptation potential of sustainable farming systems*, Rome: Food and Agriculture Organizations of the United Nations.

Olivier, J.G.J. and Peters, J.A.H.W. (2010) *No growth in total global CO_2 emissions in 2009*, Bilthoven, The Netherlands: Netherlands Environmental Assessment Agency.

Reinvang, R. and Peters, G. (2008) *Norwegian consumption, Chinese pollution: An example of how OECD imports generate CO_2 emissions in developing countries*, Oslo and Trondheim: WWF Norway and Norwegian University of Science and Technology.

Remmen, A., Jensen, A. and Frydendal, J. (2007) *Life cycle management: A business guide to sustainability*, Paris: United Nations Environment Programme.

REN21 (Renewable Energy Policy Network for the 21st Century) (2010) *Renewables 2010 global status report* (revised edition), REN21, www.ren21.net/Portals/97/documents/GSR/REN21_GSR_2010_full_revised%20Sept2010.pdf

Seligsohn, D., Heilmayr, R., Tan, X. and Weischer, L. (2009) *China, the United States, and the climate change challenge*, WRI Policy Brief, Washington, DC: World Resources Institute.

Sorrell, S. (2007) *The rebound effect: An assessment of the evidence for economy-wide energy savings from improved energy efficiency*, London: UK Energy Research Centre.

Tukker, A., Huppes, G., Guinée, J., Heijungs, R., de Koning, A., van Oers, L., Suh, S., Geerken, T., van Holderbeke, M., Jansen, B. and Nielsen, P. (2006) *Environmental Impact of Products (EIPRO): Analysis of the life cycle environmental impacts related to the final consumption of the EU-25*, Seville: Joint Research Centre, Institute for Prospective Technological Studies, European Commission.

Tuncer, B. and Schroeder, P. (2009) *A key solution to climate change: Sustainable consumption and production: Making the link*, Wuppertal, Germany: SWITCH Asia Network Facility, www.switch-asia.net/switch-learn/scp-booklets.html

UNDP China (United Nations Development Programme China) (2010) *China human development report, 2009/10: China and a sustainable future: Towards a low carbon economy and society*, Beijing: China Translation and Publishing Corporation.

UNEP (United Nations Environment Programme) (2008) *Kick the habit: A UN guide to carbon neutrality*, Nairobi: UNEP.

Wang, E. and Song, J. (2008) 'The political economy of retail change in Chinese cities', *Environment and Planning C: Government and Policy*, vol 26, pp 1197-226.

Warhurst, M. and Slater, B. (2010) *Measuring resource use: A vital tool in creating a resource-efficient EU*, London: Friends of the Earth England.

Zhao, W. and Schroeder, P. (2010) 'Sustainable consumption and production: trends, challenges and options for the Asia–Pacific region', *Natural Resources Forum*, 34: 4–15. doi: 10.1111/j.1477-8947.2010.01275.x

Worldwatch Institute (2004) *The state of consumption today*, Washington, DC: Worldwatch Institute.

WSSD (World Summit on Sustainable Development) (2002) *Plan of implementation*, New York, NY: WSSD.

WWF-UK (World Wide Fund-UK) (2004) *To whose profit? Evolution building sustainable corporate strategy*, Godalming, Surrey: WWF-UK.

WWF-UK (2008) *One planet mobility: A journey towards a sustainable future*, Godalming, Surrey: WWF-UK, www.wwf.org.uk/what_we_do/changing_the_way_we_live/transport/?2326/One-Planet-Mobility-report

Zheng, L. and Mao L. (2009) 'Nuclear power to rise 10-fold by 2020', *China Daily*, 2 July, www.chinadaily.com.cn/china/2009-07/02/content_8346480.htm

NINE

Global governance, responsibility and a new climate regime

Andreas Oberheitmann and Eva Sternfeld

In its 2007 Fourth Assessment Report, the Intergovernmental Panel on Climate Change (IPCC) states that global temperatures (according to a scenario of assumptions) could rise by between 1.1 and 6.4°C during the 21st century, leading to sea-level rise, more frequent warm spells, heat waves and heavy rainfall, and an increase in droughts, tropical cyclones and extreme high tides (IPCC, 2007). To limit the increase in global mean temperature to 2°C level, and thereby limit the extensive negative impacts of climate change, carbon dioxide (CO_2) concentrations in the Earth's atmosphere should be stabilised at no more than 400-450 parts per million (ppm). In 2007, the European Commission obliged itself to this 2°C target (EC, 2007). In June 2009, at their summit in L'Aquila, the G8 countries also agreed to this target, followed later by members of the Major Economies Forum, including China, India, Indonesia, Mexico, South Africa and South Korea (Rahmstorf, 2009).

Although the 'Copenhagen Accord' – the final document of the 15th Conference of the Parties (COP15) to the Kyoto Protocol, held in Copenhagen, Denmark in December 2009 – also stipulated this 2°C target, the conference failed to agree on a new post-Kyoto agreement for addressing climate change. Especially in Europe, it is widely believed that the main reason for this failure was that both the United States (US) and China did not come forward with a substantial climate change mitigation commitment. This raises the question of China's role in global environmental governance. In order to understand, from the Chinese perspective, the process of negotiating a successor to the Kyoto Protocol, in this chapter we begin by analysing China's role in global environmental governance. We then discuss the most important recent proposals for a post-Kyoto climate regime as presented by different authors.

The French Centre National de la Recherche Scientifique et al (CNRS/LEPII-EPE et al, 2003) compiled and contrasted different post-Kyoto approaches, such as 'per-capita convergence', 'soft landing', the 'Brazilian proposal' and the 'ability to pay'. The 'per-capita convergence' approach is seen as having advantages because it is a simple concept that allows for full emissions trading. In contrast, Russa and Criquib (2007) proposed a 'soft-landing scheme' allowing for a smooth transition of developing countries to green economies. They do not touch on per-capita emissions. During negotiation of the Kyoto Protocol, the delegation of Brazil presented an approach for the allocation of emissions reduction obligations among Annex I (developed-country) Parties based on the impact of their cumulative historical emissions from 1840 (UNFCCC, 1997). The Brazilian proposal was not adopted but did receive support, especially from developing countries. The Project Team of the Development Research Centre of the State Council of China (2009) proposed a regime based on cumulative emissions, similar to the Brazilian approach, rather than one based on per-capita emissions. According to this proposal, every country would receive an absolute emission budget for 2050. How this budget is kept is left to the individual countries. All of these approaches have a common weakness: They *at the same time* (a) do not acknowledge the historical responsibilities of industrialised countries for the historical greenhouse gas (GHG) emissions and the responsibility of developing countries for a large fraction of the current future emissions and (b) do not provide for a fair distribution of emissions rights.

Global environmental governance and responsibility in China

With regard to international climate change policies, China insists on the principle of 'common but differentiated responsibility' (CBDR): differentiated responsibility in terms of a country's level of economic development and the historical responsibility of industrialised countries. During the first decade of the 2000s, economic development – and the emissions of GHGs that have accompanied it – has taken place much faster than people expected when negotiations for the Kyoto Protocol were being held in 1997. In the late 1990s, it was assumed that China would overtake the US as the nation with the highest CO_2 emissions around 2030, but this actually occurred in 2007 (BP, 2008). Now that it is the world's largest emitter of CO_2, China is expected to take a more prominent role in global environmental governance. On the other hand, the average level of per-capita emissions in China is currently around 4 tonnes of CO_2, which is still considerably below the Western European average (about 8 tonnes per capita) and well below that of the US (about 19 tonnes per capita). However, China is going to catch up with Europe and Japan (9.5 tonnes) before 2030 even in terms of per-capita emissions.

COP15 failed to reach an agreement on a post-Kyoto system in large part because the US would not agree to strong targets for limiting its GHG emissions. The US only proposed a 4% reduction in its GHG emissions by 2020 (compared to 1990) – even though in Kyoto in 1997 it agreed to a reduction of 7%. This made it extremely difficult for China to come up with a substantial contribution of its own. Although the present leadership seems to be responsive to climate change policy issues, it is not willing to sacrifice economic development to an absolute emissions-reduction target.

On 28 January 2010, China submitted its proposed climate mitigation action to the United Nations Framework Convention on Climate Change (UNFCCC). By this the country reaffirmed earlier announced policies, first presented on 22 September 2009 by Chinese President Hu Jintao at the United Nations Climate Change Summit in New York (NDRC, 2009b, p 1):

1. A reduction in carbon intensity by a notable margin by 2020 against 2005. In December 2009 in Copenhagen this 'notable margin' was defined as a target to improve carbon intensity by 40–45%.
2. An increase in the non-fossil fuel share of primary energy supply to 15% by 2020 against 2005.
3. An increase in forest coverage of 40 million hectares, and of forest stock volume of 1.3 billion square metres by 2020 against 2005.
4. The promotion of Green Economy, Low Carbon Economy, Circular Economy and technology development.

Thus, China's climate policy is based on its energy policy and the reinterpretation of targets for improving energy efficiency in terms of their relevance for climate protection. Taking the current goals for economic growth (that is, quadrupling gross domestic product [GDP] per capita by 2020 compared to 2000), China's policy is not sufficient to reduce its total CO_2 emissions. Even if efficiency goals are successfully implemented, Chinese CO_2 emissions in 2020 will increase by more than 50%.

As for increasing the share of non-fossil energy, China certainly needs to raise current development targets. Although the country has seen a rapid development of renewable and nuclear energy in recent years, by 2008 the share of non-fossil energy to primary energy consumption was only 8.9%, a slight increase compared to 2005 (7.1%) (National Bureau of Statistics of China, 2009, p 243). Under current plans, 86 gigawatt (GW) of nuclear power will be installed by 2020, compared to 7 GW in 2005; 300 GW of hydropower (115 GW in 2005); 30 GW of wind energy (1.3 GW in 2005); and 40 billion cubic metres (m^3) of biogas will be produced by 2020 (8 billion m^3 in 2005). Together, this amounts to about 400 million tonnes of standard coal equivalent (tsce) of non-fossil energy production by 2020. Compared to the 2007 *World energy outlook* forecast of the International Energy Agency (IEA, 2007), in 2020 China will have a primary energy supply of 4 billion tsce. Thus, the share of non-fossil fuels will only reach about 10-11% of total primary energy supply in 2020. As for forestation, China has set out ambitious goals. In 2008, China's forested area was 174.9 million hectares, and forest stock amounted to 12.5 billion square metres (National Bureau of Statistics of China, 2009, p 416). The envisaged growth in forests is 22.9% against 2005, with a growth of forest stock of 10.4%.

The promotion of 'green economy', 'low-carbon economy', 'circular economy' and 'technology development' cannot be quantified. However, following these concepts is a promising way to achieve the goals of a substantive reduction of carbon intensity and to achieve a sustainable development in China (see Chapter Eight). To cope with climate change, in recent years the Chinese government has issued several action plans and legislation. The most important include the following:

- *The Renewable Energy Law of the People's Republic of China* (Standing Committee of the National People's Congress of China, 2005);
- *China's scientific and technological actions on climate change* (Ministry of Science and Technology of China et al, 2007);
- *China's National Climate Change Programme* (NDRC, 2007a);
- *China's medium- and long-term development plan for China* (NDRC, 2007b);
- *China's policies and actions for addressing climate change* (White Paper) (State Council of the People's Republic of China, 2008);
- *Implementation of the Bali roadmap: China's position on the Copenhagen climate change conference* (NDRC, 2009a).

All of these plans and legislation serve environmental protection goals as well as energy security objectives (see Chapter One). Climate protection is embedded within policies for sustainable development, and equal emphasis is given to mitigation and adaptation, as well as to support for science and technology. The 11th Five-Year plan especially aims at contributing to climate change mitigation by accelerating the building of a resource-conserving society. For example, the White Paper by the State Council of the People's Republic of China (2008) states that the control of GHG emissions shall be achieved by striving to mitigate GHG emissions through:

- accelerating the transformation of the country's economic development pattern;
- strengthening policy guidance concerning energy conservation and efficient utilisation;
- intensifying administration of energy conservation in accordance with the law;
- speeding up development;
- demonstration and application of energy conservation technologies;
- giving full play to the role of new market-based mechanisms for energy conservation;
- enhancing public awareness of the importance of energy conservation; and
- accelerating the building of a resource-conserving society.

Through these measures, the energy consumption per-unit GDP was expected to drop by about 20% by 2010 compared to that of 2005, and CO_2 emissions would consequently be reduced. By 2009, China's energy intensity dropped by 15.6% against 2005. However, in the first quarter of 2010, it rose by 3.2%. The biggest culprits are the protected state industrial enterprises that consume 70% of the energy and generate 70% of the emissions. To reach the promised target by the end of 2010, the government took measures and simply stopped or restricted energy supply in certain areas. By autumn 2010, a 15.9% energy-intensity reduction was reached.

The interaction between global environmental agendas and China's national environmental/energy policy issues is weak. As a developing country, China does not have a quantitative GHG emissions-reduction obligation under the Kyoto Protocol. China is required to report on its national circumstances and policies on climate change in national communications to the secretariat of the UNFCCC, and it is supposed to pursue its own national policies taking global climate change issues into account. Given that China is responsible for almost half of the incremental CO_2-emissions increase worldwide since the late 1990s (BP, 2008), in the medium term it should give up its reluctance to take on more obligations and thus more environmental responsibility on a global scale.

Factors associated with resource economics exercise a strong influence on China's domestic climate policy. From the mid-1980s, Chinese environmental policy developed thematically, instrumentally, institutionally and regionally. The field of environmental policy broadened according to growing environmental problems in various sectors (for example, urban pollution and nuclear safety). The degree of institutionalisation increased. This led to competition and conflicts with other policy fields, especially economic development policy. Environmental non-governmental organisations started to play a role, in addition to that of the Ministry of Environmental Protection.

The instruments of environmental policy are turning away from command-and-control measures towards the use of economic instruments that give incentives to economic entities to change their behaviours. And environmental policy has become internationalised. These result from China's increasing role in the world, and the growing international responsibility attached to this role (Oberheitmann, 2008).

China's 11th Five-Year Plan (for 2006-2010) and the Medium- and Long-Term Development Plan for Renewable Energy for 2020 presented by the National Development and Reform Commission (NDRC) in September 2007 aimed at reducing the energy intensity of the entire economy and increasing the use of renewable sources of energy (see Table 9.1). This serves to increase the country's energy security while also promoting global environmental protection (Oberheitmann and Sternfeld, 2009). The 12th Five-Year Plan will likely also include a target for reducing carbon intensity.

The 11th Five-Year Plan envisaged reducing energy consumed per unit of GDP by 20% in 2010 as compared to 2005. This is equivalent to reducing the volume of CO_2 emissions by approximately 1.5 billion tonnes relative to a 'business-as-usual' scenario, while experiencing an 8% increase in economic growth. In 2020, using 8% more energy from renewable sources would be equivalent to saving approximately 0.8-1.3 billion tonnes of CO_2, depending on what suppositions are made about economic growth. The amount of 0.8 billion tonnes is roughly equivalent to the entire volume of genuine CO_2 emissions caused by Germany in 2007 (0.857 billion tonnes of CO_2) (*Welt Online*, 2008). If current NDRC goals for the development of non-fossil energies are employed to calculate the potential that these measures have to mitigate CO_2 emissions, a value of approximately 480 million tonnes is obtained for 2010 and around 1 billion tonnes for 2020 (Table 9.1). In terms of improving energy security of supply, the saving of 1 billion tonnes of CO_2 is equivalent to a saving of fossil fuel of about 350 million tonnes of coal or 400 million tonnes of crude oil.

Table 9.1: Current situation, government targets and estimated share in reducing CO_2 emissions by using renewable sources of energy in China (2005-20)

	Status quo	NDRC goals	Reductions in CO_2 emissions (million tonnes)	NDRC goals	Reductions in CO_2 emissions (million tonnes)
	2005	2010		2020	
Large-scale hydroelectric power plants (GW)	80	120	278	225	522
Small-scale hydroelectric power plants (GW)	35	60	139	75	174
Solar power (GW)	0.07	0.3	0	2	1
Solar power systems for water purification (million square meters)	80	150	9	300	18
Wind power (GW)	1.3	5	4	30	23
Electricity from biomass (GW)	2.3	No data	No data	20	15
Biogas (billion m³)	8	19	39	40	83
Solid biomass fuel (pellets) (million tonnes)	No data	1	1	50	68
Bioethanol (billion litres)	1.4	2	5	17.8	42
Biodiesel (billion litres)	0.05	0.2	1	6	16
Geothermal power generation (GW)	0.045	No data	No data	0.25	1
Direct use of geothermal energy (million tsce)	1.1	No data	No data	8	23
Tidal power plants (GW)	0.001	No data	No data	Up to 5	Up to 4
Sum total	–	–	477	–	990

Source: Oberheitmann and Sternfeld (2009)

Current options of a new post-Kyoto regime

The Kyoto Protocol has to be reaffirmed or replaced by a new climate agreement by the end of 2012. However, in December 2009, COP15 did not bring about major steps towards a new climate regime. Between 4 and 9 October 2010, the fourth round of United Nations climate talks in 2010 were held in Tianjin, China for the preparation of COP16 which was held on 29 November and 10 December 2010 in Cancun, Mexico. Although, in Tianjin, negotiators produced a draft decision text that was submitted to the Cancun conference, less progress was made in discussions of the continuation of Kyoto Protocol. Thus, to reach an agreement on a post-Kyoto regime would have been one of the biggest challenges for COP16 in Cancun.

Different approaches to future climate architecture have been discussed (see Box 9.1). According to the Centre National de la Recherche Scientifique (CNRS/LEPII-EPE et al, 2003), the international architecture of a post-Kyoto regime may evolve in two different directions:

- a set of rules or targets that define how all Parties' emissions quotas develop over a long period (a 'full participation' regime);
- an incremental but rule-based approach to extending the climate regime, with a gradual expansion of the Annex I group of countries adopting binding quantified emissions-limitation or -reduction objectives, whether absolute or dynamic (an 'increasing participation' or 'multi-stage' regime).

According to this distinction, the 'per-capita convergence', the 'soft landing' and the 'global preference score' approaches belong to the first type of architecture, while the 'Brazilian proposal', 'ability to pay' and 'multi-stage' approaches belong to the second. These concepts vary considerably. Due to these differences, each has its own strengths, weaknesses and remedies (see Table 9.2).

Box 9.1: Overview of the main current approaches to a post-Kyoto regime

- Per-capita convergence in emissions endowments

This approach, based mainly on the egalitarian principle, has been developed into a dynamic perspective by defining emissions endowments based on convergence of per-capita emissions under a contracting global GHG emissions profile. In such a convergence regime, all countries participate in the climate regime with emissions quotas converging to equal per-capita levels at a chosen date in the future.

- Soft landing in emissions growth

Aiming principally at reaching a global target while limiting the constraint imposed on each world region, this approach proposes progressively stabilising emissions in developing countries, with the timing of the reduction of current emissions growth rates based on per-capita emissions and income levels. For Annex I countries, continued emissions reductions are required, according to an 'extended Kyoto' trend.

- Global preference score approach

This scheme defines a mixed indicator for endowment that combines a grandfathering entitlement method and a per-capita approach. A 'Preference Score Share' is calculated by adding the relative emissions shares of each obtained using the two methods by country, weighted by the share of world population assumed to prefer the first or second approach (basically Annex I countries versus non-Annex I countries).

- Historical contributions to climate change or the 'Brazilian proposal'

During the negotiations on the Kyoto Protocol, Brazil made a proposal to link the relative contribution of industrialised parties to their relative contribution to the global mean temperature rise, based on the responsibility principle.

- Ability to pay

This principle was developed as a scheme to progressively integrate non-Annex I countries into a system of global emissions reductions with an initial per-capita GDP threshold, and subsequent levels of reduction to meet long-term climate targets depending on each country's per-capita GDP.

- Multi-stage approach

This approach divides countries into different groups, with different levels of responsibility or types of commitment (stages). The number of countries involved and their level of commitment gradually increase over time according to predefined participation rules.

Source: CNRS/LEPII-EPE et al (2003)

Table 9.2: Strengths, weaknesses and possible remedies of different post-Kyoto approaches

	Strengths	Weaknesses	Possible remedies
Per-capita convergence in emission endowments	Simple concept Allows for full emission trading	Possible implementation problems for developing countries Possible surplus emissions Could lead to large reductions for some countries	Include adjustment factors Adjust convergence year Limit the use of emission trading Allow for regional per-capita convergence approaches with internal redistribution
Soft landing in emissions growth	Smooth transition Allows for full emission trading	No direct relation to equity principles Possible implementation problems for developing countries No specification of reduction stage	Introduce a participation threshold Define a reduction stage
Global preference score Approach	Simple concept Allows for full emission trading Funds for less developed countries	Extreme results Extra costs for Annex I/middle-income developing countries Possible implementation problems in developing countries Incompatible with UNFCCC	Extend policy delay/include adjustment period Give more weight to emissions than population in voting Include adjustment factors
Historical contribution to climate change	Acceptance by developing countries very likely Formal status under UNFCCC	Focus on responsibility only Extreme results Relatively complex approach Inflexible (in original form)	Use other responsibility indicator (eg cumulative emissions from 1950 or 1990)
Ability to pay	Results in a balanced distribution of costs	Based on capability only Abstract parameters	Simplify approach

	Strengths	Weaknesses	Possible remedies
Multi-stage approach	Covers different equity principles Flexible concept offering room for negotiation Compatible with Kyoto Protocol and UNFCCC	Many parameters Intensity targets reduce certainty about environmental effectiveness and complicate implementation	Limit number of stages Use dual targets concept Ex-post trading for developing countries with intensity targets Use other burden-sharing schemes than per-capita emissions

Sources: CNRS/LEPII-EPE et al (2003); Tickell (2008)

As one of the latest developments in this discussion, in March 2009 a research group of the State Council Development Research Centre published an article in the Chinese *Economic Research Journal* proposing a regime with cumulative emissions similar to the Brazilian approach, albeit not one with a per-capita basis (Project Team of the Development Research Centre of the State Council of China, 2009). They proposed that every country should receive an absolute emissions budget for 2050. How that budget is kept is left to individual countries, and it is proposed that excess emission rights can be traded.

All of these approaches to a new climate regime have weaknesses. They do not take into consideration that, on the one hand, developed countries are responsible for the current CO_2 concentration in the atmosphere and, on the other hand, developing countries such as China and India are to a large extent responsible for the current additional CO_2 emissions that are now starting to accumulate in the atmosphere (which is partly accounted for in the Brazilian proposal). Furthermore, these approaches do not provide for a fair distribution of emission rights in *per-capita convergence in emissions endowments*, which is done in per-capita approaches, albeit without accounting for historical emissions. Against this background, in this chapter we present a new approach that takes into account the weaknesses of the other individual concepts by combining the 'per-capita convergence' and the 'Brazilian proposal' approaches to achieve a climate regime that is based on per-capita cumulative CO_2 emission rights to reach the 2°C target, or a 400-450 ppm concentration of CO_2 in the atmosphere, based on CO_2 emissions between 1750 and 2007. The main difference to the Brazilian approach is that our approach is based on a per-capita distribution of CO_2 emissions rights according to a fixed year for population rather than an absolute budget. Our approach also takes into account a longer time period, starting in 1750 rather than 1840. To fully comply with the UNFCCC principle of CBDR, the early emissions of the Annex I countries have also to be taken into account.[1]

China in a climate regime for staying within the 2°C target

In our proposed post-Kyoto climate change regime, the accumulated world CO_2 emissions in a defined year consist of the CO_2 emissions from primary fossil energy consumption plus emissions from 'bunkers' (ships and airplanes),[2] the flaring of gas and cement production reduced by the natural absorption of anthropogenic CO_2 emissions over 1,000 years ago. In reality, only some of the emissions are absorbed every year; most of the CO_2 remains in the atmosphere for 1,000 years (Oberheitmann, 2010). Table 9.3 shows accumulated world CO_2 emissions.

Table 9.3: Development of accumulated world CO_2 emissions (1750-2007) (million tonnes)

Year	Africa	Asia-Pacific	China	India	Middle East	Central & South America	North America	Europe and Eurasia	World	OECD	Annex-I countries	Non-Annex-I countries
1750	0	0	0	0	0	0	0	9	9	9	9	0
1850	39	0	0	0	0	0	191	4,593	4,823	4,784	4,784	39
1900	71	267	0	126	0	30	11,008	33,546	44,921	42,961	44,673	249
1950	1,855	6,999	1,881	2,314	456	1,560	96,437	118,329	225,636	201,018	216,088	9,548
1960	3,248	14,606	5,114	3,234	1,052	3,860	126,344	153,232	302,343	255,956	282,963	19,380
1970	5,489	32,009	11,536	5,087	3,335	7,510	168,560	210,667	427,571	339,628	388,523	39,047
1980	9,680	66,338	24,937	7,966	8,224	13,188	226,306	292,777	616,513	458,162	539,378	77,134
1990	16,432	115,454	46,293	13,096	14,790	20,286	286,255	381,809	835,025	580,732	699,614	135,412
2000	24,666	192,694	81,003	21,921	24,926	29,507	355,771	458,320	1,085,884	717,616	855,785	230,098
2005	29,729	244,025	105,632	27,664	31,846	34,903	393,785	495,962	1,230,250	791,878	936,768	293,482
2006	30,827	256,623	112,411	29,000	33,466	36,091	401,478	503,850	1,262,334	807,051	953,364	308,970
2007	31,973	269,930	119,696	30,431	35,130	37,349	409,303	512,900	1,296,586	822,329	970,034	326,552

Note: OECD = Organisation for Economic Co-operation and Development.

Source: Oberheitmann (2010)

Calculating the cumulative CO_2 ($CO_{2,cum}$) emissions as a proxy for the CO_2 concentration in the atmosphere, a concentration of 400 ppm CO_2 represents about 1,600 billion tonnes of $CO_{2,cum}$ emissions, and 450 ppm represents about 2,300 billion tonnes of $CO_{2,cum}$. In 2007, the Annex I countries represented 74.8% of the world $CO_{2,cum}$ emissions, with the Organisation for Economic Co-operation and Development (OECD) countries representing 63.4% of the total. Non-Annex I countries were only responsible for 25.2% of the accumulated emissions, of which China represented 9.2%. In 2007, with 119.7 billion tonnes of $CO_{2,cum}$, China already nearly exceeded the cumulative CO_2 emissions of Germany (85.1 billion tonnes of $CO_{2,cum}$) and France (35.5 billion tonnes of $CO_{2,cum}$) put together. Taking the 2007 world population of 6,552 million as the constant reference over time, every human being on Earth would have emissions rights of 247 tonnes of $CO_{2,cum}$ for the 400 ppm concentration in the atmosphere and 355 tonnes of $CO_{2,cum}$ for a 450 ppm concentration.

Table 9.4 shows the accumulated CO_2 emission consumption per capita worldwide and by selected countries. Taking about 247 tonnes of $CO_{2,cum}$ per capita (at 400 ppm) and 355 tonnes of $CO_{2,cum}$ per capita (at 450 ppm) as a yardstick, it is quite obvious that the industrialised countries have greatly exceeded their emissions budget per capita. For example, in 2007, US citizens consumed 1,218 tonnes of $CO_{2,cum}$ per capita and Germans 1,035 tonnes of $CO_{2,cum}$, far above the OECD average (688 tonnes of $CO_{2,cum}$ per capita). In 2007, China only consumed 91 tonnes of $CO_{2,cum}$ per capita. Although the responsibility for mitigation of climate change is a national obligation here, there might be significant differences between states and sub-state regions. For example, US 'states' such as California are much more advanced in their climate change mitigation policies than the US as a country in total.

In this chapter, energy demand, CO_2 emissions, CO_2 concentration in the atmosphere, and the impact on global mean temperature and sea level rise are estimated and forecasted with the econometric log-linear Global Energy Demand and Greenhouse Gas Emissions Model (GED-GHG Model) (Oberheitmann, 2010). The GED-GHG Model uses primary energy demand data from the *BP statistical review of world energy* (BP, 2008) and data on other renewable energy demand (that is, geothermal, solar, wind, wood and waste) from the US Energy Information Administration (EIA, 2008) from 1965 to 2007 for 70 countries, plus GHG emissions data (CH_4 – methane, N_2O – nitrous oxide, PFCs – perfluorocarbons, HFCs – hydrofluorocarbons, SF_6 – sulphur hexafluoride) for OECD countries and 'countries in transition' (that is, former communist states) in Central and Eastern Europe from the UNFCCC (2008).

Table 9.4: Development of accumulated world CO_2 emissions per capita (1950-2007) (Tonnes per year)

Country	1950	1960	1970	1980	1990	2000	2005	2006	2007
Africa	10	13	15	20	27	31	33	34	34
Asia-Pacific	5	9	16	27	40	57	69	71	74
China	4	8	14	25	40	64	81	86	91
India	6	7	10	12	16	21	25	26	27
Japan	1	19	68	151	230	329	382	393	405
Middle East	14	22	51	89	114	147	168	172	177
Central & South America	11	22	33	46	57	71	78	79	81
Europe and Eurasia	178	207	258	368	453	529	567	575	584
Germany	431	504	596	738	888	956	1012	1023	1035
North America	484	525	598	702	793	879	911	920	929
US	580	639	751	908	1048	1,172	1,199	1,207	1,218
World	89	100	116	139	160	180	192	195	198
OECD	293	329	387	473	557	630	670	679	688
Annex-I countries	251	289	357	455	553	674	720	730	740
Non-Annex-I countries	6	10	15	24	34	48	58	60	62

Source: Oberheitmann (2010)

In our approach for this chapter, a growing population over time should not lead to an increase in the total emissions budget of a country. Instead, it should result in incentives for increasing energy efficiency, the promotion of renewable energy sources or possibly adoption of a proactive population-growth policy (this can be ethically questionable, however). Hence, after 2007, the CO_2 emissions per capita for each country are calculated by the division of the country's accumulated CO_2 emissions in a given year divided by its population. Table 9.5 shows the development of accumulated CO_2 emissions in the world. In the business–as–usual scenario (BAU), accumulated CO_2 emissions worldwide reach about 3290 billion tonnes of CO_2 in 2050. These emissions represent a CO_2 concentration in the atmosphere of 519 ppm. China takes a share of 23.4% of accumulated world emissions.

In the high scenario, accumulated worldwide CO_2 emissions reach 3,460 billion tonnes of $CO_{2,cum}$, a concentration of about 530 ppm. China's emissions represent a 25.4% share. A low scenario provides for cumulative worldwide CO_2 emissions of about 3,100 billion tonnes of $CO_{2,cum}$ and a concentration of about 500 ppm. China's share is 21.0% of world emissions.

Table 9.5: Development of accumulated world CO_2 emissions (2010-50) (billion tonnes of $CO_{2,cum}$)

Country	2010	2020	2030	2040	2050	% of world (2050)
			BAU			
Africa	40	50	60	70	80	2.4
Asia-Pacific	310	480	700	950	1250	38.0
China	140	240	380	560	770	23.4
India	40	50	70	100	130	4.0
Japan	60	70	90	100	110	3.3
Middle East	40	60	80	100	120	3.6
Central & South America	40	50	60	80	90	2.7
Europe and Eurasia	540	630	730	840	950	28.9
Germany	90	100	110	120	130	4.0
North America	430	520	610	700	800	24.3
US	390	470	540	630	710	21.6
World	1,400	1,790	2,240	2,740	3,290	100.0
OECD	870	1,040	1,210	1,390	1,570	47.7
Annex-I countries	1,020	1,210	1,410	1,610	1,820	55.3
Non-Annex-I countries	380	580	830	1130	1470	44.7
			HIGH			
Africa	40	50	60	70	80	2.3
Asia-Pacific	310	490	720	1,010	1,380	39.9
China	140	250	400	600	880	25.4
India	40	50	80	100	130	3.8
Japan	60	70	90	100	120	3.5
Middle East	40	60	80	100	130	3.8
Central & South America	40	50	60	80	90	2.6
Europe and Eurasia	540	630	740	850	980	28.3
Germany	90	100	110	120	130	3.8
North America	430	520	610	710	810	23.4
US	390	470	550	630	720	20.8
World	1,400	1,800	2,260	2,820	3,460	100.0
OECD	870	1,040	1,210	1,400	1,590	46.0
Annex-I countries	1,020	1,210	1,410	1,630	1,850	53.5

Country	2010	2020	2030	2040	2050	% of world (2050)
Non-Annex-I countries	380	580	850	1,190	1,610	46.5
					LOW	
Africa	40	50	60	70	80	2.6
Asia-Pacific	310	470	660	870	1,100	35.6
China	140	240	350	490	650	21.0
India	40	50	70	90	120	3.9
Japan	60	70	90	100	110	3.6
Middle East	40	60	80	100	120	3.9
Central & South America	40	50	60	80	90	2.9
Europe and Eurasia	540	630	730	820	930	30.1
Germany	90	100	110	120	130	4.2
North America	430	520	610	700	780	25.2
US	390	460	540	620	700	22.7
World	1,400	1,780	2,190	2,630	3,090	100.0
OECD	870	1,030	1,200	1,370	1,540	49.8
Annex-I countries	1,020	1,210	1,400	1,590	1,790	57.9
Non-Annex-I countries	380	570	790	1,040	1,310	42.4

Source: Oberheitmann (2010)

Finally, Table 9.6 shows the development of accumulated CO_2 emissions per capita in the world, based on the 2007 population. (To better compare it with the 400 ppm and 450 ppm thresholds, these two figures are highlighted.) In the BAU scenario, worldwide the 400 ppm threshold is reached by 2015 and the 450 ppm threshold by 2031. According to our simulations, China has to stabilise its $CO_{2,cum}$ emissions on the 2026 level for 400 ppm or at the 2035 for 450 ppm. On average, all non-Annex I countries will reach this target by 2045. In the high scenario of economic growth, China will reach the 400 ppm threshold by 2025 and the 450 ppm threshold by 2034 (worldwide: 400 ppm by 2015, 450 ppm by 2031). In the low scenario, global concentrations of 400 ppm will be reached by 2016 and 450 ppm by 2033. China's accumulated CO_2 emissions per capita will reach the 247 tonnes of $CO_{2,cum}$ level (for 400 ppm) by 2028 and the 355 tonnes of $CO_{2,cum}$ level (for 450 ppm) by 2038.

On average, Annex I countries would have to reduce their accumulated CO_2 emissions per capita to their 1950 level. In 2007, that would have meant reducing per-capita accumulated emissions from 740 tonnes of $CO_{2,cum}$ to 247 tonnes of $CO_{2,cum}$. Multiplied with the 2007 Annex I country population (1.310 billion), this results in a CO_2 emissions–reduction commitment of 646.2 billion tonnes of $CO_{2,cum}$ to stay within the 400 ppm limit, or 505.1 billion tonnes of $CO_{2,cum}$ for the 450 ppm level (provided there were no new CO_2 emissions after 2007). As additional CO_2 has been emitted after 2007, and more emissions into the atmosphere will certainly occur because an economy cannot switch to a zero-carbon path overnight, new incremental CO_2 emissions have to be taken into account. Table 9.7 shows the emissions-reduction targets and subsequent mitigation costs

Table 9.6: Development of accumulated world CO_2 emissions per capita (2010-50)[a] (tonnes of $CO_{2,cum}$)

	2010	2020	2030	2040	2050
	BAU				
Africa	38	49	61	73	84
Asia-Pacific	86	133	191	263	344
China	109	185	289	422	582
India	31	47	66	88	112
Japan	439	556	673	788	897
Middle East	200	287	387	497	617
Central & South America	88	113	139	165	192
Europe and Eurasia	614	720	835	959	1,088
Germany	1,070	1,188	1,309	1,432	1,556
North America	985	1,180	1,385	1,596	1,809
US	1,290	1,537	1,798	2,068	2,343
World	214	273	341	419	502
OECD	728	866	1,011	1,160	1,309
Annex-I countries	781	924	1,074	1,231	280
Non-Annex-I countries	72	111	158	216	86
400 ppm	*247*	*247*	*247*	*247*	*247*
450 ppm	*355*	*355*	*355*	*355*	*355*
	HIGH				
Africa	38	50	62	74	86
Asia-Pacific	86	134	197	278	380
China	109	188	300	457	665
India	31	47	67	91	119
Japan	439	557	676	796	912
Middle East	200	289	391	507	634
Central & South America	88	113	140	167	194
Europe and Eurasia	614	721	840	971	1114
Germany	1,070	1,189	1,310	1,434	1,560
North America	985	1,182	1,389	1,606	1,829
US	1,290	1,539	1,803	2,081	2,368
World	214	274	346	430	528

	2010	2020	2030	2040	2050
OECD	728	867	1,015	1,169	1,327
Annex-I countries	782	925	1,079	1,242	1,413
Non-Annex-I countries	72	112	162	227	307
400 ppm	247	247	247	247	247
450 ppm	355	355	355	355	355
LOW					
Africa	38	49	61	71	82
Asia-Pacific	86	130	182	239	303
China	109	180	268	372	490
India	31	46	64	84	104
Japan	439	553	667	775	876
Middle East	200	285	379	482	593
Central & South America	88	112	137	163	188
Europe and Eurasia	614	717	826	940	1,057
Germany	1,070	1,188	1,308	1,429	1,551
North America	985	1,177	1,376	1,578	1,781
US	1,290	1,534	1,786	2,045	2,308
World	214	271	334	401	472
OECD	728	864	1,003	1,145	1,286
Annex-I countries	781	921	1,066	1,213	1,363
Non-Annex-I countries	72	109	151	198	250
400 ppm	247	247	247	247	247
450 ppm	355	355	355	355	355

Note: Based on the 2007 population.

Source: Oberheitmann (2010)

for the Annex I countries in three economic growth scenarios, and the 400 ppm and 450 ppm CO_2 concentration caps, for the start of the mitigation measures in 2010 and 2020.

Starting in 2010, the emissions reduction obligations of the Annex I countries sum up to about 682 billion tonnes of $CO_{2,cum}$ for the 400 ppm target and about 541 billion tonnes of $CO_{2,cum}$ for the 450 ppm target. Assuming mitigation costs of US$50 per tonne of CO_2, this translates into US$34 trillion and US$27 trillion respectively in mitigation costs for all Annex I countries. Per capita, this amounts to US$20,000–26,000, which is about two to three times what the German government has reserved as guarantees and government spending for the current international financial crisis. Clearly, early action for climate change mitigation is preferable. For the 400 ppm CO_2 concentration target, the emissions–reduction requirements of the Annex I countries

Table 9.7: Emissions-reduction targets and costs for Annex-I countries in different economic growth scenarios and CO_2 concentration caps up to 2050 (2010 and 2020) (billion tonnes of $CO_{2,cum}$ and US$)

400 ppm

Start of reduction measures	Reduction target (billion tonnes $CO_{2,cum}$)			Reduction costs (trillion US$)			Reduction costs per capita (US$)		
	BAU	HIGH	LOW	BAU	HIGH	LOW	BAU	HIGH	LOW
2010	681.9	682.0	681.8	34.1	34.1	34.1	26,000	26,000	26,000
2020[a]	867.2	868.7	864.2	37.9	38.0	37.8	29,000	29,000	28,900

450 ppm

Start of reduction measures	Reduction target (billion tonnes $CO_{2,cum}$)			Reduction costs (trillion US$)			Reduction costs per capita (US$)		
	BAU	HIGH	LOW	BAU	HIGH	LOW	BAU	HIGH	LOW
2010	540.8	540.9	540.7	27.0	27.0	27.0	20,600	20,600	20,600
2020[a]	726.1	727.6	723.2	31.8	31.8	31.6	24,300	24,300	24,200

Note: [a] Net present value (interest rate = 2.5%).

Source: Oberheitmann (2010)

sum up to be about a 27% higher level in 2020 compared to actions starting in 2010. Again, assuming mitigation costs of US$50 per tonne of CO_2, this translates into an additional US$9 trillion in total mitigation costs in the scenarios for later action in 2020. Per capita, this is about US$7,000 more. Allowing for an atmospheric CO_2 concentration of 450 ppm, which represents a higher probability of reaching or even overshooting the 2°C target, the costs of a delay in climate change mitigation measures are even larger than in the 400 ppm case. Starting in 2020 rather than 2010 means that mitigation costs of about 35% more. However, the total reduction costs and costs per capita are lower than in the 400 ppm case because the CO_2 emissions-reduction obligations of Annex I countries are about 16–21% smaller.

Long term, these massive reductions in CO2 emissions can only be realised by 'negative' emissions – by a combination of renewable energy production (for example, biofuels) which are by definition zero emission and combining it with the capture and storage of these fossil-fuel emissions out of the atmosphere (that is, carbon capture and storage [CCS]). As a result, the emissions are becoming 'negative'.

However, CCS is an expensive option and still in the developmental stage, even for coal-based power generation. CCS for biofuels is even earlier in its development. In addition, with respect to biofuels, the issue of competition with food crops has to be solved, especially against the background of a growing world population.

In a growing world economy (the 'high' scenario in the preceding tables), on the one hand, there is even more difficulty in reaching these negative emissions as energy demand tends to grow. However, on the other hand, only a growing economy provides for sufficient investment capital. Slower growth in the world economy (the 'low' scenario) would reduce the growth of energy demand, but governments might be more reluctant to make long-term investments in negative emissions because they might see a trade-off between those investments and economic growth, and they might be worried about the implications for their international competitiveness if there is not a global approach.

However, our proposed new post-Kyoto regime allows for international emissions trading. If countries have not reached their limit for accumulated per-capita CO_2 emissions, they could sell them to other countries short of emissions rights. The same is true for certificates accruing from other flexible mechanisms under the Kyoto Protocol, such as the Clean Development Mechanism (Article 12 of the Protocol), Joint Implementation (Article 6) and Land-use, Land-Use Change and Forestry (Article 3, para 4). Against the background of the problems mentioned before, this would be a more feasible option for the Annex I countries, at least in the medium term. Whether the non-Annex I countries would agree on this is of course a political issue. Currently, they may have remaining emissions rights that they could sell. However, when their economies reach their budget threshold in the future, which for China would occur around 2025, emissions rights would be scarce.[3]

Conclusion

Climate change is one of the most severe global problems of the 21st century. Currently, China's share of global CO_2 emissions is about 20%, exceeding that of the US. Assuming different growth paths for the Chinese economy, by 2050 this share might increase to 45% in the 'high' scenario of the model described above. In the current Kyoto regime, as a developing country China does not have quantitative emissions-reduction obligations. However, China was responsible for almost 50% of new CO_2 emissions between 1997 and 2007. It should therefore take on a more prominent role in climate change mitigation and global environmental governance. COP15 in Copenhagen in December 2009 failed to a large extent because the US and China, together responsible for 40% of global CO_2 emissions, did not come forward with substantial-enough emissions-limitation targets. The US proposed emissions reduction that did not even reach the amount fixed for it in the Kyoto Protocol in 1997, making it difficult for China to put forward a more substantial target. If these two mega-players do not reach a consensus, and continue to take the reluctance of the other as an excuse to avoid their own substantial moves, there will be no global success in the mitigation of climate change.

Against this background, a new cooperative climate regime is necessary to meet the world's energy and environmental problems. However, the approaches that are being discussed have common weaknesses: (a) they do not acknowledge the responsibilities of the industrialised countries for their historical GHG emissions and the responsibility of developing countries for a large fraction of the future emissions and (b) they do not provide for a fair distribution of emissions. Taking these shortcomings into account, the new climate regime proposed in this chapter is based on cumulative CO_2 emissions. Figure 9.1 shows the development of cumulative CO_2 emissions per capita in the three scenarios (business as usual, high and low).

Early action to mitigate climate change is of the essence. A delay in mitigation measures of only 10 years after 2010 would increase the mitigation costs for Annex I countries by around 30%. Delayed action would also increase the probability of accelerating CO_2 emissions as a result of triggered feedbacks (not considered in the models), such as release of methane trapped under melting permafrost and acidification of oceans (Worldwatch Institute, 2009).

Figure 9.1: Accumulated CO_2 emissions per capita in different scenarios of GDP growth (2010-50) (tonnes per capita)

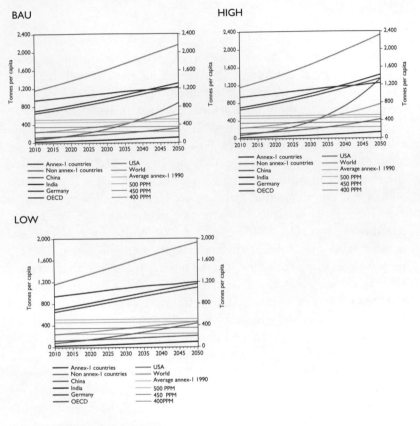

Source: Authors' own calculations

From this we can conclude that China's increasing GHG emissions present a growing challenge for climate change mitigation. Being responsible for almost half of additional global CO_2 emissions, China is under increasing international pressure to reduce its emissions. However, the failure of COP15 in 2009 showed that there will only be a successful international approach if both China and the US – together being responsible for more than 40% of global CO_2 emissions – come up with substantial emissions-reduction targets. A new post-Kyoto regime could provide for environmental equity if it is based on cumulative per-capita emissions rights leading to a cap in CO_2 emissions at an amount that, by 2050, will limit global warming to 2°C. Environmental equity in responsibility can be achieved if both the historical CO_2 emissions of the industrialised countries (since 1750) are taken into account along with the growing CO_2 emissions of newly industrialising countries such as China (since the 1980s). An international trading system based on this new regime could induce increasing low-carbon technology transfer and it could provide financial support for China and other developing countries to develop their own eco-efficient innovations.

Notes

[1] The approach undertaken here was developed independently from the budget approach of the German Advisory Council on Climate Change (WBGU), published in July 2009 (WBGU, 2009). The allocation scheme presented here differs from WBGU because it comprises the cumulative emissions from 1750 onwards, whereas WGBU only cumulates the budget from 1990 to achieve the global 2°C goal by 2050.

[2] Only up to 1964; from 1965, bunkers were included in the data for primary energy consumption (BP, 2008).

[3] The approach presented in this chapter has limits. Especially on the data side, the non-CO_2 emissions listed in the Kyoto Protocol (that is, CH_4, N_2O, HFCs, PFCs and SF_6) have to be accounted for and calculated for all of the non-Annex I countries. Due to a lack of data, the approach presented here is only based on cumulative CO_2 emissions, rather than on all GHG emissions. On the mitigation cost side, increasing marginal abatement costs have to be taken into account. For reasons of simplicity, constant costs are assumed here. Furthermore, the analysis should also target the impact of different paths of GDP of other important non-Annex I countries (for example, Brazil, Indonesia and South Africa) on their obligations in the proposed post-Kyoto regime.

References

BP (2008) *BP statistical review of world energy*, London: BP, www.bp.com/productlanding.do?categoryId=6929&contentId=7044622

CNRS/LEPII-EPE (Centre National de la Recherche Scientifique/ Laboratoire d'Économie de la Production et de l'Intégration Internationale), RIVM/MNP (National Institute for Public Health and the Environment), ICCS-NTUA (Institute of Communications & Computer Systems-National Technical University of Athens) and CES-KUL (Centre for European Studies-Katholieke Universiteit Leuven) (2003) 'Greenhouse gas reduction pathways in the UNFCCC process up to 2025: policymakers summary', Mimeo.

Department of Climate Change, National Development & Reform Commission of China (2010) Letter including domestic mitigation action, 28 January 2010, http://unfccc.int/files/meetings/cop_15/copenhagen_accord/application/pdf/chinacphaccord_app2.pdf

EC (European Commission) (2007) *Limiting global climate change to 2 degrees Celsius: The way ahead for 2020 and beyond*, Communication of the Commission to the Council, the European Parliament, the European Economic and Social Committee and the Committees of the Regions, COM(2007) 2 final, Brussels: EC.

EIA (Energy Information Administration) (2008) International energy data, Washington, DC: EIA, www.eia.doe.gov/emeu/international/contents.html

IPCC (Intergovernmental Panel on Climate Change) (2007) *Climate change 2007: Synthesis report: Contribution of Working Groups I, II and III to the Fourth Assessment Report of the Intergovernmental Panel on Climate Change* (Core Writing Team, Pachauri, R.K and Reisinger, A. [eds]), Geneva: IPCC.

Ministry of Science and Technology, National Development and Reform Commission, Ministry of Foreign Affairs, Ministry of Education, Ministry of Finance, Ministry of Water Resources, Ministry of Agriculture, State Environmental Protection Administration, State Forestry Administration, Chinese Academy of Sciences, China Meteorology Administration, National Natural Science Foundation, State Oceanic Administration, China Association for Science and Technology (2007) *China's scientific and technological actions on climate change*, Mimeo.

National Bureau of Statistics of China (2009) *China statistical yearbook*, Beijing: National Bureau of Statistics of China.

NDRC (National Development and Reform Commission) (2007a) *China's National Climate Change Programme*, Beijing: NDRC.

NDRC (2007a) *China's medium- and long-term development plan for China*, Beijing: NDRC.

NDRC (2009a) *Implementation of the Bali roadmap: China's position on the Copenhagen climate change conference*, Beijing: NDRC.

NDRC (2009b) *China's policies and actions for addressing climate change: The progress report 2009,* Beijing: NDRC.

Oberheitmann, A. (2008) 'Environmental policy reform in China', in T. Heberer and G. Schubert (eds) *Institutional change and political continuity in contemporary China* (pp 269-96), London and New York, NY: Routledge.

Oberheitmann, A. (2010) 'A new post-Kyoto climate regime based on per-capita cumulative emissions rights – rationale, architecture and quantitative assessment of the implication for the CO_2 emissions from China, India and the Annex I countries by 2050', *Mitigation and Adaptation Strategies for Global Change,* vol, no 2, pp 137-68.

Oberheitmann, A. and Sternfeld, E. (2009) 'Climate change in China: the development of China's climate policy and its integration into a new international post-Kyoto climate regime', *Journal of Current Chinese Affairs,* vol 38, no 3, pp135-64.

Project Team of the Development Research Centre of the State Council of China (2009) 'Greenhouse gas emissions reduction: a theoretical framework and global solution', *Economic Research Journal,* vol 44, no 3, pp 4-14.

Rahmstorf, S. (2009) ,2 Grad in L'Aquila', *Wissenslogs,* 10 July, www.wissenslogs.de/wblogs/blog/klimalounge/debatte/2009-07-10/2-grad-aquila

Russa, P. and Criquib, P. (2007) 'Post-Kyoto CO_2-emission reduction: the soft landing scenario analysed with POLES and other world models', *Energy Policy,* vol 35, pp 786-96.

Standing Committee of the National People's Congress of China (2005) *The Renewable Energy Law of the People's Republic of China,* Beijing: Standing Committee of the National People's Congress of China.

State Council of the People's Republic of China (2008) *China's policies and actions for addressing climate change,* White Paper, Beijing: State Council of the People's Republic of China.

Tickell, O. (2008) *Kyoto2: How to manage the global greenhouse,* London: Zed Books.

UNFCCC (United Nations Framework Convention on Climate Change) (1997) *Paper No 1: Brazil: Proposed elements of a protocol to the United Nations Framework Convention on Climate Change,* Bonn: UNFCC.

UNFCCC (2008) 'GHG data from UNFCCC', Bonn: UNFCCC, http://unfccc.int/ghg_data/ghg_data_unfccc/items/4146.php

WBGU (German Advisory Council on Climate Change) (2009) 'Solving the climate dilemma: the budget approach', Berlin, Mimeo.

Welt Online (2008) 'Deutschland erreicht fast das Ziel von Kyoto', *Welt Online*, 9 March, www.welt.de/politik/article1779449/Deutschland_erreicht_fast_das_Ziel_von_Kyoto.html

Worldwatch Institute (2009) *State of the world 2009: Into a warming world*, Washington, DC: Worldwatch Institute.

Part Four
Conclusion

TEN

Chinese responsibility for climate change

Paul G. Harris

Is China responsible for climate change? The preceding chapters show that the answer to this question depends on a number of factors, such as the timescale being assessed, China's capabilities and its level of development, whether we seek answers about practical or ethical-normative issues, and indeed how we define 'China' in this context – among other considerations. In this chapter I highlight some these factors before focusing on one that is becoming increasingly important from both practical and normative perspectives: the growing role of the Chinese people, specifically the growing number of them joining the ranks of the world's affluent classes.[1]

One issue that permeates analyses and discussions of China's (and other developing countries') role in climate change is historical responsibility. If we consider China's *practical* contribution to the problem of climate change – which many will say infers *responsibility* under certain circumstances – the timeframe we are considering becomes quite important. Almost regardless of one's ethical viewpoint, on a practical level we cannot say that China is as responsible for historical emissions of greenhouse gases (GHGs) as are the developed countries of the West if the historical period we are considering begins with the Industrial Revolution. The material benefits of that revolution largely passed China by until quite recently; until the latter part of the 20th century, China was too poor to have a very large impact on the Earth's climate, at least relative to major industrialised countries. However, if we think in terms of the *recent* past – say, from the late 1970s when China opened to the world and its economic growth began to take off – the question of whether it has been responsible for climate change takes on a new and very important dimension. China's contributions to climate change started to have profound practical significance in recent decades, and over the last 10 years and more its contribution has been enormous – and for the last half decade it has contributed more to the problem than any other country.

Nevertheless, some will still argue (as the Chinese government does) that its 'responsibility' remains very low (or non-existent) because the country's *per-capita* emissions have been low historically and remain low relative to most developed countries. That said, one cannot deny that China's GHG emissions are affecting the global climate in profound ways, and even its per-capita emissions now exceed the global average. If China lacks the same moral responsibility for the impacts of its emissions as do richer countries, we cannot deny that pollution coming from within China's borders is indeed a major part of the problem. What is more, when we think about the future, China's responsibility grows in both practical and normative importance. Even if one concludes that China's responsibility for climate change *today* is quite low, it will be hard to reach the same conclusion in the *future*, not least because the Chinese government is fully aware of the consequences for the Earth's climate of the country's economic development and growth – unlike countries in the West, which are to a significant extent locked into polluting infrastructures developed before the world became aware of the problem of climate change. Fundamentally, arguments that the Chinese government uses to attribute responsibility for climate change to the West, particularly those based on the West's historical emissions, will be used against China by future generations.

Another way of looking at China's responsibility for climate change is to consider its capabilities. When China was a predominantly poor country, one would be hard pressed to blame it legitimately for future climate change. However, at its current level of development – not to mention its national wealth in coming years – reflected in its ability to respond aggressively to climate change and other environmental challenges (given its newfound economic and technological prowess), clearly China is now capable of acting on climate change if the government so wishes. Put another way, China is no longer a traditional 'developing country'. While parts of China remain very poor, others are extraordinarily wealthy. China's ability to adopt environmentally sustainable ways of developing has grown considerably in recent years, meaning that the government has a choice about whether the country will develop in ways that make it less responsible for causing future climate change, at least in practical terms. What is more, in so far as we can attribute some of China's GHG emissions to exports – that is, to demand for material products from the developed world – the equation is changing. Demand within China is growing rapidly as the expanding middle class consumes in ways reminiscent of the boom times in post-Second World War America. Consequently, even the good argument that much of China's pollution in recent decades could be attributed to the West will become less convincing with time.

Another way of thinking about China's responsibility for climate change is in terms of the role it plays in the world's efforts to address the problem. If the Chinese government makes practical contributions to solutions, particularly to furthering international cooperation, its responsibility arguably declines. If it obstructs robust action on climate change, as it was accused of doing at the 2009 Copenhagen conference, arguably its responsibility for the problem increases. In so far as China is a participant in the corrosive and ultimately self-destructive 'blame game' among countries – a game in which China demands that the United States (US) and other developed countries reduce their emissions of GHGs substantially before China agrees to take on obligations to limit its own emissions, and developed countries (notably the US) refuse to do so on the basis of China not doing so – it is an obstacle to progress and international cooperation to tackle climate change. This is not to suggest that China has as much responsibility for this problem as do the US and other developed countries, but rather to point out that we must acknowledge that China can, if it chooses, do more to solve the problem through international cooperation than it is doing at present.

These are just some of the considerations examined in the preceding chapters. Building on another idea discussed by other contributors, in the remainder of this final chapter I suggest that a determination of whether – or how much – China is responsible for climate change depends on how we define 'China'. If we define it in terms of the Chinese 'state' and its government, as the Chinese and other governments, as well as most observers, tend to do, history plays a big role and China's responsibility for climate change is mitigated. However, if we define China as the Chinese people, and then look closely at their role, our answer to the question of whether China is responsible for climate change becomes more complicated. Identifying and specifying China's responsibility is a function of both the country and the people who live within it.

Responsibilities of states *and* responsibilities of people

When thinking about the role of China and people living there in the context of climate change, attention has understandably been focused on the many millions of poor Chinese. Surely they cannot be expected to take on much or any responsibility for climate change, not least because each of them contributes relatively little to the problem. This is the view that the Chinese government wants us to take when we think about China's responsibility for climate change. However, while most Chinese do not have any (or much) responsibility for climate change, a significant proportion of them do. The latter include the growing middle and upper classes of Chinese who are living lives remarkably akin to those of most people in the developed world – and polluting just as much, if not more so. Regardless of what we might conclude about *China's* past responsibility for climate change, recent changes in affluence there mean that a segment of the *Chinese people* do have responsibilities for climate change, including to reduce their consumption and pollution, and perhaps even to aid those who are suffering from climate change or will do so in the future.[2]

To illustrate the importance of considering the role of *people* in China, in addition to the role of 'China' as a state, imagine a map of the world that reflects the international politics of climate change. That map would be a typical depiction of states within well-defined political boundaries. If we were to layer *current* GHG emissions on top of this political map of the world – imagine that countries with high overall emissions are coloured red, those with moderate emissions are yellow and those with low emissions are green – China and the US would be red, as would much of Europe and Japan, while middle-income countries, such as those in Latin America, would be largely yellow, and nearly all of Africa and much of South Asia would be green. Imagine further a map of the world showing *historical* GHG emissions. On this map, China's colour would change from red to yellow given its relatively low historical emissions, India might change from yellow to green, and most of Africa would remain solidly green.

These three maps would provide most of the information one needs to understand the international politics of climate change because they would show us national boundaries coinciding with the participants in climate change negotiations; they would tell us a fair bit about how countries are contributing to the problem now, thus showing us which ones are most important for global solutions to climate change; and they would show us which countries are most responsible for historical emissions, thereby revealing perhaps the most contentious aspect of climate diplomacy: which countries are historically 'at fault' and which believe that it would be unjust to expect them to accept responsibility for addressing climate change.

Now, instead of this political map of the world with GHG emissions layered on top, imagine a physical map of the Earth without any political boundaries whatsoever, with all land surfaces coloured in brown and the oceans in blue. Imagine two billion tiny red dots – one for each of the two billion most affluent people on the planet – spread across this borderless map. Not surprisingly, hundreds of millions of those tiny dots would be clustered in North America, Europe, Japan and Australia. We would see large red splotches collocated with New York, London, Tokyo and Sydney. Smaller but still quite large and prominent collections of dots would be spread, sometimes in waves, throughout the developed world. These collections and waves of red dots across the global North would correspond with about half of the world's current GHG emissions (see, for example, den Elzen and Höhne, 2008).[3]

While much of those parts of the world map corresponding to the developing world would have relatively few red dots, and the poorest parts of the world would have wide swathes of land devoid of them, there would also be a surprising number of large (and, as it happens, growing) collections of red dots in many parts of the developing world, and especially in areas that correspond with the newly industrialising countries. These red splotches would be collocated with Beijing, Shanghai, Hong Kong, Rio de Janeiro, Mexico City, Jakarta and Bangkok, with waves of red along the coastal areas of China and into the suburbs of major cities of the developing world. These red splotches and waves would correspond with perhaps (roughly speaking) something approaching a quarter of the world's current GHG emissions, with the relative size of these emissions growing rapidly compared to those of people in the developed world.[4]

If we now compare this physical map of GHG emissions with the map of political boundaries, the issue of climate change comes into a new light. We see that the diplomacy of climate change has been, to a substantial degree, misplaced: it does not correspond with the environmental geography of climate change, which would more accurately reveal where the people who pollute the atmosphere live. While the political map, including one overlaid with national historical emissions of GHGs, would suggest that China has very limited responsibility for climate change and therefore may be morally entitled to sit on the sidelines and wait for the developed countries to act on their responsibilities for the problem, the map showing the world's affluent polluters would reveal that hundreds of millions of them live in China, meaning that they or the Chinese government (or both, depending on one's perspective) share responsibility for climate change, at the very least for contributing to pollution that will make it worse in the future. This puts China's new status as the world's largest national source of GHG pollution in a new light. If we focus on political boundaries, China appears to have very little responsibility for GHG pollution today, but if we focus on who is actually doing the polluting, surely many Chinese are in fact to blame, along with most people in the developed world.

If we ask ourselves where the dots corresponding to affluent consumers (GHG polluters, in effect) are located, we can see that the red splotches of the Western world have spread into the developing world, especially China. We can see that climate diplomacy and resulting policies, which still focus on political boundaries and specifically view developing countries and all people in them as beyond the bounds of mandatory GHG cuts, fail to capture much of the red. To be sure, it was only two or three decades ago that the individual sources of climate change fell much more clearly within the borders of developed countries – the red splotches in China would have been very much smaller than today. But things have changed substantially in recent years. As hundreds of millions of people in China (and some other developing countries) have joined the global consumer class (Myers and Kent, 2004), the collections of red dots of affluent GHG emitters there have quickly grown much larger. This will be very much the trend in coming decades.

This means that if we focus much more on the world's affluent *people* instead of only on affluent states, responsibility for climate change spreads around the globe, particularly to China. One important implication of this is that policies to address climate change will have to include hundreds of millions of affluent people in China, alongside most people in the developed world and affluent people in other large developing countries, if those policies are to capture the impacts of as many of the sources of global warming as will be necessary to mitigate future impacts significantly and if they are to identify the people (and governments) that should help those who will be most harmed by climate change.

Chinese responsibility and a new politics of climate change

A major reason that so little has been done about climate change, even as the world's GHG pollution grows by leaps and bounds, is the world's preoccupation with *responsibility of states* for the problem. The Chinese government has been complicit in this preoccupation. At the heart of the problem are national interests, or more precisely how those national interests are perceived by governments, politicians and diplomats, and how they are shaped by special interests within states. The narrowly perceived national interests that have guided climate diplomacy are not consistent with global interests or indeed with the long-term interests of most countries, including China. Climate change has become another tragedy of the commons, albeit on a scale much larger than any other. As long as protection and promotion of states' interests remain the aim of the climate change agreements among governments, the tragedy will likely continue in the form of more muddling along, reminiscent of the Copenhagen conference, that will do far too little relative to the scale of the problem.

How can the world escape this tragedy? One major solution to climate change may be to shift away from statist conceptions of who is responsible for climate change – which countries have caused the problem, which of them ought to cut GHG pollution the most, which ones owe money to others in this context – to more encompassing, global or 'cosmopolitan' conceptions of climate change-related responsibilities. Doing this would focus more attention on the world's affluent consumers, including the growing number of them in China, as the fundamental causes of climate change and, through changes in their behaviours, among the potential solutions to the problem. Looking at climate change in this new way would focus more attention on the red splotches described above, and less on political boundaries. It would mean more attention being given to consumers and polluters in the developed world, to be sure, but also much more attention on the developing world's new consumers – including the hundreds of millions of newly affluent people in China – who are living and polluting just like people in much of North America and Europe.

What is required, then, is a move away from debates about which *countries* are responsible for climate change towards debates about which *people* are responsible for the problem and for helping those people who are suffering from it and will do so in the future (see Harris, 2010b). This does not reduce the responsibilities of the countries and governments of the developed world, but it does increase the responsibility of many people in China. What is vitally important about this more global/cosmopolitan approach to climate responsibility is that it would, paradoxically, give China an opportunity to take the *lead* on solving this problem, in the process breaking the international political deadlock. The Chinese government could take the lead by explicitly placing climate-related restrictions on its most affluent citizens, starting by, for example, heavily taxing luxury purchases (and using the resulting funds to help poor Chinese cope with climate change) or outlawing heavily polluting private cars. Importantly, China would not be taking on any new *national* obligations; new obligations would be on affluent *people* within China, not on the Chinese state. This is vitally important because it avoids the issue of the historical obligations of rich-world countries. China would not be doing anything to renounce the principle of common but differentiated responsibility (CBDR) of countries whereby rich ones have acknowledged that they are most responsible for climate change historically and therefore have greater responsibility to address it.

Instead, by taking this kind of lead, China would be acknowledging that there is CBDR *among people*, too. By restricting the GHG pollution of its most affluent residents, the Chinese government would show that some people in China are acting even while too few in the developed world are doing so. In effect, China would constrain GHG emissions within its borders for climate-related reasons without having to take on new state-to-state obligations (which it has thus far refused to do for the reasons outlined in previous chapters). Western governments, and indeed most people in the West, would be left with no place to hide – they could no longer complain that Chinese people are failing to act on climate change. Leaders of the developed countries could then point their compatriots to what is happening in China and ask why people in a poorer country are taking the lead while people of the West continue to pollute as much as they have done for decades. The political implications could be potentially enormous.

Conclusion

Where does this leave us? The principle of CBDR is the cornerstone of China's view of its responsibility for climate change. At the 2009 Copenhagen conference, Chinese Premier Wen Jiabao said that:

> [t]he principle of 'common but differentiated responsibilities' represents the core and bedrock of international cooperation on climate change, and it must never be compromised.... Developed countries must take the lead in making deep quantified emission cuts and provide financial and technological support to developing countries. This is an unshirkable moral responsibility as well as a legal obligation that they must fulfil. (Wen, 2009)

However, while the Chinese government has yet to acknowledge it, China's *common* responsibility for climate change is on the rise as its overall wealth and level of development increase and its contribution to the problem increases. Indeed, because China is now the largest national source of GHG pollution, on a practical level no other country is more responsible for the additional future impacts of climate change from current emissions. Consequently, China's growing *national* contributions will give rise to demands that it take on more of the 'common responsibility' for climate change normally attributed to the developed countries.

What is more, CBDR *of people* is an overlooked but unavoidable factor which will put growing pressure to China's government to increase its efforts to limit and, quite soon, reduce its GHG emissions. Although China's per-capita GHG emissions remain well below those of developed countries, the number of affluent people in China has grown substantially in recent decades, meaning that there is, in effect, a 'Germany within China' given that the number of people in Germany and other developed countries number fewer than the newly affluent people in China (Harris, 2010b, pp 141-6). Comparisons of consumption-based emissions statistics and data on national income-distribution suggest that per capita emissions of the richest 10% of the people in China are well above those of the poorest 10% of Americans, putting these affluent Chinese on par with per-capita emissions in some European countries (Hertwich and Peters, 2009; UNDP, 2009, pp 195-6). These evolving statistics will make it increasingly difficult for China to claim that the principle of CBDR inoculates it – or at least several hundred million Chinese people – from the moral obligation to take on more responsibility for climate change, and more specifically to take on binding GHG limitations. The fact is that millions of newly affluent people in China are doing just what people in the West are rightly being blamed for, meaning that pressure will likely build on China from both the developed world and the least developed countries to agree to a GHG ceiling in the medium term, followed by GHG cuts before too long (see Harris, 2010b, pp 124-9).

On the whole, I believe that we can answer the question of whether China is responsible for climate change with an affirmative answer. Where once it would be difficult to justify saying that China shares responsibility for this problem, the opposite is now true. While one might still argue that, under some assumptions (for example, by looking at long-term historical GHG emissions), China lacks much responsibility, being persuasive about this is becoming increasingly difficult. China's responsibility for climate change, and that of millions of affluent people living in China, is increasing rapidly as we move into the future. China shares common responsibility. That common responsibility remains less than developed states, but it is much more than the responsibility of very poor countries. China's *differentiated* national responsibility is growing as it becomes wealthier, and the differentiated responsibility of affluent Chinese people is similar to that of affluent people everywhere, including in the West. Thus, one possible future for Chinese policy on climate change – a future that could put China in the lead on this issue – would be for China to match its demands for CBDR *among countries* with a recognition that requirements for CBDR *among people* necessitate GHG emissions reductions by at least several tens of millions (if not a few hundred million) affluent people in China.

The fundamental conclusion at which I arrive is quite simple, but no doubt extremely controversial in China: China cannot act on its responsibility for climate change, nor can it transition to the most environmentally sustainable future that is possible, if it remains obsessed with itself as an insular, sovereign state first and foremost. To be sure, more work needs to be done to understand China's responsibility for climate change from a range of views, including practical and normative perspectives. More daunting, perhaps, will be convincing the government and people of China that they should accept much more responsibility for climate change – and that they should shoulder this responsibility through international cooperation and domestic policies that stem and, before too long, reverse the rising tide of GHG pollution from within China's borders.

Notes
[1] Parts of this chapter build on Harris (2010a).

[2] It goes without saying that responsible individuals in China include affluent non-citizens there (for example, affluent expatriate workers, migrants, diplomats and visitors).

[3] Assuming that individuals are considered to account for industrial, agricultural and other pollution coming from their consumption of materials, power, food and so forth (cf Hertwich and Peters, 2009).

[4] For data and trends, see, for example, Baer et al (2008, 2009). The remaining global emissions can be attributed to roughly four billion people who contribute relatively little per capita and ought not in most cases be expected to reduce their GHG emissions until sustainable alternatives are readily available to them.

References

Baer, P., Athanasiou, T. and Kartha, S. (2008) *The Greenhouse Development Rights Framework: The right to development in a climate constrained world* (2nd edition), Berlin: Heinrich Böll Foundation.

Baer, P., with Athanasiou, T., Kartha, S. and Kemp-Benedict, E. (2009) 'Greenhouse development rights: a proposal for a fair global climate treaty', *Ethics, Place and Environment*, vol 12, no 3, pp 267-81.

den Elzen, M. and Höhne, N. (2008) 'Reductions of greenhouse gas emissions in Annex I and non-Annex I countries for meeting concentration stabilisation targets', *Climatic Change*, no 91, pp 249-74.

Harris, P.G. (2010a) 'Misplaced ethics of climate change: political vs. environmental geography', *Ethics, Place & Environment*, vol 13, no 2, pp 215-22.

Harris, P.G. (2010b) *World ethics and climate change: From international to global justice*, Edinburgh: Edinburgh University Press.

Hertwich, E.G. and Peters, G.P. (2009) 'Carbon footprint of nations: a global, trade-linked analysis', *Environmental Science and Technology*, vol 43, no 16, pp 6414-20.

Myers, N. and Kent, J. (2004) *The new consumers*, London: Island Press.

UNDP (United Nations Development Programme) (2009) *Human development report 2009*, New York, NY: UNDP.

Wen, J. (2009) 'Build consensus and strengthen cooperation to advance the historical process of combating climate change', Address at the Copenhagen Climate Change Summit by Wen Jiabao, Premier of the State Council of the People's Republic of China, Copenhagen, 18 December.

Index

Note: The following abbreviations have been used: t = table; f = figure; n = note

A

'ability to pay' 196, 202, 203t, 204t
Ad-hoc Group for the Modelling and Assessment of Contributions of Climate Change (MATCH) 89f, 91 92
adaptation 8, 9, 10, 26, 36, 38, 49, 174
funding 103, 104, 108, 111, 113, 115
Africa 158t
Agenda 21 47
Alliance of Small Island States (AOSIS) 82, 83f, 85
allowance-based methodology 77–8
alternative energies 162, 182–4, 197–8, 201t
Annex I countries 81, 87, 88, 90, 91, 92, 93n, 135, 196, 206
CO_2 emissions 210–11, 212, 213t, 214, 215–16
AOSIS *see* Alliance of Small Island States
Aristotle 74–5
Asia 158t, 176
Asia-Pacific Partnership on Clean Development and Climate 173
atmospheric lifetime 149, 150t, 151, 153, 161
Australia 99–100

B

bio-capacity 52, 55, 59
biofuels 136, 138, 145, 198, 201t, 214
black carbon 16–17, 149, 158, 159f, 161t, 162, 163n
  per-capita emissions 150t, 151, 152f
  radiative forcing 149, 151, 154, 155f, 156, 162
border tax adjustments (BTAs) 15, 100, 113–14, 115, 116

Brazil 115
'Brazilian proposal' 196, 202, 203t, 204t, 205
'bunker fuel' emissions 72, 104, 206, 217n
'business-as-usual' scenario 38, 59, 102, 104, 134, 200, 208, 210
Byrd-Hagel Resolution (1997) 104

C

Canada 104, 147
capability principle 157, 158t, 159f, 160, 161t, 164n, 224–5
carbon capture and storage techniques (CCS) 132, 136, 137–8, 214
carbon dioxide (CO_2) emissions 8, 51, 63n, 94n, 129, 148, 149
  carbon intensity 182, 197
  developing/developed countries 164n
  energy sector 175
  'first polluter' 6–7, 14, 48, 50, 127
  fossil fuels 135, 154, 155f, 158, 159f, 161t, 200
  heavy-industry sector 175
  household consumption 177–8
  'luxury emissions' 38
  per-capita emissions 18, 77, 81f
  per unit of production 12
  radiative forcing 150t, 151, 152f, 153
  responsibility 153–4, 155f, 156–7, 200
  stabilization 195
  2°C target 206t, 207, 208t, 209t, 210t, 211–12t, 213t, 214–15
  urban dwellers 185
carbon tariffs 15, 101, 115–16, 117
CAS *see* Chinese Academy of Sciences